John Stevens

Troubleshooter Englisch

Typische Fehler vermeiden

Hueber Verlag

3. 2. 1. | Die letzten Ziffern
2018 17 16 15 14 | bezeichnen Zahl und Jahr des Druckes.
Alle Drucke dieser Auflage können, da unverändert,
nebeneinander benutzt werden.
1. Auflage

Basiert auf ISBN 978-3-19-107918-5, 978-3-19-057918-1 und 978-3-19-007918-6
Umschlaggestaltung: creative partners gmbh, München
Umschlagillustration: Martin Guhl, Stein am Rhein, Schweiz
Zeichnungen: Irmtraud Guhe, München
Layout: appel media, Oberding
Satz: Sieveking · Agentur für Kommunikation, München
Druck und Bindung: Kessler Druck + Medien GmbH & Co. KG, Bobingen
Printed in Germany
ISBN 978-3-19-357918-8

Art. 530_18332_001_01

Vorwort

Was Sie mit diesem Buch erreichen können

Sie sprechen bereits Englisch, aber es schleichen sich immer wieder typische Fehler ein? Sie sind sich z.B. manchmal nicht sicher, ob Sie die richtige Zeitform oder das richtige Wort gewählt haben? Zwei Formen sind sich ähnlich und Sie müssen sich für eine entscheiden, wissen aber nicht 100-prozentig für welche?

Mit diesem Übungsbuch können Sie gezielt Ihr Englisch von lästigen Fehlern befreien. *Troubleshooter Englisch* bietet Grammatik, Wortschatz und Sprachgebrauch zum praktischen und schnellen Wiederholen und Üben, ermöglicht die Analyse und Korrektur fehleranfälliger Bereiche, und fördert die korrekte und authentische Kommunikation.

Wie das Buch aufgebaut ist

Troubleshooter Englisch ist in drei Teile eingeteilt: *Common Mistakes in English Grammar* (S. 5–122), *True and False Friends* (S. 123–247) und *Phrases for Everyday Communication* (S. 249–398). Das detaillierte Inhaltsverzeichnis, das vor jedem der drei Teile abgedruckt ist (S. 6, 124 und 250), gibt genauere Auskunft. Alle drei Teile haben einen integrierten Lösungsschlüssel, mit dem Sie Ihre Arbeit kontrollieren und notfalls berichtigen können.

Wie Sie mit dem Buch arbeiten können

Über das jeweilige Inhaltsverzeichnis finden Sie die Themen, die Sie gezielt üben möchten. Das Buch ist aber auch insgesamt so abwechslungsreich gestaltet, dass Sie es entsprechend Ihrer Zeiteinteilung von Kapitel zu Kapitel und Seite zu Seite nach und nach bearbeiten können.

Das Buch eignet sich für Selbstlerner, die wichtige Sprachstrukturen üben und festigen wollen, aber auch als zusätzliches Übungsmaterial in allen Bildungseinrichtungen.

Viel Spaß und viel Erfolg
wünscht Ihr Hueber-Team

1

Common Mistakes in English Grammar

Inhalt Teil 1

Übungen

Seite

A. Einfache Form und Verlaufsform

1. I'm just finishing my lunch.
2. I live in Hameln.
3. A phone call
4. *Have* and *having*
5. They aren't taking a holiday this year.
6. I don't like the sound of all this.
7. Trends
8. It seems very cold.
9. I was still having breakfast.
10. I need a drink.

A1 I'm just finishing my lunch.

Was passt zusammen?

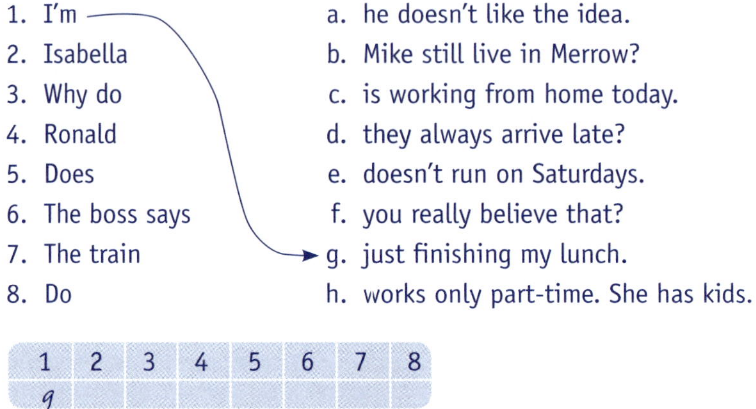

1. I'm	a. he doesn't like the idea.
2. Isabella	b. Mike still live in Merrow?
3. Why do	c. is working from home today.
4. Ronald	d. they always arrive late?
5. Does	e. doesn't run on Saturdays.
6. The boss says	f. you really believe that?
7. The train	g. just finishing my lunch.
8. Do	h. works only part-time. She has kids.

1	2	3	4	5	6	7	8
g							

A2 I live in Hameln.

Unterstreichen Sie die richtige Form.

1. I (a.) am living / (b.) live in Hameln. I've lived there all my life.
2. A friend of ours from Canada (a.) is staying / (b.) stays with us at the moment.
3. (a.) Are you enjoying / (b.) Do you enjoy the party? – Yes, thanks. I (c.) am having / (d.) have a great time.
4. (a.) I am not having / (b.) I don't have lunch in the canteen usually. I nearly always (c.) am bringing / (d.) bring something to eat from home.
5. Jackie (a.) has / (b.) is having a part-time job in a lawyer's office. But she's going to have a baby soon.
6. People (a.) aren't wanting / (b.) don't want to hear bad news. That's why politicians (c.) promise / (d.) are promising heaven on earth.

A3 A phone call

Ergänzen Sie. Zwei Ausdrücke werden nicht benötigt.

arrives • I can see • I don't think so • ~~I'm just walking~~
is just arriving • is shining • It snows • It's snowing • seem

◆ Where are you? Are you at the station yet?
● Yes, (1.) *I'm just walking* into the station building now.
◆ You're late, aren't you?
● (2.) ________________. It's 9.47, and their train is due at 9.49. It might be late because of the weather anyway.
(3.) ________________ hard here at the moment.
◆ The sun (4.) ________________ here.
● OK, I'm at the arrivals and departures board. A lot of people (5.) ________________ to be waiting. There are quite a few delays posted, but Ann & Ian's train is on time. Platform 5. Oh, (6.) ________________ it now. The train (7.) ________________.

A4 *Have* and *having*

Ergänzen Sie *I have* oder *I'm having*.

1. Sorry, *I have* no time this weekend.
2. ____________ an argument with my internet provider on the other line. I'll call you back.
3. ____________ lunch with Diana next Tuesday.
4. ____________ a really great holiday. The hotel, the beach, the people – all just great.
5. ____________ a party on 10th May. Can you come?
6. ____________ a lot to do this morning.
7. ____________ three children, two boys and a girl.

A5 They aren't taking a holiday this year.

Sortieren Sie die Teile und bilden Sie Sätze. Achtung:
Nicht alle Teile werden benötigt!

1. a holiday / aren't taking / don't take / they / this year

   They aren't taking a holiday this year.

2. does / is / mean / meaning / this symbol / what

   ____

3. Joanna / is trying / to lose / tries / some weight

   ____

4. doesn't eat / isn't eating / meat / she

   Ann's a vegetarian. ______________________________

5. is just closing / just closes / the tourist office

   ____

6. closes / earlier / is closing / it / in the winter

   ____

7. gets better / slowly / is getting better / the situation

   ____

8. am not / I / remember / don't / anything / remembering

   ____

A6 I don't like the sound of all this.

Ergänzen Sie die richtige Gegenwartsform.

1. I (not / like) ___*don't like*___ the sound of all this.
2. We (not / know) ________________ why he did it.
3. Ron and Claire (not / speak) ________________________ to each other at the moment.
4. Jem (make) ________________ real progress.
5. We (need) ________________ more time.
6. The paperback version (not / cost) ________________ so much.
7. I (not / mind) ________________ what you do.
8. What (you / do) ________________? – I (try) _______________ to repair this door handle.
9. Jan and Ed have split up. Ed (live) _____________ temporarily with me.
10. Temperatures (rise) _______________ worldwide.
11. Who (you / wait) ______________________ for?
12. What (this word / mean) __________________________?

A7 Trends

Korrigieren Sie.

1. People ~~go~~ ___*are going*___ on shorter holidays.
2. Winters ~~become~~ ________________ warmer and wetter in many parts of the globe.
3. The price of oil ~~rises~~ ________________ again.
4. More fathers ~~take~~ ________________ time off to care for their children.
5. People ~~worry~~ ________________ about the economy more.
6. Employers ~~give~~ ________________ more short-term contracts.
7. People ~~buy~~ ________________ smaller cars that use less fuel.
8. More and more people ~~live~~ ________________ a second life online.

A8 It seems very cold.

Korrigieren Sie.

1. It is ~~seeming~~ ___*seems*___ very cold. Is the heating not on?
2. ~~Are you remembering~~ ______________________ what happened?
3. She's very rich. She ~~is owning~~ ________________ six hotels.
4. No, this ~~isn't belonging~~ ______________________ to me.
5. I ~~am not seeing~~ ______________________ what you are trying to say.
6. ~~Were you understanding~~ ________________________ what he just said?

A9 I was still having breakfast.

Korrigieren Sie – falls nötig.

1. They fixed a fault in the computer system so I couldn't work.

   They were fixing a fault in the computer system so I couldn't work.

2. We didn't eat till they arrived.

   We ______________________ till they ________________.

3. We still sat at the table at midnight.

   We ______________________ at the table at midnight.

4. We saw a flash of light, then we heard a loud explosion.

   We ____________ a flash of light, then we ___________ a loud explosion.

5. I listened to music and had headphones on, so I didn't hear anything.

   I _____________ to music and _____________ headphones on, so I _____________ anything.

6. The boss walked in when we discussed his new hairstyle.

   The boss _____________ when we _______________ his new hairstyle.

7. It rained hard, so I decided to take a taxi.

   It _____________ hard, so I _____________ to take a taxi.

8. I still had breakfast when the taxi arrived.

   I ______________________ breakfast when the taxi ____________.

A10 I need a drink

Übersetzen Sie.

1. Ich brauche etwas zu trinken.

   I need a drink.

2. Es hängt alles davon ab, was es kostet.

   ____

3. Ich arbeite zurzeit von zu Hause.

   ____

4. Ich lerne Spanisch.

   ____

5. Als ich hinkam *(arrive)*, warteten schon über 50 Menschen.

   ____

6. Sie bauen ein neues Hotel.

   ____

7. Normalerweise stehe ich samstags später auf.

   ____

8. Aber heute arbeite ich.

   ____

B. Present Perfect und Vergangenheit

1. I've seen the report.
2. A or B?
3. We went to Amsterdam last weekend.
4. I've seen this film.
5. I've never eaten kangaroo.
6. When did this come?
7. An email
8. Delaying tactics
9. Have you ever ...?
10. Finders, keepers

B1 I've seen the report.

Was passt zusammen?.

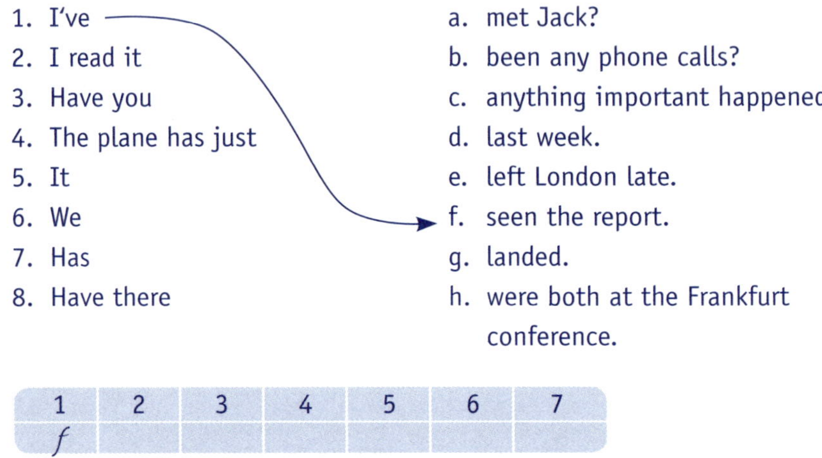

1. I've
2. I read it
3. Have you
4. The plane has just
5. It
6. We
7. Has
8. Have there

a. met Jack?
b. been any phone calls?
c. anything important happened?
d. last week.
e. left London late.
f. seen the report.
g. landed.
h. were both at the Frankfurt conference.

1	2	3	4	5	6	7
f						

B2 A or B?

Was passt: a oder b?

1. The meeting has just (a.) began / (b.) begun.
2. I've never (a.) fell / (b.) felt so good.
3. We (a.) flew / (b.) flown to Chicago, not New York.
4. I've completely (a.) forgot / (b.) forgotten.
5. She's (a.) spend / (b.) spent quite a lot of time in China.
6. We (a.) swam / (b.) swum out to an island.
7. Who (a.) laid / (b.) lay the table?
8. I (a.) laid / (b.) lay down, but I couldn't sleep.

1	2	3	4	5	6	7	8
b							

B3 We went to Amsterdam last weekend.

Streichen Sie den falschen Satz durch.

1. Wir sind letztes Wochenende nach Amsterdam gefahren.
a. ~~We have been to Amsterdam last weekend.~~
b. We went to Amsterdam last weekend.

2. Wir waren noch nie vorher dort.
a. We've never been there before.
b. We were never there before.

3. Wir waren schon einmal in Den Haag.
a. We've been to Den Haag before.
b. We were in Den Haag before.

4. Wir haben auf einem Hausboot gewohnt.
a. We've stayed in a houseboat.
b. We stayed in a houseboat.

5. Es war wunderschön.
a. It's been wonderful.
b. It was wonderful.

6. Wir haben viel gesehen und hatten viel Spaß.
a. We saw a lot and had a great time.
b. We've seen a lot and had a great time.

7. Wir sind in diesem Frühjahr bisher schon zwei Mal verreist.
a. We've been away twice so far this spring.
b. We were away twice so far this spring.

B4 I've seen this film.

Ergänzen Sie wie im Beispiel.

1. I've seen this film.

   ____*I saw it*____ last week with Hugh.

2. I've done this journey many times.

   ________________ for the first time in 2005.

3. We've begun to pack.

   ______________________________ yesterday.

4. I've spoken to Jill.

   ________________ to her on Monday.

5. I haven't slept very well.

   ________________ only three hours last night.

6. Jack has shown the visitors round.

   ________________ when they arrived.

7. I've rung the embassy.

   ________________ yesterday too.

8. I've paid the bill.

   ________________ two days ago.

9. Someone has stolen my parking space.

   ________________ on Tuesday too.

B5 I've never eaten kangaroo.

Ergänzen Sie.

decided • didn't • didn't • ~~eaten~~ • had • have eaten
said • tasted • thought • was

Have you ever (1.) *eaten* kangaroo meat? I (2.) ________ some last month when I (3.) ________ on holiday in New South Wales. It (4.) ________ strange, and I (5.) ________ really like it. But I (6.) ________ want to hurt my Australian hosts' feelings, so in true British fashion I (7.) ________ that I (8.) ________ it was "very interesting". I (9.) ________________ worse things before, but I (10.) ________ that next time some-one offers me some I will say no.

B6 When did this come?

Ergänzen Sie.

◆ When (1. this / come) *did this come*?
● Someone (2. bring) ________________ it about ten minutes ago.
◆ Why (3. you / not open) ________________ it?
● Because it's addressed to you.
◆ But I (4. not order) ________________ anything from a company called Webspan.
● Maybe you (5. do) ________________, but you (6. forget) ________________.
◆ I (7. be) ________________ very busy lately, but I (8. not become) ________________ that forgetful!

B7 An email

Ergänzen Sie Present Perfect, Vergangenheit oder Gegenwart.

Thank you for your suggestion. I (1. discuss) *have discussed* it with my colleagues and (2. be) ________________ pleased to tell you that we (3. decide) ________________ that we (4. think) ________________ it is a very good idea.
We have been partners for over 10 years now. During this time we (5. have) ________________ some difficult periods, especially since the credit crisis (6. break out) ________________ in late 2008. We (7. always look for) ________________ solutions that (8. serve) ________________ both parties, and feel that you (9. again find) ________________ one which is good for both of us.

B8 Delaying tactics

Ergänzen Sie die passenden Verben im Present Perfect.

be • buy • check • ~~drink~~ • eat • give • give up • read

(1.) *I've drunk* two cups of coffee, (2.) ________________ my emails, and (3.) ________________ the latest news online, (4.) ________________ my plants some water, (5.) ________________ to the canteen and (6.) ________________ and (7.) ________________ a chocolate bar – (8.) ________________ smoking. So I suppose I'll have to start work now ...

B9 Have you ever ...?

Ergänzen Sie die Fragen. Antworten Sie *Yes, I have* bzw. *No, I haven't.*

1. cut
   Have you ever cut your own hair? ____________
2. drive
   ____________ a sports car? ____________
3. drink
   ____________ real champagne? ____________
4. ride
   ____________ a camel? ____________
5. buy
   ____________ a diamond ring? ____________
6. wear
   ____________ a fur hat? ____________
7. sing
   ____________ in a karaoke bar? ____________
8. eat
   ____________ seaweed[1]? ____________

[1]Seetang

B10 Finders, keepers[1]

Ergänzen Sie.

(1. you / ever find) *Have you ever found* a large amount of money in the street? I have. It (2. be) ___________ a few years ago, in a country that shall remain nameless[2], but which I (3. visit) ________________________ many times in my life and which I (4. always love) ________________________ very much. It (5. be) ___________ Eastertime, and we (6. be) ___________ there on a week's holiday. It (7. be) ___________ still cold at home, and we just (8. want) ___________ to get away from the long cold winter. I (9. often dream) ________________________ of spending the winter in a warm southern country, but I (10. never have) _______ ________________ the money, and I don't expect I ever will.

Anyway, I (11. find) ____________ this 100 euro note in the street. I (12. not think) ___________________ it was right to keep it, so I (13. take) ______________________ it to the police. The first problem was that nobody (14. speak) ____________ English, and they (15. have to) _________________________ go and find the local school teacher. I (16. explain) ________________________ to her what had happened, and she (17. interpret[3]) ________________________ for the policeman. He shrugged his shoulders[4] and (18. say) ____________ something I of course (19. not understand) ________________________. The teacher (20. tell) ___________________ me that the policeman (21. not want) ________________________ any bother[5], and I should keep the money. That had never happened to me before, and (22. never happen) ________________________ again since then!

[1]Wer's findet, dem gehört's [2]das ungenannt bleiben soll [3]dolmetschen
[4]zuckte mit den Schultern [5]irgendwelche Scherereien

C. Present Perfect mit *since*, *for* und *how long*

1. *For* or *since*?
2. What's right?
3. We're old friends.
4. How long?

C

C1 *For* or *since*?

Kreuzen Sie an.

	since	for	
1.	☒	☐	2007
2.	☐	☐	two and a half years
3.	☐	☐	yesterday afternoon
4.	☐	☐	ten hours
5.	☐	☐	ten hours ago
6.	☐	☐	I don't know when
7.	☐	☐	ages
8.	☐	☐	sometime last year
9.	☐	☐	a short while
10.	☐	☐	a short while ago
11.	☐	☐	a long time
12.	☐	☐	as long as I can remember

C2 What's right?

Kreuzen Sie an.

1.	☐	a.	I have lived here for a long time.
	☐	b.	I have lived here since a long time.
2.	☐	a.	How long do you know Mike?
	☐	b.	How long have you known Mike?
3.	☐	a.	She hasn't been really fit ever since she had that accident.
	☐	b.	She isn't really fit ever since she had that accident.
4.	☐	a.	I need some help, just for half an hour.
	☐	b.	I've needed some help, just for half an hour.

C3 We're old friends.

Korrigieren Sie.

1. I ~~know~~ Jim since university.

   I have known Jim since university.

2. Mrs Franzen ~~is~~ ill ~~since~~ three weeks.

   Mrs Franzen ______________ ill ______________ three weeks.

3. How long ~~do~~ you ~~know~~ this?

   How long ______________________________ this?

4. This situation ~~is developing since~~ a long time.

   This situation ______________________________ a long time.

5. Things ~~calm down~~ since Watson ~~has left~~ the company.

   Things ______________ since Watson ______________ the company.

6. The company ~~is~~ active in Asia ~~since~~ over 30 years.

   The company ______________ active in Asia ______________ over 30 years.

7. How long ~~does~~ this problem ~~exist~~?

   How long ______________________________?

8. How long ~~are you~~ with the company?

   How long ____________________ with the company?

C4 How long?

Ergänzen Sie die Fragen wie im Beispiel.

1. live
   How long have you been living here?
2. work
   ______________________________ for this company?
3. drive
   ______________________________ a car like that?
4. learn
   ______________________________ English?
5. wait
   ______________________________?
6. try
   ______________________________ to reach me?
7. sit
   ______________________________ there?
8. train
   ______________________________ for the marathon?
9. plan
   ______________________________ this?

D. Verneinung mit und ohne *do*

1. I'm not ready.
2. A or B?
3. We're in a hurry.
4. Why not?
5. Not a cold climate
6. No, that's not right.
7. I don't ...

D1 I'm not ready.

Was passt zusammen?

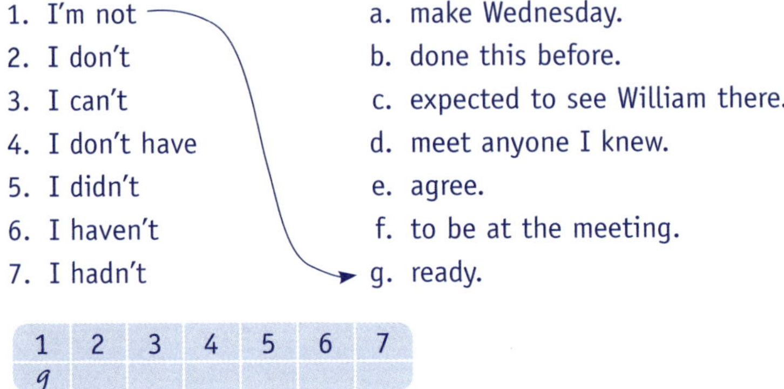

1. I'm not
2. I don't
3. I can't
4. I don't have
5. I didn't
6. I haven't
7. I hadn't

a. make Wednesday.
b. done this before.
c. expected to see William there.
d. meet anyone I knew.
e. agree.
f. to be at the meeting.
g. ready.

1	2	3	4	5	6	7
g						

D2 A or B?

Was passt: a oder b?

1. We ... see them again for a long time.
   a) aren't going to b) don't
2. I ... much sport.
   a) don't b) don't do
3. I'm sorry, but I ... much English.
   a) don't speak b) speak not
4. You've misunderstood me. I ... that!
   a) meant not b) didn't mean

1	2	3	4

D3 We're in a hurry.

Ergänzen Sie wie im Beispiel.

1. We're late.

   But we ___*aren't*___ very late.

2. I know the first man.

   But I ________________ the other one.

3. We walked over twenty miles on the first day.

   But we ________________ so far on the next two.

4. I have plenty of time.

   But I ________________ much money!

5. I've made a mistake.

   I ________________ this kind of mistake for a long time.

6. I can speak a little Spanish.

   But I ________________ any Portuguese.

7. They'll give us something to drink.

   But they ________________ us anything to eat.

8. I do the washing.

   But I ________________ the ironing.

D4 Why not?

Ergänzen Sie.

can't • didn't • don't • haven't • ~~isn't~~ • won't

1. Why *isn't* this stupid machine working?
2. Why _________ this stupid machine do what it's supposed to do?
3. Why _________ I spend a bit more money and buy something that was a bit more reliable?
4. Why _________ I just take it back to the shop and try and change it?
5. Why _________ they write instruction manuals that a normal person can understand?
6. Why _________ they updated the software?

D5 Not a cold climate

Korrigieren Sie – falls nötig.

1. It's not a very wet climate.

   korrekt
2. It rains not often.

   ____
3. We have not many frosts.

   ____
4. You haven't to have a lot of thick coats.

   ____
5. We've not had snow for years.

   ____

D6 No, that's not right.

Sortieren Sie die Teile und bilden Sie Sätze. Jeweils ein Wort wird nicht benötigt!

1. city / don't / I / in / live / not / the

   I don't live in the city.
2. before / ever / happened / hasn't / never / this

   ____
3. didn't / do / I / not / this

   ____
4. coming / don't / Frank / isn't / why

   ____
5. decide / decided / didn't / till / we / yesterday

   ____
6. do / don't / making / more / preparation/ why / you

   ____
7. absolutely / agree / don't / I / not

   ____
8. doesn't / in / passes / Torquay / stop / the / train

   ____

D7 I don't ...

Übersetzen Sie.

1. Ich mag dieses Zimmer nicht.

____

2. Wir wissen nicht, was passiert ist.

____

3. Er macht keinen Sport.

____

4. Zurzeit arbeite ich nicht.

____

5. Das ist doch nicht wirklich passiert?!

____

6. Ich habe nicht gewartet. Es war spät.

____

7. Wir wollten kein Taxi nehmen.

____

8. Er hat nicht viel Talent.

____

E. Fragen und Frageanhängsel

1. Who are you?
2. A or B?
3. How did you get there?
4. When do we arrive?
5. Questions, questions, questions
6. An interview
7. Which provider?
8. Talking to a lab technician
9. Right?
10. Right again?
11. That surprises me.

E

E1 Who are you?

Was passt zusammen?

1. Who are
2. What sort of car
3. When does
4. Who
5. Who do
6. What did
7. Why have
8. What colours
9. Which colour

a. the match start?
b. knows the answer?
c. they invited that idiot?
d. are there?
e. has she got?
f. it cost?
g. is best, do you think?
h. you?
i. you know here?

1	2	3	4	5	6	7	8	9
h								

E2 A or B?

Was ist richtig: a oder b?

1. When ... the problem start?
   a) did b) has
2. Who ... the presentation?
   a) did give b) gave
3. What ...? Maybe I can help.
   a) do you need b) need you
4. Which hotel ... for you?
   a) they booked b) did they book

1	2	3	4

E3 How did you get there?

Ergänzen Sie die Frage.

1. ◆ How (get) *did you get* here?
   ● I came by car.
2. ◆ (like) ____________ Italian food?
   ● Oh yes! I love it!
3. ◆ (take) ____________ anyone with you?
   ● Yes, I'm taking Fran and Megan.
4. ◆ (do) ____________ anything interesting?
   ● Not really. We had a very lazy two days.
5. ◆ What (should / wear) ____________ ?
   ● It doesn't really matter. They're always very informal.
6. ◆ Who (cook) ____________ in your family when you were a kid?
   ● Actually it was mostly my dad.
7. ◆ Who (ask) ____________ when you needed advice?
   ● That was usually my mum.
8. ◆ Who (go shopping) ____________ in your family?
   ● I do!

E4 When do we arrive?

Streichen Sie den falschen Satz durch.

1. Wann kommen wir an?
a. ~~When we arrive?~~
b. When do we arrive?

2. Was bedeutet dieses Wort?
a. What does this word mean?
b. What means this word?

3. Wen kennst du?
a. Who know you?
b. Who do you know?

4. Wie viel muss ich bezahlen?
a. How much do I have to pay?
b. How much do I must pay?

5. Brauchen Sie ein Taschentuch?
a. Do you need a handkerchief?
b. Need you a handkerchief?

6. Wer schreibt die Einladungen?
a. Who is writing the invitations?
b. Who does write the invitations?

E5 Questions, questions, questions

Was passt zusammen?

1. Does Tina know about the meeting?
2. Will you be at Sandra's party?
3. Has the water boiled?
4. Did you get my message?
5. Can you see OK from where you're sitting?
6. Are you ready?
7. Did they reach an agreement?
8. Have the tickets come?

a. Yes, it has.
b. Yes, I did thanks.
c. Almost. Are you?
d. Not really. Can you?
e. No, I won't, I'm afraid.
f. No, I'm afraid they didn't.
g. Yes, they came in this morning's post.
h. Yes, she does.

1	2	3	4	5	6	7	8
h							

E6 An interview

Ergänzen Sie.

- ◆ So where (1. you be) ___*were you*___ last night between 10.30 and midnight?
- ● At home, in bed.
- ◆ (2. anyone can) ________________ confirm[1] that? (3. you be) ________________ with anyone?
- ● That's none of your business!
- ◆ It may be in your interest to have a witness[2].
  When (4. you hear) ________________ about the break-in at your office?
- ● This morning. My secretary called me.
- ◆ What time (5. you get) ________________ this call?
- ● I don't know, 8.15, 8.30.
- ◆ (6. he know) ________________ that the company is in serious financial difficulties?
- ● He's my secretary. I don't tell him everything.
- ◆ How long (7. you be) ________________ in debt[3]?
- ● What does all this have to do with the break-in?
- ◆ That's what I am trying to find out.
  What (8. you do) ________________ after you got the call?
- ● I called my insurance company.
- ◆ Why (9. you do) ________________ that?
- ● Because that's what I didn't do the last time the offices were broken into! It was a big mistake.

[1]bestätigen [2]Zeuge [3]verschuldet

E7 Which provider?

Ergänzen Sie die Frage.

1. Which provider (you / use) *do you use*?
2. Which providers (be) ______________ the most popular?
3. How many people (you / interview) __________________________ in last month's survey?
4. How many people (come) ______________ to last month's presentation?
5. What (interest) ______________ people most at conferences like this?
6. What (people / like) _____________________ about conferences like this?
7. Who (phone) ______________ the police? Was it you?
8. Who else (you / inform) ______________? Did you tell Mr Roberts?
9. Where (you / be) ______________? I've been looking for you everywhere.
10. Where (you / sit) ______________? I didn't see you.

E8 Talking to a lab technician

Ergänzen Sie.

- ◆ Where (1. you come) *do you come* from?
- ● The north of England.
- ◆ And what (2. you do) ______________?
- ● I'm a lab technician.
- ◆ What sort of company (3. you work) ______________ for?
- ● A food manufacturer.
- ◆ (4. you be) ______________ with them a long time?
- ● Three years.
- ◆ (5. it be) ____________ an interesting job?
- ● It's OK.
- ◆ (6. you have to) __________________ study or train a long time to get your qualifications?
- ● Quite a long time, but I didn't go to university.
- ◆ (7. you be) _________ married? (8. you have) ______________ children?
- ● It's no on both of those.
- ◆ (9. you always live) ______________________ where you live now?
- ● No, I grew up near London.

E9 Right?

Was passt zusammen?

1. This is a lovely hotel,
2. A Danish company bought it,
3. You speak some French,
4. They haven't decided yet,
5. You can't swim,
6. Reg lives in Horsham,
7. The tyres need replacing,
8. It won't make a lot of difference,

a. don't you?
b. have they?
c. doesn't he?
d. don't they?
e. will it?
f. didn't they?
g. isn't it?
h. can you?

1	2	3	4	5	6	7	8
g							

E10 Right again?

Ergänzen Sie das passende Frageanhängsel.

1. You don't like Phelps, ___do you___?
2. We're going to be late, ____________________?
3. It didn't cost as much as last time, ____________________?
4. You'll be coming, ____________________?
5. John wasn't there, ____________________?
6. Gerda always looks so good, ____________________?
7. You eat meat, ____________________?

E11 That surprises me.

Ergänzen Sie.

1. ◆ We're all rather worried.
   ● ____*Are you*____? I don't think there's any reason to be.
2. ◆ I can't believe that robots can do this job.
   ● ____*Can't you*____? They can do amazing things these days.
3. ◆ I don't want to go.
   ● ________________? Whyever not? It's going to be a great event.
4. ◆ She loves anything exotic – oriental, African, Arabic.
   ● ________________? I hope she eats 'normal' European food, too.
5. ◆ I know this film.
   ● ________________? I've never seen it before.
6. ◆ They keep asking for more money.
   ● ________________? Well, I would just refuse.
7. ◆ We ran out of petrol.
   ● ________________? So how did you get here?
8. ◆ The snow didn't last.
   ● ________________? So no skiing?

F. Zukunftsformen

1. I'll ...
2. I'll have fish.
3. A or B?
4. All right?
5. More than one option

F

F1 I'll ...

Korrigieren Sie.

1. ~~Wait, I help you.~~

   Wait, I'll help you.

2. ~~I give you a hand.~~

   ____

3. ~~I lend you the money.~~

   ____

4. ~~I give you a lift.~~

   ____

5. Just a moment, ~~I get Simon for you.~~

   Just a moment, ______________________________

6. ~~He calls you back.~~

   ____

7. ~~I see if she's here.~~

   ____

8. ~~They let you know~~ as soon as possible.

   ______________________________ as soon as possible.

F2 I'll have fish.

Ergänzen Sie.

◆ Are you ready to order?
● I think so. Amy? Have you decided?
■ (1. have) *I'll have* the fish, please.
◆ And what would you like with that? Salad or vegetables?
■ (2. take) ______________ vegetables, please.
◆ And you, sir?
● I think (3. have) ______________ the steak.
◆ Certainly, sir. And how would you like it?
● Medium, please. No, (4. have) ______________ it rare.
◆ Certainly. And what would you like to drink?
● I think (5. we try) ______________ the South African red. Is that OK with you, Amy?
■ Sure.
◆ It's a very nice wine, I can really recommend it. A bottle?
● Yes, please.
■ And (6. we take) ______________ a bottle of mineral water, too.
◆ Sparkling or still?
■ Still, please.
◆ Any starters?
■ (7. not have) ______________ anything, thanks.
● Nor me, thanks. (8. we have) ______________ a dessert instead.

F3 A or B?

Was stimmt: a oder b?

1. a) I expect we meet again in Frankfurt.
   b) I expect we'll meet again in Frankfurt.
2. a) He doesn't want to stay the night because he's leaving on a business trip the next morning.
   b) He will not stay the night because he's leaving on a business trip the next morning.
3. a) I have a feeling that something awful happens.
   b) I have a feeling that something awful is going to happen.
4. a) What do you do this Friday? Do you have time then?
   b) What are you doing this Friday? Do you have time then?
5. a) We don't go away this Christmas.
   b) We're not going away this Christmas.
6. a) We leave the dog with Karen's parents as usual.
   b) We'll be leaving the dog with Karen's parents as usual.

1	2	3	4	5	6
b					

F4 All right?

Kreuzen Sie alle richtigen Lösungen an.

1. When we're in London next month,

- ☐ a. we'll be staying with friends.
- ☐ b. we're going to stay with friends.
- ☐ c. we're staying with friends.
- ☐ d. we stay with friends.

2. The weather forecast doesn't sound too good.

- ☐ a. I expect it rains at the weekend.
- ☐ b. I expect it'll rain at the weekend.
- ☐ c. I expect it's going to rain at the weekend.
- ☐ d. I expect it's raining at the weekend.

3. He's no longer a youngster!

- ☐ a. He'll be 50 next year.
- ☐ b. He'll be being 50 next year.
- ☐ c. He's 50 next year.
- ☐ d. He's going to be 50 next year.

4. How much wine should I get?

- ☐ a. How many people are coming?
- ☐ b. How many people are going to be coming?
- ☐ c. How many people come?
- ☐ d. How many people will be coming?

F5 More than one option

Ergänzen Sie eine passende Zukunftsform.

1. The meeting tomorrow (only be) __________________ two hours.
2. Maybe there (not be) __________________ enough time to discuss everything.
3. We (move) __________________ house next month.
4. This time next week I (lie) __________________ on the beach.
5. By this time next week we (do) __________________ most of the work.
6. When (you take) __________________ your exam?
7. I suppose (you have) __________________ next Friday off.
8. Maybe the recession (not be) __________________ as bad as all the experts are forecasting.
9. There's no point in rushing. The train (leave) __________________ by now.

G. Aktiv und Passiv

1. Record holders etc.
2. Who did it?
3. A or B?
4. From active to passive
5. Tourist questions
6. Who and/or what?
7. Who did it?

G1 Record holders etc.

Ergänzen Sie.

a film • a ~~horror story~~ • a play • a series of children's books

J.K. Rowling • ~~Steven King~~ • Steven Spielberg • William Shakespeare

1. THE DARK TOWER Stephen King — *a horror story by Steven King*

2. Harry Potter and the Philosopher's Stone; Harry Potter and the Chamber of Secrets; Harry Potter and the Prisoner of Azkaban ____________________

3. Jurassic Park ____________________

4. Macbeth ____________________

Und nun korrigieren Sie.

Michael Schumacher   Steffi Graf

5. The record for tennis Grand Slam singles titles is held ~~from Margaret Court~~.
   It ____________________.

6. The record for Formula 1 championships is held ~~from Juan Fangio~~.
   It ____________________.

G2 Who did it?

Was passt zusammen?

1. Someone has
2. Over 1000 hits
3. We are being
4. Over one million euros have
5. The road was
6. A far higher number of sales had
7. English is
8. Many of these places had not

a. asked to accept pay cuts.
b. been discovered as tourist destinations.
c. widened last year.
d. left a message on the answering machine.
e. been expected.
f. were recorded on the website within the first two hours.
g. been spent.
h. spoken all over the world.

1	2	3	4	5	6	7	8
d							

G3 A or B?

Was passt: a oder b?

1. We ... made to feel very unwelcome.
   a) was b) were
2. 'Yesterday' was a famous song ... the Beatles.
   a) by b) from
3. I couldn't get into the room because it ... .
   a) was being cleaned b) was cleaned
4. Where ...? I seem to recognize that tree.
   a) has this photo been taken b) was this photo taken?
5. Bags ... at reception.
   a) can be left b) can left
6. A new model ...
   a) has just been launched b) is just launched
7. Reminders ... next week.
   a) will be sent out b) will send out
8. A lot of changes ... since then.
   a) are made b) have been made
9. ...
   a) By who was the brochure designed?
   b) Who was the brochure designed by?
10. We ... refreshing cold drinks when we arrived.
    a) were being offered b) were offered

1	2	3	4	5	6	7	8	9	10
b									

G4 From active to passive

Wandeln Sie wie im Beispiel um.

1. Someone has made a serious mistake.
   A serious mistake has been made.
2. They'll tell us tomorrow.
   We ______________________________ tomorrow.
3. They're still testing the system.
   The system ______________________________
4. They didn't invite us.
   We ______________________________
5. Someone was filming the event.
   The event ______________________________
6. They are re-printing the book.
   The book ______________________________
7. They ate up all the food in minutes!
   All the food ______________________________ in minutes!
8. Nobody had expected such a huge crowd.
   Such a huge crowd ______________________________
9. They are monitoring all phone calls and emails.
   All phone calls and emails ______________________________

G5 Tourist questions

Übersetzen Sie.

1. Wann wurde das Schloss errichtet?

   When was the castle built?

2. Wann ist das Hotel eröffnet worden?

3. Wann werden die Koffer abgeholt (werden)?

4. Wo sind die Tickets ausgestellt [*issue*] worden?

5. Wie sind Sie informiert worden?

6. Wird der Briefkasten heute geleert [*empty*] (werden)?

7. Warum sind die Betten nicht gemacht worden?

8. Hat man unsere Bestellung vergessen?

9. Wird ein Trinkgeld erwartet?

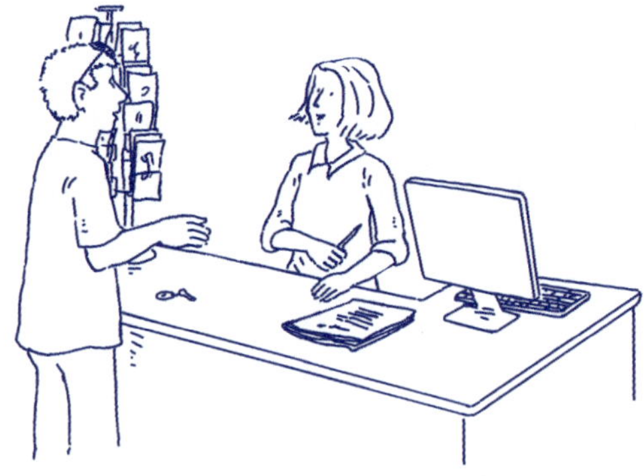

G6 Who and/or what?

Was ist richtig: a, b oder a und b?

1. We had to answer lots of questions.

   a. We were asked lots of questions.
   b. Lots of questions were asked.

2. Someone explained the rules to us.

   a. The rules were explained to us.
   b. We were explained the rules.

3. They offered me help with the removal costs as part of the deal.

   a. Help with the removal costs was offered as part of the deal.
   b. I was offered help with the removal costs as part of the deal.

4. They gave us very little time to make up our mind.

   a. Us was given very little time to make up our mind.
   b. We were given very little time to make up our mind.

5. They promised me assistance.

   a. Assistance was promised.
   b. I was promised assistance.

6. They suggested that we should re-think the packaging.

   a. It was suggested that we should re-think the packaging.
   b. We were suggested to re-think the packaging.

7. They described the whole process in great detail.

   a. The whole process was described in great detail.
   b. We were described the whole process in great detail.

G7 Who did it?

Ergänzen Sie die Rückfragen, indem Sie das Passiv verwenden.

1. A famous British architect designed the museum.
   Sorry. Who was it designed by ?
2. They've deposited the key with the neighbours.
   Sorry, who ______ with?
3. The interim manager will inform the workforce.
   Sorry. Who ______?
4. Local business people are sponsoring the event.
   Sorry, who ______?
5. The CEO signed the letter.
   Sorry, who ______?
6. The company has been taken over by a foreign investor.
   Sorry, who ______?
7. Edison invented it.
   Sorry, who ______?
8. The government is going to bail the company out[1].
   Sorry, who ______?

[1]eine Bürgschaft übernehmen für

H. Infinitiv und Gerundium

1. A or B?
2. Do you enjoy cooking?
3. They aren't taking a holiday this year.
4. Would you like ...?
5. I saw it happen.
6. She accused me.
7. *By, instead, without, ...*
8. What are you afraid of?
9. A or B?

H1 A or B?

Was passt: a oder b?

1. a) I hope to be able to come.
   b) I hope being able to come.

2. a) We've just finished repairing the broken window.
   b) We've just finished to repair the broken window.

3. a) I suggested calling Alexander and asking him.
   b) I suggested to call Alexander and ask him.

4. a) I'd like trying to learn Dutch.
   b) I'd like to try and learn Dutch.

5. a) We've decided to wait.
   b) We've decided waiting.

6. a) I've given up to try.
   b) I've given up trying.

7. a) You can't avoid making mistakes on a project like this.
   b) You can't avoid to make mistakes on a project like this.

8. a) I refuse taking no as an answer.
   b) I refuse to take no as an answer.

9. a) I don't mind paying a bit extra if the quality is good.
   b) I don't mind to pay a bit extra if the quality is good.

10. a) I can't imagine doing your job.
    b) I can't imagine to do your job.

11. a) We're looking forward to see you again.
    b) We're looking forward to seeing you again.

1	2	3	4	5	6	7	8	9	10	11
a										

H2 Do you enjoy cooking?

Ergänzen Sie die richtige Form.

1. ◆ Do you enjoy (cook) ___cooking___ for a big crowd?
   ● Yes, I do. And I like (try out) ______________ new recipes.

2. ◆ Don't do it! You'll risk (make) ______________ an enemy of the man. And that's something you'd regret (do) ______________ till the end of your days.
   ● What would you recommend (do) ______________ then?

3. ◆ We need to practise (do) ______________ this in a hurry.
   ● Yes, we don't want (make) ______________ any mistakes.

4. ◆ Can you remind me (ask) ______________ Jill for the address?
   ● I can't promise (remember) ______________.

5. ◆ It's no use (worry) ______________.
   ● No, you're right. There's no point (get) ______________ anxious.
   ◆ Just stop (worry) ______________ and hope for the best.

6. ◆ I was looking forward to (enjoy) ______________ a nice long lazy weekend. I felt like (stay) ______________ in bed all weekend. But then Martin decided (do) ______________ a blitz on the garden.

H3 They aren't taking a holiday this year.

Sortieren Sie die Teile und bilden Sie Sätze. Achtung: Je ein Teil wird nicht benötigt!

1. badly / behaving / he / liking / seems / to like

   He seems to like behaving badly.

2. a lift / I / giving / offered / them / to give

3. at the café / don't / me / meeting / mention / to meet

4. admit / being / I / there / to be

5. asking for / help / I / really dislike / to ask

6. can't / carry on / like this / meeting / to meet / we

7. closing / discussed / the factory in Poland / they / to close

8. about it / claims / having / he / known / nothing / to have

H4 Would you like ...?

Korrigieren Sie.

1. ~~Would you like that I help you?~~
   Would you like me to help you?
2. ~~Would you like that we wait for you?~~
   ______________________________ for you?
3. ~~I'd like that you go to the conference for us.~~
   ______________________________ to the conference for us.
4. ~~I want that you completely re-do this.~~
   ______________________________ completely re-do this.
5. ~~Does he really expect that I work every weekend?~~
   ______________________________ every weekend?
6. ~~I need that you pick up the children from school.~~
   ______________________________ the children from school.
7. ~~Would you like that I shut the window?~~
   ______________________________ the window?
8. ~~Do you want that I take Sven to the airport?~~
   ______________________________ Sven to the airport?
9. ~~I'd love that he makes just one mistake.~~
   ______________________________ just one mistake.

H5 I saw it happen.

Unterstreichen Sie die richtige Form.

1. I saw it (a.) happen / (b.) to happen.
2. We've decided not (a.) book / (b.) to book in advance.
3. Just don't let this (a.) happen / (b.) to happen again!
4. Can you get someone (a.) clear up / (b.) to clear up the room?
5. We'd better (a.) leave / (b.) to leave fairly soon because of the traffic.
6. I'll make them (a.) pay / (b.) to pay for this!
7. They won't let me (a.) park / (b.) to park any closer.
8. Did you hear the police cars (a.) pass by / (b.) to pass by?

1	2	3	4	5	6	7	8
a							

H6 She accused me.

Was passt zusammen?

1. She accused me
2. Banks were criticized
3. The protesters were prevented
4. They thanked us
5. I'm very proud
6. There's no real alternative
7. Is there any chance
8. We've had little success

a. from entering the building by the police.
b. of doing it all by myself.
c. to flying. It's too far away.
d. of finding a flat for under 600 euros?
e. of trying to manoeuvre her out of her job.
f. for looking after their cat.
g. in finding a replacement for Sarah Johnson.
h. for lending to people who weren't credit-worthy.

1	2	3	4	5	6	7	8
e							

H7 *By, instead, without, ...*

Wandeln Sie wie im Beispiel um.

1. If you book online, you can save quite a bit. (by)
   You can save quite a bit by booking online.
2. Let's not go on the bus, but let's take a taxi. (instead)
   ______ instead of ______
3. I asked the question. I didn't even think. (without)
   ______ without ______
4. If you read a lot, you can improve your vocabulary. (by)
   ______ by ______
5. Scan the attachment for viruses, then open it. (before)
   Before ______
6. We drove all the way. We didn't stop. (without)
   ______ without ______
7. I won't have coffee, I'll take tea for a change. (instead)
   Instead ______
8. He invested in the stock market and lost a lot of money. (by)
   ______ by ______

H8 What are you afraid of?

Ergänzen Sie.

at • for • in • of • on

1. I'm always afraid _of_ making a mistake.
2. I'd be interested _____ finding out more.
3. Sandra's good _____ dealing with this sort of problem.
4. I got tired _____ waiting and left.
5. Are you in favour _____ commissioning an independent review?
6. I don't believe _____ being soft on beginners.
7. Do you have any specific reason _____ asking this?
8. I'm grateful to you _____ informing me so promptly.
9. I'd like to congratulate you _____ making such a good choice.
10. Is there any point _____ continuing with this?

H9 A or B?

Was stimmt: a oder b?

1. a) I must remember calling Janine and ask her how she got on at her interview. — b) I must remember to call Janine and ask her how she got on at her interview.
2. a) Have you forgotten losing our way when we went there the first time? — b) Have you forgotten to lose our way when we went there the first time?
3. a) I forgot paying the bill, and now they've sent a reminder. — b) I forgot to pay the bill, and now they've sent a reminder.
4. a) Don't you remember meeting them in Amsterdam once, quite by chance? — b) Don't you remember to meet them in Amsterdam once, quite by chance?
5. a) I stopped on the way down once to stretch my legs. — b) I stopped on the way down once stretching my legs.
6. a) I've stopped even opening all these junk-mail newsletters. — b) I've stopped even to open all these junk-mail newsletters.
7. a) I meant to ask you: have you got your money back yet? — b) I meant asking you: have you got your money back yet?
8. a) Flying with a budget airline usually means getting up in the middle of the night. — b) Flying with a budget airline usually means to get up in the middle of the night.

1	2	3	4	5	6	7	8
b							

I. *if*-Sätze

1. *If* or *when*?
2. With or without *will*?
3. If I know ...
4. What's wrong?
5. I'll deal with it.
6. If ..., then ...

I1 *If* or *when*?

Ergänzen Sie.

1. I'm meeting Ann next week. _When_ I see her, I'll tell her what you need.
2. Would it be OK ________ I came a little later?
3. I'll do the plan ________ I have all the data. That should be by tomorrow at the latest.
4. ________ Jonathan agrees, we can borrow his boat.
5. ________ the weather stays fine, we could have a barbecue.
6. ________ it's fine, we often have a barbecue.
7. I don't know what I would do ________ I didn't have you to help me.
8. ________ you get stuck, give me a call.
9. ________ I'm not there, just take a taxi.

I2 With or without *will*?

Unterstreichen Sie die richtige Form.

1. When I sleep in old buildings, I (a.) seem / (b.) will seem to dream more.
2. (a.) We eat / (b.) We'll eat when Jack gets here. He said he'd be here by seven.
3. When I see Mervin, (a.) I check / (b.) I'll check if he's got everything he needs.
4. If they find out, (a.) there's / (b.) there will be hell to pay.

I3 If I know ...

Was passt zusammen?

1. If I know the answer by this evening,
2. What would you have done
3. What will you do
4. They'll be here by six
5. They'd be here by six
6. They would have been here by six
7. What would you do
8. If I knew the answer,
9. If I had known the answer then,

a. if your firm moved its base to another country?
b. if there are no problems with the traffic.
c. if they left at four.
d. if I hadn't warned you?
e. if they hadn't had that breakdown.
f. I'll let you know.
g. if the weather's bad?
h. I wouldn't have to ask you!
i. we would have been saved a lot of trouble.

1	2	3	4	5	6	7	8	9
f								

I4 What's wrong?

Korrigieren Sie.

1. ~~It would be better if I would have more time.~~

   _______ *It would be better if I had more time.* _______

2. ~~If you will want, I can come back later.~~

   ____________________, ________ come back later.

3. ~~If I would have seen you, I had stopped.~~

   ____

4. ~~It made me feel happier if I would be more prepared.~~

   ________ feel happier, ____________ more prepared.

5. ~~If it wouldn't been cheaper, I didn't buy it from a foreign company.~~

   ________________________ from a foreign company.

6. ~~Where would you live if you can choose?~~

   ____

7. ~~They hadn't invited me to the meeting if Hannah didn't said something.~~

   ________________ to the meeting ________________
   something.

8. ~~We fly on a weekday if we would have the choice.~~

   __________ on a weekday ________________ the choice.

I5 I'll deal with it.

Ergänzen Sie die richtige Form.

1. I (deal) ___*will deal*___ with it this weekend if I have time.
2. She says she (be) ______________ back at work on Monday if all goes well.
3. If he had recognized the warning signs, he (not be) ______________ ___________ so surprised at what happened.
4. If you (not drink) ______________ wine in the evenings, you would sleep much better.
5. If Ronald (call) ______________, can you ask him to leave a message, please?
6. What (you / do) ______________________ if they had said there were no places left?
7. If I (have) ______________ their mobile number, I could give them a call.
8. If we (can) ______________ sell our house for a decent price, we might move.
9. Think how much better things would be if everyone (have) ______________ their own room.
10. If I (not see) ______________ it with my own eyes, I (not believe) _________________________ it!
11. If Noel (not go) ______________ to that exhibition, he (never meet) ____________________________ Sophie.
12. If I (not read) ______________ the book, I (not understand) ___________________________ the movie.

I6 If ..., then ...

Übersetzen Sie.

1. Wenn der Bus nicht bald kommt, gehe ich zu Fuß.

   ____

2. Ich hätte nicht ja gesagt, wenn ich Zweifel gehabt *[be in doubt]* hätte.

   ____

3. Ich würde dir helfen, wenn ich wüsste wie.

   ____

4. Wenn er mich noch einmal Fritzi nennt, bringe ich ihn um!

   ____

5. Wenn wir verloren hätten, wäre es nicht das Ende der Welt gewesen.

   ____

6. Es wäre schrecklich, wenn wir das Wetter kontrollieren könnten.

   ____

7. Auch wenn sie es mir schenken würden, würde ich es nicht haben wollen.

   ____

8. Wenn ich die richtige Kleidung mitgenommen hätte, hätte ich nicht die ganze Woche gefroren.

   ____

9. Wenn die Firma nicht diese riskanten Investitionen getätigt hätte, wäre sie nicht bankrott gegangen.

   ____

J. Modalverben

1. Does Bernd have to ...?
2. I can't swim.
3. *Mustn't* or *needn't*
4. Can do!
5. I've been able to contact him.
6. *Have to*
7. All right?
8. *Can, may,* etc.
9. A or B?

J1 Does Bernd have to ...?

Was passt zusammen?

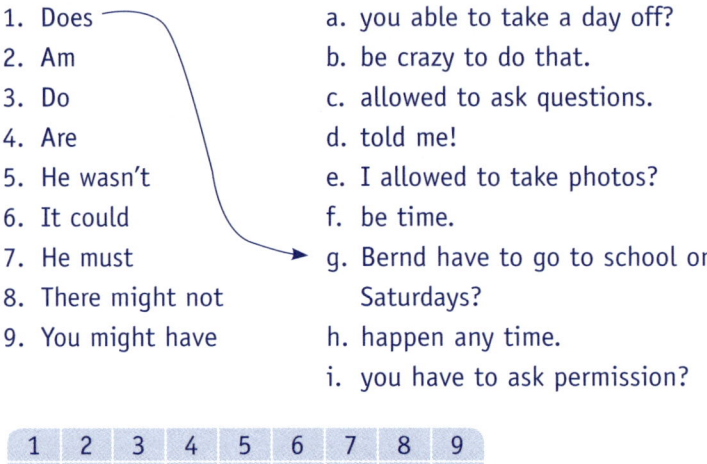

1. Does
2. Am
3. Do
4. Are
5. He wasn't
6. It could
7. He must
8. There might not
9. You might have

a. you able to take a day off?
b. be crazy to do that.
c. allowed to ask questions.
d. told me!
e. I allowed to take photos?
f. be time.
g. Bernd have to go to school on Saturdays?
h. happen any time.
i. you have to ask permission?

1	2	3	4	5	6	7	8	9
g								

J2 I can't swim.

Ergänzen Sie.

~~can't~~ • couldn't • might not • mustn't • shall • will • would

1. I'm very embarrassed about the fact that I ___can't___ swim.
2. ____________ I see if he's there?
3. We ____________ be able to come. I'll let you know tomorrow.
4. You ____________ do that! There'll be all hell to pay if they find out.
5. Anna ____________ come because she was away on business.
6. ____________ you agree that this is not the best time to try and sell?
7. I just heard the door. That ____________ be Andy.

J3 *Mustn't* or *needn't*

Ergänzen Sie.

1. You ___________ laugh. It's a serious matter.
2. You ___________ hurry. We've still got lots of time.
3. I ___________ forget to take a camera.
4. The Thompsons ___________ worry. Nobody is going to build a supermarket in a neighbourhood like this.
5. Frank and Joel ___________ attend. I know they have more important things to deal with.
6. Something like that ___________ cost a lot of money.

J4 Can do!

Ergänzen Sie das fehlende Wort.

1. Ich kann Französisch.
   I can ______ French.
2. Bitte schreib du die Karte. Du kannst es so gut.
   You write the card please. You can ______ it so well.

J5 I've been able to contact him.

Ergänzen Sie die richtige Form.

could have • ~~couldn't~~ • haven't been able to • wasn't able to
weren't able to • won't be able to

1. I've managed to speak to Jack at last. I *couldn't* get hold of him yesterday.
2. From next week you ______________________ park here any more. They're going to start building on the site.
3. I'm still looking for a present. I ______________________ find anything suitable yet.
4. We would have loved to stay longer, but we ________________. We had to get back.
5. Sven wasn't at the meeting, so I ________________ ask him.
6. The effects ________________ been much worse. We were very lucky.

had to • ~~will have to~~ • will have to • won't have to

7. It's no good. We *will have to* ask for more time.
8. I ________________ wait over two hours. I was furious!
9. You ________________ be more careful in future.
10. Don't worry. You ________________ say anything.

J6 *Have to*

Korrigieren Sie.

1. I ~~hadn't to~~ wait very long.
   I *didn't have to* wait very long.

2. What ~~have we to~~ do?
   What ______________________ do?

3. When ~~have we to~~ be there?
   When ______________________ be there?

4. Why ~~must you~~ say that? That was stupid.
   Why ______________________ say that? That was stupid.

5. The work ~~mustn't~~ be handed in till Monday.
   The work ______________________ be handed in till Monday.

6. I was really quite surprised. We ~~mustn't~~ show any ID.
   I was really quite surprised. We __________________ show any ID.

7. How long ~~had you to~~ wait?
   How long ______________________ wait?

8. If your flight's at 6.30 tomorrow morning, ~~mustn't~~ you get up very early?
   If your flight's at 6.30 tomorrow morning, ______________________ get up very early?

J7 All right?

Kreuzen Sie alle richtigen Lösungen an.

1. I'm afraid I can't let you in just like that.
   - ☐ a. Can I see your ID, please?
   - ☐ b. Could I see your ID, please?
   - ☐ c. May I see your ID, please?

2. I'm afraid I have to ask you to leave.
   - ☐ a. It isn't allowed to use mobile phones here.
   - ☐ b. You can't to use mobile phones here.
   - ☐ c. You aren't allowed to use mobile phones here.

3. They seem to have changed things.
   - ☐ a. We've never been allowed to park here before.
   - ☐ b. We've never can park here before.
   - ☐ c. We've never could park here before.

4. Where's Jack? He organized this meeting.
   - ☐ a. He can't have forgotten, can he?
   - ☐ b. He can't have forgotten, has he?
   - ☐ c. He mustn't have forgotten, must he?

5. I don't think we can just march in and help ourselves.
   - ☐ a. We had better to ask first.
   - ☐ b. We ought to ask first.
   - ☐ c. We should ask first.

J8 *Can, may,* etc.

Ergänzen Sie in der richtigen Zeitform.

1. Es kann sein, dass sie unsere Pässe sehen wollen.
   They ___________ want to see our passports.
2. Es könnte sein, dass ich nicht komme.
   I ___________ not come.
3. Es kann morgen regnen. Wir wissen es nicht.
   It ___________ rain tomorrow. We don't know.
4. Konnten sie den Fehler finden?
   _________________ find the fault?
5. Musstet ihr etwas unterschreiben?
   _________________ sign anything?
6. Auf diesen Augenblick habe ich lange warten müssen.
   I _________________ wait a long time for this moment.
7. Es darf nicht passieren.
   It _________________ happen.
8. Ich weiß nicht, mit wem sie spricht. Es kann Peter sein.
   I don't know who she's talking to. It ___________ be Peter.

J9 A or B?

Was stimmt: a oder b?

1. a) When you lost your job, it must be very difficult for you.
   b) When you lost your job, it must have been very difficult for you.

2. a) I may can help you. Ask me again tomorrow.
   b) I may be able to help you. Ask me again tomorrow.

3. a) Fantastic. You must be feeling over the moon!
   b) Fantastic. You must feeling over the moon!

4. a) Things could been worse, so I shouldn't complain.
   b) Things could have been worse, so I shouldn't complain.

5. a) To have to sit and watch and not be able to do anything was the hardest part.
   b) To must to sit and watch and not be able to do anything was the hardest part.

1	2	3	4	5
b				

K. Artikel und Begleiter

1. On Monday
2. Twice a month
3. A or B?
4. They argued and argued.
5. I'm a teacher.
6. A or B?
7. St. Pancras Station
8. A friend
9. Love
10. All right?

K1 On Monday

Was passt zusammen?

1. You can tell me when I see you on
2. We meet on the
3. The next meeting is on
4. We meet for
5. We don't meet so often in the
6. There's a break in

a. the second of March.
b. summer.
c. brunch.
d. August.
e. first Saturday in the month.
f. Friday.

1	2	3	4	5	6
f					

K2 Twice a month

Korrigieren Sie.

1. We meet ~~twice in the month~~.
   We meet *twice a month*.
2. Fresh rolls are baked ~~four times in the day~~.
   Fresh rolls are baked ______________________.
3. There's a bus to the local town only ~~twice in the week.~~
   There's a bus to the local town only ______________________.
4. It's the sort of thing that happens ~~once in the lifetime~~.
   It's the sort of thing that happens ______________________.

K3 A or B?

Was stimmt: a oder b?

1. a) Our son is training as a teacher.
   b) Our son is training as teacher.

2. a) My boss is a workaholic.
   b) My boss is workaholic.

3. a) Why are you always in a such hurry?
   b) Why are you always in such a hurry?

4. a) What a beautiful day!
   b) What for a beautiful day!

5. a) What a beautiful weather!
   b) What beautiful weather!

6. a) Tony is a golfer.
   b) Tony is golfer.

7. a) He's a member of several clubs.
   b) He's member of several clubs.

8. a) Please have a seat.
   b) Please take seat.

1	2	3	4	5	6	7	8
a							

K4 They argued and argued.

Was passt zusammen?

1. They argued all weekend, almost without
2. We need to look at the system as
3. What do you do for
4. I haven't seen Amy for
5. Let's just stay at home for
6. Oh dear, what

a. a living?
b. a long time.
c. a whole.
d. a break.
e. a pity.
f. a change.

1	2	3	4	5	6
d					

K5 I'm a teacher.

Übersetzen Sie.

1. Ich bin Lehrerin.

   I'm a teacher.

2. Es war so eine furchtbare Reise.

   ____

3. Was für ein Auto fährt er?

   ____

4. Was für ein herrliches Wetter!

   ____

5. Wir treffen uns einmal im Monat.

   ____

K6 A or B?

Was stimmt: a oder b?

1. a) Where do your children go to school?
   b) Where do your children go to the school?

2. a) They are closing school in Green Street.
   b) They are closing the school in Green Street.

3. a) When was church built?
   b) When was the church built?

4. a) Do people in this country still go to church?
   b) Do people in this country still go to the church?

5. a) At least half the people didn't notice anything.
   b) At least the half of the people didn't notice anything.

6. a) Most people were asleep.
   b) The most people were asleep.

7. a) Who got most the votes?
   b) Who got the most votes?

8. a) It's been like this all week.
   b) It's been like this the all week.

1	2	3	4	5	6	7	8
a							

K7 St. Pancras Station

Ergänzen Sie *the*, wenn es nötig ist.

1. Eurostar trains arrive at __–__ St. Pancras Station.
2. Which river runs through London? Is it ______ Thames?
3. I love ______ Alps.
4. I have no desire to climb ______ Mount Everest.
5. She lives in ______ Half Moon Street.
6. The biggest lake in Africa is ______ Lake Victoria.
7. We land at ______ Gatwick Airport, not Heathrow.
8. My favourite London park is ______ Green Park.
9. Everybody knows ______ Tower Bridge.
10. Where exactly are ______ Ardennes?

K8 A friend

Übersetzen Sie.

1. Tim ist ein Freund von mir.

   ____

2. Andrea ist eine Kollegin von Julia.

   ____

3. Ein Bruder von Jack fährt einen alten Jaguar.

   ____

4. Nachbarn von uns haben ein Haus in Spanien.

   ____

K9 Love

Ergänzen Sie die Übersetzung.

1. Die Liebe hält nie, oder?
   ____Love____ never lasts, does it?
2. Welches Land ist der Geburtsort der Demokratie?
   Which country is the birthplace of ________________?
3. Die Geschichte unserer Stadt begann vor 800 Jahren.
   ________________ of our town began 800 years ago.
4. Es hat mehrere große Präsidenten in der amerikanischen Geschichte gegeben.
   There have been several great presidents in
   ________________.
5. Das Leben und der Tod gehören zusammen.
   ________________ and ________________ belong together.
6. Wann hast du von dem Tod erfahren?
   When did you hear about ________________?
7. Das Leben ist ein Abenteuer.
   ________________ is an adventure.
8. Wie die Zeit vergeht!
   How ________________ flies!
9. Welche Partei ist nicht für die Freiheit?
   Which party does not stand for ________________?
10. Schau: die Schönheiten der Natur!
    Look: the beauties of ________________!

K10 All right?

Kreuzen Sie alle richtigen Lösungen an.

1.
- ☐ a. I know nearly all people in this room.
- ☐ b. I know nearly all the people in this room.
- ☐ c. I know the people in this room nearly all.

2.
- ☐ a. I know all in our street.
- ☐ b. I know every in our street.
- ☐ c. I know everyone in our street.

3.
- ☐ a. Both skiers were injured.
- ☐ b. Both the skiers were injured.
- ☐ c. The both skiers were injured.

4.
- ☐ a. Neither hotel has any rooms left.
- ☐ b. Neither of the two hotels has any rooms left.
- ☐ c. The hotels have neither any rooms left.

5.
- ☐ a. Nobody of us knew about it.
- ☐ b. None of us knew about it.
- ☐ c. No one of us knew about it.

L. Singular und Plural

1. Boxes
2. A or B?
3. Where are my glasses?

L1 Boxes

Wandeln Sie wie im Beispiel um.

1. What's this box doing here?
   What are these ___boxes___ doing here?
2. A new business has been opened.
   Several new ______________ have been opened.
3. Do you have the address?
   Do you have the ______________?
4. Can you make a copy, please?
   Can you make some ______________, please?
5. I don't want a green tomato, I want a ripe one!
   I don't want green ______________, I want ripe ______________!
6. Jason is my brother-in-law.
   Jason and Alan are my ______________________.
7. There's an interesting new series on TV.
   There are several interesting new ______________ on TV.
8. What criterion are you using?
   What ______________ are you using?
9. We have a fox, a mouse and a sheep.
   We have ______________, ______________ and ______________.
10. I have a tooth that's causing problems.
    I have two ______________ that are causing problems.

L2 A or B?

Was stimmt: a oder b?

1. a) We've just received an interesting new information.
   b) We've just received some interesting new information.

2. a) Let me give you an advice.
   b) Let me give you a piece of advice.

3. a) Her hair was a different colour when I saw her last.
   b) Her hairs were a different colour when I saw her last.

4. a) This furniture is old, but comfortable.
   b) These furniture are old, but comfortable.

5. a) The damage was enormous.
   b) The damages were enormous.

6. a) These spaghetti are cold!
   b) This spaghetti is cold!

7. a) It was a difficult task.
   b) It was a difficult work.

8. a) She speaks a very good English.
   b) She speaks very good English.

9. a) Progress is slow.
   b) Progress are slow.

10. a) This room is absolute chaos!
    b) This room is an absolute chaos!

L3 Where are my glasses?

Übersetzen Sie.

1. Wo ist meine Brille?
   Where *are my glasses* ____________?

2. Wo ist die Polizei?
   Where ______________________________?

3. Ich habe drei Hosen gepackt.
   I've packed three ________________________.

4. Die USA haben große Probleme.
   The USA ______________ great problems.

5. In Zeiten wie diesen sind sechs Prozent Zinsen viel.
   In times like these six per cent interest ____________ a lot.

6. Die Schere ist auf dem Tisch.
   __________________ on the table.

7. Die Ware kommt morgen.
   __________________ coming tomorrow.

8. Die Nachrichten sind gut.
   __________________ good.

9. Die Treppe ist steil.
   __________________ steep.

M. Adjektiv und Adverb

1. A or B?
2. *Bad* and *badly*
3. Odd one out
4. *Careful* or *carefully*?
5. Right or wrong?
6. Trends
7. A or B?
8. Here or there?
9. Every day

M1 A or B?

Was passt: a oder b?

1. Have you spoken to Jenny ...?
   a) late b) lately
2. We arrived back very ... yesterday evening.
   a) late b) lately
3. I feel ... tired.
   a) incredible b) incredibly
4. Have you ever seen such an ... performance?
   a) incredible b) incredibly
5. How ... do you know them?
   a) good b) well
6. I hadn't been feeling very ... so I went to the doctor's.
   a) good b) well
7. I was never very ... at maths.
   a) good b) well
8. This sort of weather is ..., even for this part of the world.
   a) extreme b) extremely
9. The service is ... unreliable.
   a) extreme b) extremely
10. It was ... to see some new faces at last.
    a) wonderful refreshingly b) wonderfully refreshing

1	2	3	4	5	6	7	8	9	10

M2 *Bad* and *badly*

Was passt zusammen?

1. I slept
2. I had a really
3. I've never stayed in such a
4. The man in the next room snored
5. At four o'clock there was a
6. It was
7. I felt pretty
8. I complained

a. noisy hotel room.
b. sudden loud noise.
c. badly last night.
d. suddenly there. I don't know what it was.
e. noisily all night long.
f. angrily to the management.
g. bad night.
h. angry.

1	2	3	4	5	6	7	8
c							

M3 Odd one out

Streichen Sie, was nicht passt.

1. quickly – ~~friendly~~ – especially – happily
2. slowly – carefully – well – madly
3. fast – early – hard – happy
4. automatically – basically – ethnically – publicly

M4 *Careful* or *carefully*?

Ergänzen Sie die richtige Form.

careful

1. Listen ___*carefully*___ to what I have to say.
2. Be ______________ what you do with that knife.

excited

3. You look ______________. Is something about to happen?
4. We heard a car pull up outside, and Janine looked ______________ out of the window.

particular

5. Was there any ______________ colour you were looking for?
6. The sofa was a ______________ horrid colour.

lovely

7. This tastes ______________.
8. It's a ______________ meal.

anxious

9. ______________ glances passed between them, but neither of them said anything.
10. You seem ______________. What's the matter?

M5 Right or wrong?

Korrigieren Sie den *kursiv* gedruckten Teil, falls nötig.

1. Three people arrived *early*, nobody arrived late.

   korrekt

2. You are very *good informed*.

   ____

3. In this sort of job you really have to work *hardly*.

   ____

4. His first wife died *tragicly* in a car accident.

   ____

5. The country has a *goodly* developed economy.

   ____

6. It was *hardly* necessary to point out Ferrow's mistake yet again.

   ____

7. The children are all very *good behaved*.

   ____

8. He's a very *good-natured* dog and would never bite anyone.

   ____

M6 Trends

Korrigieren Sie.

1. Sales are much ~~badder~~ ______________ than in the same period last year.
2. They are 20% ~~more low~~ ______________.
3. It's not getting ~~easyer~~ ______________ to make forecasts.
4. Things were much ~~more better~~ ______________ ten years ago.
5. We've sold the ~~lest~~ ______________ number of units in our luxury range.
6. They are of course much ~~expensiver as~~ ________________________ mass-market models.
7. The downturn has come much ~~sooner as~~ _____________ expected.
8. Many of my colleagues are much ~~more surprised as I~~ ______________________________.
9. They don't have the same kind of overview ~~like I~~ ________________________.
10. This is not the ~~most easyest~~ _____________ business to be in in a time of crisis.

M7 A or B?

Was passt: a oder b?

1. a) You must always be prepared!
   b) You must be prepared always!
2. a) I usually am ready first.
   b) I am usually ready first.
3. a) We don't often watch TV.
   b) We don't watch often TV.
4. a) She drinks never alcohol.
   b) She never drinks alcohol.
5. a) I had an accident yesterday.
   b) I had yesterday an accident.
6. a) I'm still waiting for a reply.
   b) I'm waiting still for a reply.
7. a) They've announced just some job losses.
   b) They've just announced some job losses.
8. a) I do every day the same. It's so boring.
   b) I do the same every day. It's so boring.
9. a) She's flying next week to Trinidad.
   b) She's flying to Trinidad next week.
10. a) There probably won't be enough time.
    b) There won't probably be enough time.

1	2	3	4	5	6	7	8	9	10
a									

M8 Here or there?

Markieren Sie die richtige Stellung.

1. (easily) We can (a.) _X_ reach (b.) ____ Chicago by nightfall.
2. (slowly) The rain (a.) ____ is (b.) ____ starting to clear.
3. (usually) The process (a.) ____ doesn't take (b.) ____ this long.
4. (certainly) I (a.) ______ don't (b.) ______ agree.
5. (rapidly) He (a.) ______ found (b.) ______ a replacement.
6. (eventually) I (a.) ______ got (b.) ______ to sleep.
7. (soon) You'll (a.) ______ forget (b.) ______ the whole thing.
8. (soon) You'll (a.) ______ have forgotten (b.) ______ the whole thing.

M9 Every day

Übersetzen Sie.

1. Ich nehme jeden Tag meine Medizin.

   ____

2. Ich sehe dich wahrscheinlich bald wieder.

   ____

3. So ein altes Auto kaufe ich nie wieder!

   ____

4. Sie verließ vor zehn Minuten das Büro.

   ____

N. Präpositionen

1. A or B?
2. *At, in* or *on*?
3. Not before lunch
4. A or B?
5. Right or wrong?
6. A or B?
7. In my opinion
8. I'm tired of it.
9. A, B, C or D?

N1 A or B?

Was stimmt: a oder b?

1. a) Brighton is at the coast.
   b) Brighton is on the coast.

2. a) There wasn't a cloud at the sky.
   b) There wasn't a cloud in the sky.

3. a) Everest is the highest mountain in the world.
   b) Everest is the highest mountain of the world.

4. a) Is the Dead Sea below sea level?
   b) Is the Dead Sea under sea level?

5. a) Who were you at the phone with for so long?
   b) Who were you on the phone to for so long?

6. a) Come and sit beside me.
   b) Come and sit besides me.

7. a) What are you doing at Christmas?
   b) What are you doing on Christmas?

8. a) We'll be by Janet's parents at Christmas Day.
   b) We'll be with Janet's parents on Christmas Day.

1	2	3	4	5	6	7	8

N2 *At, in* or *on*?

Ergänzen Sie.

1. I suggest we meet _*at*_ the entrance.
2. The party is _____ Jane's house.
3. I shall be _____ the office all day.
4. The company's headquarters are _____ 17 Spring Gardens.
5. _____ the weekend I like to get out of town.
6. They have a cottage _____ the country.
7. There's somebody _____ the door.
8. There were some expensive-looking prints _____ the wall.
9. I've spent the whole day _____ my computer.
10. I shall be _____ a conference in Bilbao next week.
11. How much time do you spend _____ the internet?
12. Who's the person _____ this photo?
13. Mason is _____ the doctor's. He's not feeling well.
14. I had to stop _____ the traffic lights.
15. Actually I hate lying _____ the beach.

N3 Not before lunch

Ergänzen Sie.

1. I'll meet you _____ lunch, not before.
2. We'll see you _____ Monday.
3. When there is a full moon, it's not really dark _____ night.
4. I sometimes sit next to her _____ lunch.
5. What are you doing _____ 1st May?
6. Isn't your birthday _____ June?
7. I haven't spoken to him _____ last week.
8. It happened while I was _____ work.
9. What's _____ TV tonight?
10. Have you always lived _____ this address?
11. I would love to live _____ the sea.
12. My office is _____ the third floor.
13. I have no time _____ the moment, I'm afraid.
14. I moved here _____ the age of 12.
15. I've lived here now _____ over 20 years.

N4 A or B?

Was stimmt: a oder b?

1. a) We should get to the airport by ten past seven.
   b) We should get to the airport till ten past seven.

2. a) I waited by seven o'clock, but he didn't call back.
   b) I waited till seven o'clock, but he didn't call back.

3. a) I have to finish this by Monday evening.
   b) I have to finish this till Monday evening.

N5 Right or wrong?

Korrigieren Sie den *kursiv* gedruckten Teil, falls nötig.

1. The opening ceremony is *at 10.30 in the morning.*
   ______ *korrekt* ______
2. He usually has the children *on the last Saturday in the month.*
   ______
3. I'm sure the topic will come up sometime *while the meeting.*
   ______
4. It all happened *for several years.*
   ______
5. It should arrive *till Tuesday* at the latest.
   ______
6. I'll be here *up to at least eight.*
   ______
7. We should know *within the next week.*
   ______
8. We live *nearby Oxford.*
   ______

N6 A or B?

Was stimmt: a oder b?

1. Von wem ist das Buch? Kenne ich den Autor?
   a) Who is the book by?
   b) Who is the book from?
2. Wir sind alle gegen den Vorschlag.
   a) We are all against the suggestion.
   b) We are all contra the suggestion.
3. Wie viel Wein sollten wir pro Person einplanen?
   a) How much wine should we plan per person?
   b) How much wine should we plan pro person?
4. Es wurde wegen des Wetters verschoben.
   a) It was postponed because the weather.
   b) It was postponed because of the weather.
5. Es kommt auf die Chefin an. Sie entscheidet.
   a) It's on the boss. She decides.
   b) It's up to the boss. She decides.
6. Wir erwarten bis zu 500 Personen.
   a) We're expecting until 500 people.
   b) We're expecting up to 500 people.
7. Es kann nicht bis morgen warten.
   a) It can't wait by tomorrow.
   b) It can't wait till tomorrow.
8. Ich muss bis morgen eine Antwort haben.
   a) I have to have an answer by tomorrow.
   b) I have to have an answer till tomorrow.
9. Sie bauen sowohl Fabriken als auch Hotels.
   a) They build factories as well as hotels.
   b) They build factories as well than hotels.

N7 In my opinion

Ergänzen Sie.

about • above • at • besides • except • in • of • on (2x) • to

1. ___In___ my opinion this is all going to cost too much.
2. Everyone was there ______ Tina, who was on holiday.
3. We are ahead ______ schedule, which is absolutely fantastic!
4. How much do visitors spend ______ average?
5. If I don't get there ______ time, start without me.
6. According ______ Mr Watkins this is "absolutely normal".
7. I'm calling ______ the email you sent.
8. I'm having to do Pia's job ______ my own.
9. It's ______ all the cost that is worrying me.
10. There were ______ least 80 applicants for the job.

N8 I'm tired of it.

Ergänzen Sie.

1. We got tired ___of___ going to the same place every year.
2. You're very good ______ explaining things.
3. The city is famous ______ its museums.
4. But it's always crowded ______ tourists.
5. What are you interested ______?

N9 A, B, C or D?

Markieren Sie die richtige Antwort.

1. Who do you know here ... Alice?
   a. apart from   b. beside   c. except   d. next to
2. We live ... Hamburg.
   a. by   b. in the near of   c. near   d. nearby
3. I have no intention ... letting you go off with all our knowhow.
   a. at   b. for   c. of   d. on
4. What's the point ... arguing?
   a. at   b. in   c. on   d. to
5. I'm really very proud ... you.
   a. at   b. in   c. of   d. on
6. They accused me ... stealing the code.
   a. at   b. for   c. from   d. of
7. I'll let you know well ... advance.
   a. at   b. by   c. in   d. on
8. We've sold way ... what had been forecast.
   a. ahead   b. beyond   c. more   d. up

0. Dies und das

1. Relative clauses
2. A or B?
3. Indirect speech
4. A, B or C?
5. A or B?

01 Relative clauses

Kreuzen Sie alle richtigen Lösungen an.

1. Who is the guy ...?
   - ☐ a. I saw you with
   - ☐ b. that I saw you with
   - ☐ c. which I saw you with
   - ☐ d. who I saw you with

2. 2300 were sold, ... were later returned.
   - ☐ a. 110 of that
   - ☐ b. 110 of which
   - ☐ c. of that 110
   - ☐ d. 110 of those

3. The teacher ... class gets the best exam results wins an award.
   - ☐ a. of who
   - ☐ b. of who's
   - ☐ c. who's
   - ☐ d. whose

02 A or B?

Was stimmt: a oder b?

1. a) I used to live in Frankfurt.
   b) I used to living in Frankfurt.

2. a) He didn't use to have a beard, did he?
   b) He didn't use to having a beard, did he?

3. a) He claimed kids these days are not used to work hard.
   b) He claimed kids these days are not used to working hard.

4. a) I'm slowly getting used to get up at 4.
   b) I'm slowly getting used to getting up at 4.

03 Indirect speech

Wandeln Sie im Beispiel um.

1. "Teresa called."
   Raymond told me that Teresa ___*called / had called*___.
2. "We won't have time."
   Jacob insisted that ______________________.
3. "I'm leaving tomorrow."
   On Saturday she said that ______________________.
4. "Please take a seat."
   She asked me ______________________.
5. "Has Rebecca been invited?"
   Tony wanted to know ______________________.
6. "Do you speak Portuguese?"
   They asked me ______________________.
7. "I'm so excited."
   He said that ______________________.
8. "They aren't expecting us."
   Sheila was worried that ______________________.
9. "I've made a mistake."
   He knew that ______________________.
10. "Will James be there?"
    She wondered ______________________.

04 A, B or C?

Markieren Sie die richtige Antwort.

1. We're ... outside the station.
   a. meeting b. meeting ourselves c. meeting us
2. They've known ... for a very long time. *[sich]*
   a. each other b. them c. themselves
3. I'd like to introduce ... .
   a. I b. me c. myself
4. Do you have your passport with ...?
   a. you b. your c. yourself
5. Quiet! I can't ... .
   a. concentrate b. concentrate me c. concentrate myself
6. I heard footsteps behind ... .
   a. I b. me c. myself
7. Everyone will have to look after ... . *[sich selbst]*
   a. him and her b. themself c. themselves

05 A or B?

Was stimmt: a oder b?

1. The company has lost sight of (a.) it's / (b.) its customers.
2. This suitcase seems to have lost (a.) it's / (b.) its owner.
3. Oh no, (a.) it's / (b.) its raining again.
4. I don't think (a.) it's / (b.) its a pity.
5. What can you tell me about the building and (a.) it's / (b.) its history?
6. I feel (a.) it's / (b.) its time to finish.

Lösungen

A. Einfache Form und Verlaufsform

A1 2. h 3. d 4. c 5. b 6. a 7. e 8. f

A2 1. b 2. a 3. a, c 4. b, d 5. a 6. b, c

> ▶ **Verlaufsform (mit *-ing*):**
>
> eine gerade ablaufende Tätigkeit, eine vorübergehende Situation, eine noch nicht abgeschlossene Entwicklung.
> **Einfache Form:** Dauerzustand oder Gewohnheit.
>
> Verben, die einen Zustand, d.h. keine Tätigkeit ausdrücken, können nicht in der Verlaufsform stehen.

A3 2. I don't think so. 3. It's snowing 4. is shining 5. seem 6. I can see 7. is just arriving

A4 2. I'm having 3. I'm having 4. I'm having 5. I'm having 6. I have 7. I have

> ▶ ***have*** drückt Tätigkeit aus: kann in der Verlaufsform stehen.
>
> ***have*** drückt Zustand aus: kann nur in der einfachen Form stehen.

A5 2. What does this symbol mean? 3. Joanna is trying to lose some weight. 4. She doesn't eat meat. 5. The tourist office is just closing. 6. It closes earlier in the winter. 7. The situation is getting better slowly. 8. I don't remember anything.

A6 2. don't know 3. aren't speaking 4. is making 5. need 6. doesn't cost 7. don't mind 8. are you doing? am trying 9. is living 10. are rising 11. are you waiting 12. does this word mean

A7 2. are becoming 3. is rising 4. are taking 5. are worrying 6. are giving 7. are buying 8. are living

> ▶ Noch nicht abgeschlossene Entwicklungen: Verlaufsform

A8 2. Do you remember 3. owns 4. doesn't belong 5. don't see 6. Did you understand

> ▶ Verben, die einen Zustand ausdrücken: keine Verlaufsform

A9 2. korrekt 3. were still sitting 4. korrekt 5. was listening; korrekt 6. korrekt; were discussing 7. was raining; korrekt 8. was still having; arrived

A10 2. It all depends (on) what it costs. 3. I'm working from home at the moment. 4. I'm learning Spanish. 5. When I arrived, over 50 people were (already) waiting. 6. They are building a new hotel. 7. Normally I get up / I normally get up later on Saturdays. 8. But I'm working today.

B. Present Perfect und Vergangenheit

B1 2. d 3. a 4. g 5. e 6. h 7. c 8. b

B2 2. b 3. a 4. b 5. b 6. a 7. a 8. b

▶ begin, began, begun; feel, felt, felt; fall, fell, fallen; fly, flew, flown; forget, forgot, forgotten; spend, spent, spent; swim, swam, swum; lay, laid, laid (*legen, decken*); lie, lay, lain (*liegen*)

B3 Richtig: 2. a 3. a 4. b 5. b 6. a 7. a

▶ Bericht über ein in der Vergangenheit abgeschlossenes Geschehen (oft mit Zeitbestimmung der Vergangenheit): nur einfache Vergangenheit möglich.
Present Perfect: Etwas hat sich irgendwann in der Vergangenheit ereignet, der genaue Zeitpunkt ist unbekannt oder unwichtig; wichtig ist das jetzige Ergebnis.
Vergangenheitsform: Etwas geschah zu einem bestimmten Zeit-punkt. – Present Perfect: Wichtig ist allein die Tatsache, dass sich etwas ereignet hat.

B4 2. I did it 3. We began 4. I spoke 5. I slept 6. He showed them round 7. I rang it/them 8. I paid it 9. Someone/They stole it

B5 2. had 3. was 4. tasted 5. didn't 6. didn't 7. said 8. thought 9. have eaten 10. decided

B6 2. brought 3. didn't you open *[damals, als es gekommen ist]* / haven't you opened *[es ist jetzt nicht geöffnet]* 4. haven't ordered *[es liegt keine Bestellung vor]* / didn't order *[gab keine Bestellung auf]* 5. did 6. have forgotten *[du weißt es jetzt nicht mehr]* / forgot *[nachdem du es tatest]* 7. have been 8. haven't become

▶ Bisweilen sind zwei Sichtweisen auf ein Geschehen möglich – als Ereignis zu einem bestimmten Zeitpunkt in der Vergangenheit (einfache Vergangenheitsform), oder als Ereignis irgendwann in der Vergangenheit mit einem jetzigen Ergebnis (Present Perfect).

B7 2. am 3. have decided *[jetziges Ergebnis]* / decided *[Entschluss zu einem bestimmten Zeitpunkt]* 4. think 5. have had *[in der ganzen Zeit bis jetzt]* 6. broke out 7. have always looked for *[in der ganzen Zeit bis jetzt]* 8. serve / have served / served 9. have again found *[jetziges Ergebnis]*

B8 2. I've checked 3. I've read 4. I've given 5. I've been 6. I've bought 7. (I've) eaten 8. I've given up

B9 2. Have you ever driven 3. Have you ever drunk 4. Have you ever ridden 5. Have you ever bought 6. Have you ever worn 7. Have you ever sung 8. Have you ever eaten

B10 2. was 3. have visited 4. have always loved 5. was 6. were 7. was 8. wanted 9. have often dreamt/dreamed 10. have never had 11. found 12. didn't think 13. took 14. spoke 15. had to 16. explained 17. interpreted 18. said 19. didn't understand 20. told 21. didn't want 22. has never happened

C. Present Perfect mit *since, for* und *how long*

C1 2. for 3. since 4. for 5. since 6. since 7. for 8. since 9. for 10. since 11. for 12. for

C2 1. a 2. b 3. a 4. a

> ▶ Zum Ausdruck eines Zustandes, der in der Vergangenheit begonnen hat und bis jetzt andauert, verwendet das Englische das Present Perfect, NICHT eine Gegenwartsform, oft zusammen mit *since* (+ Anfangszeitpunkt) und *for* (+ Zeitspanne) bzw. in Fragen mit *how long*.

C3 2. has been, for 3. have you known 4. has been developing 5. have calmed down, left 6. has been active, for 7. has this problem existed 8. have you been

C4 2. How long have you been working
3. How long have you been driving
4. How long have you been learning
5. How long have you been waiting?
6. How long have you been trying
7. How long have you been sitting
8. How long have you been training
9. How long have you been planning

> ▶ Mit der Verlaufsform des Present Perfect wird das ununterbrochene Andauern eines Vorgangs betont.

D. Verneinung mit und ohne *do*

D1 2. e 3. a 4. f 5. d 6. b 7. c

D2 1. a 2. b 3. a 4. b

D3 2. don't know 3. didn't walk
4. don't have 5. haven't made
6. can't speak 7. won't give
8. don't do

D4 2. won't 3. didn't 4. don't 5. can't 6. haven't

D5 2. It doesn't rain often. 3. We don't have ... 4. You don't have to have ... 5. korrekt

D6 2. This hasn't ever happened before. 3. I didn't do this. 4. Why isn't Frank coming? 5. We didn't decide till yesterday. 6. Why don't you do more preparation? 7. I absolutely don't agree. 8. The train doesn't stop in Torquay.

D7 1. I don't like this room.
2. We don't know what('s) happened.
3. He doesn't do any sport.
4. I'm not working at the moment. 5. That didn't really happen! / ..., did it?
6. I didn't wait. It was late. 7. We didn't want to take a taxi.
8. He doesn't have / hasn't got much talent.

E. Fragen und Frageanhängsel

E1 2. e 3. a 4. b 5. i 6. f 7. c 8. d 9. g

E2 1. a 2. b 3. a 4. b

E3 2. Do you like 3. Are you taking 4. Did you do 5. What should I wear? 6. Who cooked 7. Who did you ask 8. Who goes shopping

> ▶ *Who* ist Subjekt des Fragesatzes: keine Umschreibung mit *do*.
> *Who* ist Objekt: Umschreibung.

E4 Richtig: 2. a 3. b 4. a 5. a 6. a

E5 2. e 3. a 4. b 5. d 6. c 7. f 8. g

E6 2. Can anyone 3. Were you 4. did you hear 5. did you get 6. Does he know 7. have you been 8. did you do 9. did you do

E7 2. are 3. did you interview 4. came 5. interests 6. do people like 7. phoned 8. did you inform 9. were you 10. were you sitting

E8 2. do you do 3. do you work 4. Have you been 5. Is it 6. Did you have to 7. Are you 8. Do you have 9. Have you always lived

E9 2. f 3. a 4. b 5. h 6. c 7. d 8. e

E10 2. aren't we 3. did it 4. won't you 5. was he 6. doesn't she 7. don't you

> ▶ Bejahter Satz – verneintes Anhängsel (ggfs. *don't / doesn't / didn't* ergänzen). Verneinter Satz – bejahtes Anhängsel.

E11 3. Don't you? 4. Does she? 5. Do you? 6. Do they? 7. Did you? 8. Didn't it?

> ▶ „Echo-Fragen": Bejahter Satz – bejahte Frage. Verneinter Satz – verneinte Frage. In beiden Fällen ggfs. *do(n't) / does(n't) / did(n't)* ergänzen.

F. Zukunftsformen

F1 2. I'll give you a hand. 3. I'll lend you the money. 4. I'll give you a lift. 5. I'll get Simon for you. 6. He'll call you back. 7. I'll see if she's here. 8. They'll let you know

> ▶ Bei spontanen Entscheidungen, Angeboten und Zusagen: *will*

F2 2. I'll take 3. I'll have 4. I'll have 5. we'll try 6. we'll take 7. I won't have 8. We'll have

F3 2. a 3. b 4. b 5. b 6. b

> ▶ Gegenwartsformen, um die Zukunft auszudrücken, sind im Englischen seltener als im Deutschen. Unterschiede zwischen den Zukunftsformen:
>
> - *will:* neutrale Form, ohne Färbung durch Absicht, Plan o.ä. (Beachten Sie: Deutsch „will" = Engl. *want to*)
> - *going to:* Es besteht die Absicht, etwas zu tun; oder die Gewissheit, dass etwas passieren wird.
> - Verlaufsform der Gegenwart: Etwas ist geplant, vorgesehen, abgemacht.
> - Einfache Gegenwart: Etwas ist bestimmt durch Fahr- oder Ablaufplan.
> - Verlaufsform der *will*-Zukunft: Etwas ist so vorgesehen, wird sich so ergeben.

F4 1. a, b, c 2. b, c 3. a, c, d 4. a, b, d

F5 1. will only be / is only going to be 2. won't be / isn't going to be 3. are moving / are going to move / will be moving 4. will be lying 5. will have done 6. are you taking / do you take / are you going to take / will you take / will you be taking 7. you'll have / you'll be having / you're having / you're going to have 8. won't be / isn't going to be 9. will have left

▶ Vollendete Zukunft (Nrn. 5, 9): *will have* + Partizip Perfekt

G. Aktiv und Passiv

G1 2. a series of children's books by J.K. Rowling 3. a film by Steven Spielberg 4. a play by William Shakespeare 5. It is held by Margaret Court. 6. It is held by Michael Schumacher.

G2 2. f 3. a 4. g 5. c 6. e 7. h 8. b

G3 2. a 3. a 4. b 5. a 6. a 7. a 8. b 9. b 10. b

G4 2. will be told 3. is still being tested 4. weren't invited 5. was being filmed 6. is being re-printed 7. was eaten up 8. had not been expected 9. are being monitored

G5 2. When was the hotel opened? 3. When will the bags/suitcases be collected? 4. Where were the tickets issued? 5. How were you informed? 6. Will the letterbox / postbox be emptied today? 7. Why haven't the beds been made? 8. Has our order been forgotten? 9. Is a tip expected?

G6 1. a + b 2. a. 3. a + b 4. b 5. a + b 6. a 7. a

▶ Bei vielen englischen Verben kann das indirekte Objekt eines Aktivsatzes zum Subjekt eines Passivsatzes gemacht werden. Ausnahmen: *explain, suggest, describe.*

G7 2. has the key been deposited 3. will the workforce be informed by 4. is the event being sponsored by 5. was the letter signed by 6. has the company been taken over by 7. was it invented by 8. is the company going to be bailed out by

H. Infinitiv und Gerundium

H1 2. a 3. a 4. b 5. a 6. b 7. a 8. b 9. a 10. a 11. b

▶ In *look forward to* ist to Präposition, deshalb folgt ein Gerundium.

H2 1. trying out / to try out 2. making, doing, doing 3. doing, to make 4. to ask, to remember 5. worrying, in getting, worrying 6. enjoying, staying, to do

H3 2. I offered to give them a lift. 3. Don't mention meeting me at the café. 4. I admit being there. 5. I really dislike asking for help. 6. We can't carry on meeting like this. 7. They discussed closing the factory in Poland. 8. He claims to have known nothing about it.

H4 2. Would you like us to wait 3. I'd like you to go 4. I want you to 5. Does he really expect me to work 6. I need you to pick up 7. Would you like me to shut 8. Do you want me to take 9. I'd love him to make

H5 2. b 3. a 4. b 5. a 6. a 7. a 8. a

H6 2. h 3. a 4. f 5. b 6. c 7. d 8. g

H7 2. Let's take a taxi instead of going on the bus. 3. I asked the question without even thinking. 4. You can improve your vocabulary by reading a lot. 5. Before opening the attachment, scan it for viruses. 6. We drove all the way without stopping. 7. Instead of having coffee I'll take tea for a change. 8. He lost a lot of money by investing in the stock market.

H8 2. in 3. at 4. of 5. of 6. in 7. for 8. for 9. on 10. in

H9 2. a 3. b 4. a 5. a 6. a 7. a 8. a

▶ *remember/forget:* für Vergangenes: *-ing*-Form; für Zukünftiges: Infinitiv (jeweils vom Erzählzeitpunkt aus gesehen).
stop (aufhören) und *mean* (bedeuten): *-ing*-Form;
stop (anhalten) und *mean* (vorhaben): Infinitiv.

I. *if*-Sätze

I1 2. if 3. when 4. If 5. If 6. When 7. if 8. If 9. If

I2 1. a 2. b 3. b 4. b

I3 2. d 3. g 4. b 5. c 6. e 7. a 8. h 9. i

I4 2. If you want, I can 3. If I had seen you, I would have stopped. 4. It would make me ... if I was 5. If it hadn't been cheaper, I wouldn't have bought it 6. Where would you live if you could choose? 7. They wouldn't have invited me ... if Hannah hadn't said 8. We would fly ... if we had

I5 2. will be 3. wouldn't have been 4. didn't drink 5. calls 6. would you have done 7. had 8. could 9. had 10. hadn't seen, wouldn't have believed 11. hadn't gone, would never have met 12. hadn't read, wouldn't have understood

I6 1. If the bus doesn't come soon, I'll walk. 2. I wouldn't have said yes if I had been in doubt. 3. I would help you if I knew how to. 4. If he calls me Fritzi again, I'll kill him. 5. If we had lost, it wouldn't have been the end of the world. 6. It would be terrible if we could control the weather. 7. Even if they gave it (to) me, I wouldn't want it. 8. If I had taken the right clothing/ clothes with me, I wouldn't have frozen all week. 9. If the firm/ company hadn't made these risky investments, it wouldn't have gone bankrupt.

J. Modalverben

J1 2. e 3. i 4. a 5. c 6. h 7. b 8. f 9. d

J2 2. Shall 3. might not 4. mustn't 5. couldn't 6. Would 7. will

J3 1. mustn't 2. needn't 3. mustn't 4. needn't 5. needn't 6. needn't

▶ *mustn't* = nicht dürfen; *needn't* = nicht müssen.

J4 1. speak 2. do

J5 2. won't be able to 3. haven't been able to 4. weren't able to 5. wasn't able to 6. could have 8. had to 9. will have to 10. won't have to

J6 2. do we have to 3. do we have to 4. did you have to 5. doesn't have to 6. didn't have to 7. did you have to 8. won't you have to

J7 1. a + b + c 2. c 3. a 4. a 5. b + c

J8 1. may / might 2. might 3. may / might 4. Were they able to 5. Did you have to 6. have had to 7. mustn't 8. may / might

J9 2. b 3. a 4. b 5. a

K. Artikel und Begleiter

K1 2. e 3. a 4. c 5. b 6. d

K2 2. four times a day 3. twice a week 4. once in a lifetime

K3 2. a 3. b 4. a 5. b 6. a 7. a 8. a

K4 2. c 3. a 4. b 5. f 6. e

K5 2. It was such a terrible journey. 3. What kind/sort of car does he drive? 4. What glorious weather! 5. We meet once a month.

K6 2. b 3. b 4. a 5. a 6. a 7. b 8. a

K7 2. the 3. the 4. - 5. - 6. - 7. - 8. - 9. - 10. the

K8 1. Tim is a friend of mine. 2. Andrea is a colleague of Julia's. 3. A brother of Jack's drives an old Jaguar. 4. Neighbours of ours have a house in Spain.

K9 2. democracy 3. The history 4. American history 5. Life and death 6. the death 7. Life 8. time 9. freedom 10. nature

K10 1. b 2. c 3. a + b 4. a + b 5. b

L. Singular und Plural

L1 2. businesses 3. addresses
4. copies 5. tomatoes, ones
6. brothers-in-law 7. series
8. criteria 9. foxes, mice and sheep
10. teeth

L2 1. b 2. b 3. a 4. a 5. a 6. b
7. a 8. b 9. a 10. a

L3 2. are the police 3. pairs of trousers
4. has 5. is 6. The scissors are
7. The goods are 8. The news is
9. The stairs are

M. Adjektiv und Adverb

M1 1. b 2. a 3. b 4. a 5. b 6. b
7. a 8. a 9. b 10. b

M2 2. g 3. a 4. e 5. b 6. d 7. h
8. f

M3 2. well (einziges ohne -*ly*) 3. happy (einziges, das nicht als Adjektiv und Adverb die gleiche Form hat)
4. publicly (einziges, das nicht auf -*ically* endet)

M4 2. careful 3. excited 4. excitedly
5. particular 6. particularly
7. lovely 8. lovely 9. Anxious
10. anxious

M5 2. well informed 3. hard
4. tragically 5. well developed
6. korrekt 7. well behaved
8. korrekt

M6 1. worse 2. lower 3. easier
4. better 5. least 6. more expensive than 7. sooner than 8. more surprised than me / than I am
9. as me / as I have 10. easiest

M7 2. b 3. a 4. b 5. a 6. a 7. b
8. b 9. b 10. a

M8 2. b 3. a 4. a 5. a 6. a 7. a
8. a

M9 1. I take my medicine every day.
2. I'll probably see you again soon.
3. I'll never buy such an old car again! 4. She left the office ten minutes ago.

N. Präpositionen

N1 1. b 2. b 3. a 4. a 5. b 6. a
7. a 8. b

N2 2. at 3. at / in 4. at 5. At / *(AE:)* On 6. in 7. at 8. on
9. at 10. at 11. on 12. in
13. at 14. at 15. on

N3 1. after 2. on 3. at 4. at 5. on
6. in 7. since 8. at 9. on 10. at
11. by 12. on 13. at 14. at
15. for

N4 1. a 2. b 3. a

N5 2. korrekt 3. during the meeting
4. several years ago 5. by Tuesday
6. korrekt 7. korrekt 8. near

N6 1. a 2. a 3. a 4. b 5. b 6. b
7. b 8. a 9. a

N7 2. except 3. of 4. on 5. on
6. to 7. about 8. besides
9. above 10. at

N8 2. at 3. for 4. with 5. in

N9 1. a 2. c 3. c 4. b 5. c 6. d
7. c 8. b

0. Dies und das

01 1. a + b + d 2. b 3. d

02 1. a 2. a 3. b 4. b

03 2. they wouldn't have time 3. she was leaving / would be leaving the next day 4. to take a seat 5. if/ whether Rebecca had been invited 6. if I spoke / speak Portuguese 7. he was so excited 8. they weren't expecting us 9. he had made a mistake 10. if/whether James would be there

04 1. a 2. a 3. c 4. a 5. a 6. b 7. c

05 1. b 2. b 3. a 4. a 5. b 6. a

2 True and False Friends

Inhalt Teil 2

Übungen

A. True friends?

Englisch-deutsche Wortpaare mit ähnlicher Form und ähnlicher Bedeutung – aber nicht immer!

A1 I'll take you. *bringen / bring*

Was passt zusammen? Ordnen Sie zu.

1. I'll take you
2. Can you put
3. Can you bring me
4. I don't want to get you
5. First get the children

a. into difficulties.
b. a cloth, please?
c. to the station.
d. to safety.
e. the children to bed?

Und nun ergänzen Sie *bring* oder *take*.

6. We use _________ for a movement away from the person who is speaking.
7. We use _________ for a movement towards the person who is speaking.

A2 What a day! *bringen / bring*

Ergänzen Sie passende Übersetzungen von „bringen" aus A1.

What a day! I've been on the go for about 14 hours, non-stop. In the morning they (1.) _________ our new fitted kitchen. Of course there were problems, with pieces missing and pieces that didn't fit, which really (2.) _________ the workmen into difficulties. The whole thing took longer than expected, and two of them had to go off to another job while the third one finished off.
I (3.) _________ him to the bus-stop half an hour ago – not my job I know, but he had such a lot of stuff to carry and had really done a good job, so I took pity on him.
In between making tea for the workmen and picking up the kids from school and trying to prepare the presentation I'm giving in Berlin next week, I had to (4.) _________ Julian to the airport. He's gone to Stockholm for a week, on business. I told him not to forget to (5.) _________ something back for the kids. Yes, the kids. It's 9.15, and I've only just (6.) _________ them to bed.

A3 Are you coming? *kommen / come*

Welcher Ausdruck passt in die Lücke?

1. A group of us are going to the pub. Are you ...
   a. coming with b. coming c. by us d. with us
2. Excuse me. How do I ... to the station?
   a. come b. arrive c. get d. reach
3. His temperature is really high. I'm going to ... the doctor.
   a. ask to come b. get to come c. let come d. send for
4. The sender's address ... in the top right-hand corner.
   a. comes b. is belonging c. goes d. places
5. Where do the wine glasses ...? In this cupboard, or in the cupboard in the other room?
   a. come to b. come c. go d. stay
6. We had a very long discussion, but I'm afraid we ... far.
   a. didn't come b. didn't cover c. didn't get d. didn't reach
7. Christmas ... soon.
   a. comes b. is arriving c. is going to be d. will be here
8. Regina ... hospital next week for an operation.
   a. is coming into b. is going to c. comes to the
   d. will be coming into
9. ... while I was having my shower this morning.
   a. A great idea came b. A great idea came me
   c. I became a great idea d. I had a great idea
10. I've put on over six kilos. That ... eating too much and getting too little exercise.
    a. is because b. comes from c. comes of d. goes from

1	2	3	4	5	6	7	8	9	10

A4 I'm looking for ... *Karte / card*

Ergänzen Sie eine passende Entsprechung für „Karte".

1. At a kiosk

◆ Yes, please?

● I'm looking for a _________ of the south of England. Not just a plan of London, but the whole of the south of the country.

2. At a restaurant

◆ Was everything all right?

● Yes, it was very nice, thank you.

◆ Would you like a dessert?

● Yes, can we see the _________ again, please?

3. At a theatre booking office

◆ Yes, please?

● I would like three _________s for tomorrow evening's performance, please.

4. In a shop

◆ Isn't it Anna's birthday next week?

● Yes. I must get her a _________.

5. At a station

◆ Excuse me, can you help me with this machine? I want to buy a _________ to go to the city centre.

● That's Zone A. Just press this button here.

A5 Coming and going *gehen / go*

Wählen Sie die richtige(n) Lösung(en), um die Übersetzung zu vervollständigen.

1. Es ist nicht weit, ich gehe zu Fuß.
   It's not far, I'm going … .
   ● (kein weiteres Wort). ● by foot ● to walk

2. Wie lange geht die Sendung?
   How long does the programme …?
   ● go ● last ● take

3. Wo gehen die Kinder zur Schule?
   Where do the children …?
   ● go to school ● go in school ● walk to school

4. Die Heizung geht nicht.
   The heating … .
   ● doesn't go ● doesn't function ● isn't working

5. Wann geht Ihre Maschine?
   When …?
   ● is your flight ● does your plane go ● does your flight go

6. Geht der Bus auch sonntags?
   Does the bus … on Sundays too?
   ● drive ● run ● travel

7. Das kommt nicht in Frage. Das geht nicht.
   That's out of the question. …
   ● That's not going ● That's impossible. ● I can't make it.

A6 Oh damn! *vergessen / forget*

Welches Verb ist richtig?

1. ... the name of the street.
   a. He's forgotten   b. He's left
2. ... the piece of paper with the address on at home!
   a. He's forgotten   b. He's left
3. Jack is impossible! ... his PIN again!
   a. He's forgotten   b. He's left
4. Oh no! ... my mobile in the car!
   a. I've forgotten   b. I've left
5. There's big trouble. Williams ... the CD with all the data on the train!
   a. has forgotten   b. has left

A7 What is it? *Glas / glass*

Ergänzen Sie. Sie können die angegebenen Wörter mehrmals verwenden.

glass • honey • jar • of • olives • wine

1. a ______________

2. a ______________

3. a ______________

4. a ______________

A8 A crossword *Salat, Soße / salad, sauce*

Ergänzen Sie passende Übersetzungen von „Salat“ und „Soße“.

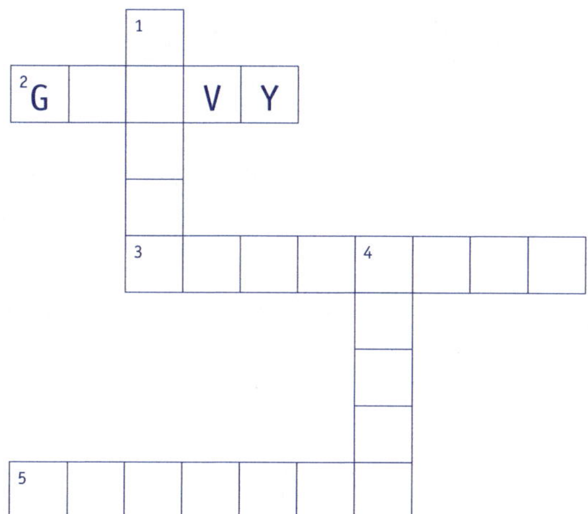

1. This dish is served with French fries and vegetables, or French fries and ... . You can help yourself from the ... bar.
2. I never make ... out of a packet, I always use the meat juices from cooking.
3. What sort of ... do you want on your salad? Italian or French?
4. One of my favourite desserts is ice-cream with chocolate ... .
5. We grow our own ... in the garden.

A9 In the kitchen *scharf / sharp*

Ergänzen Sie passende Übersetzungen von „scharf“.

1. One of the most important pieces of kitchen equipment is a set of __________ knives.
2. Glenn likes ___________ food – curries, anything with chili powder or Tabasco sauce!

A10 Definitions *Gast / guest*

Ordnen Sie zu.

customer • guest • guesthouse • host • inn
passenger • visitor

1. When you visit someone in their home, you are that person's ______________.
2. They are your ______________.
3. If they have a room especially for people who come and stay overnight, that is their ______________ room.
4. When you eat in a restaurant, you are one of the restaurant's ______________s.
5. When you stay in a hotel, you are a hotel ______________.
6. When you spend some time in another country, you are a ______________ to that country.
7. When you travel in a taxi, you are the taxi driver's ______________.
8. The place where you go for a drink or a meal with friends, and where you can also stay the night is called an ______________.
9. A ______________ is a sort of small private hotel.

A11 Life-long learning *lernen / learn*

Korrigieren Sie – falls nötig!

1. I've decided that I'm going to *learn* __________ Spanish.
2. Angela is upstairs in her room *learning* __________. She has a history test tomorrow.
3. Some people just never *learn* __________ .

A12 The test was easy *falsch / false*

Ergänzen Sie *false* oder *wrong*.

1. The test was easy, it consisted of just twenty true-__________ questions.
2. I'm sorry, but your answer is __________.
3. There's no need to worry, it was a __________ alarm.
4. I went to the __________ address.
5. The man gave the police a __________ address, but they soon found out.
6. I only got one question __________, all my other answers were correct.
7. The driver of the other car was on the __________ side of the road. That's why the accident happened.
8. I couldn't understand what I had done __________.
9. I felt such a fool. I had arrived on the __________ day!
10. This class is one for real beginners. If you already know some English, you should register for the __________ beginners' class.

A13 Time for coffee *Pause / pause*

Übersetzen Sie.

1. Um 15.00 Uhr machen wir eine Kaffeepause.
   We'll ______________________________ at three o'clock.
2. Es gab eine kurze Pause, nicht mehr als zwei Sekunden.
   ______________________________, not more than two seconds.
3. Das Theaterstück war sehr lang und es gab zwei Pausen.
   ____
4. An manchen Tagen habe ich so viel zu tun, dass ich keine Mittagspause mache.
   ____
5. Hören Sie zu und sprechen Sie in der Pause nach.
   ____
6. Die [Schul-]Pause ist nach der zweiten [Unterrichts-]Stunde.
   ____

A14 A visit to a castle *dick / thick*

Was ist richtig: a oder b? Oder sind a und b beide richtig?

The castle was really impressive, with walls nearly three metres (a.) fat / (b.) thick (1.). One of the most interesting things about it was that it had a library, with some beautiful old leather books, really (a.) fat / (b.) thick (2.) books that must have been very valuable.

We had just finished our tour and were just coming out of the front gate, when a (a.) big fat / (b.) thick (3.) car drove up. It stopped, and a man got out. He was small, but incredibly (a.) fat / (b.) thick (4.). He walked round to the other side of the car, opened the door, and a woman got out. 'Welcome to Wellesborne', he said, and gave her a (a.) big / (b.) thick (5.) kiss on her cheek. She didn't like this at all, it was clearly a (a.) big / (b.) thick (6.) mistake. But it didn't seem to bother him. He laughed and said something to the gatekeeper, who then laughed too. They were obviously (a.) close / (b.) thick (7.) friends.

1	2	3	4	5	6	7

A15 Some things are extra *extra / extra*

Übersetzen Sie. Verwenden Sie die angegebenen Ausdrücke.

extra • on purpose • separately • specially

1. Kostet das extra?

   ____

2. Ich bezahle den Wein extra.

   ____

3. Ich habe den Wein extra für dich gekauft.

   ____

4. Er hat es extra gemacht, ich bin sicher!

   ____

A16 Not long, but ... *lang / long*

Ergänzen Sie. Nicht alle angegebenen Wörter werden benötigt.

a long time • for • length • long • twenty years

1. I waited ______________, it was almost an hour.
2. ____________________ they've been going to the same place for their holidays, every year the same.
3. It was the shoulder-____________ hair that made me think it was a woman.
4. The journey time is the same ____________, whether you go by car or by train.
5. I haven't seen them for ______________, it must be over five years since we last met.

A17 Young athletes *Preis / price, prize*

Was ist richtig: a oder b?

Some of these gymnasts are very young, not more than 14 or 15 years old. They may win a lot of (a.) prices / (b.) prizes (1.), but they pay a high (a.) price / (b.) prize (2.).

A18 Ears open *(zu)hören / hear*

Ergänzen Sie die passende Form von *hear* oder *listen (to)*.

1. _______ you _______ the latest news? Another bank is in trouble.
2. I'm sorry, can you say that again? I'm afraid I wasn't __________________.
3. The train was full, but I just closed my eyes and __________________ music on my MP3 player.
4. They were shouting at each other. I should think the whole house could __________________ them.
5. I don't know how many times I've told him not to park outside our gate, but he just won't __________________!
6. __________________ closely, and you'll __________________ the difference.

A19 Is it true? *sagen / say*

Ergänzen Sie *say* oder *tell*.

1. Will you please _______ me the truth.
2. Can you _______ me the way to the station?
3. Can you _______ that again, please?
4. _______ hello.
5. I'll _______ them where they can park.
6. _______ us that joke about the DJ again.

A20 What people say *sagen / say*

Übersetzen Sie.

1. Können Sie mir sagen, was es kostet?

   ____

2. Ich sage immer die Wahrheit.

   ____

3. Sie sagte *Happy birthday,* aber es war nicht mein Geburtstag.

   ____

4. Sie ist eine sehr stille Person. Sie sagt nicht viel.

   ____

5. Was hat er euch gesagt?

   ____

6. Was hat er gesagt?

   ____

7. Er sagte, er könnte uns nichts sagen.

   ____

8. Das [Fussball-]Spiel war langweilig. – Das kannst du laut sagen!

   ____

A21 Everything under control *Kontrolle / control*

Ergänzen Sie passende Übersetzungen von „kontrollieren/Kontrolle".

1. He was driving too fast and lost _________ of the car on a bend.
2. Remember to pack the scissors in your suitcase. If you put them in your hand luggage, they'll take them away when you get to the security _________.
3. I work in the quality _________ department.
4. It's all right, there's no need to worry. I have everything under _________.
5. We travelled over 300 kilometres and our tickets were not _________ once.
6. Our work is _________ all the time – it's like working in a police state!
7. The authorities carry out random _________s of restaurants to ensure that health standards are maintained.

A22 Entertaining a visitor *Koch, kochen / cook*

Drei der *kursiv* gedruckten Ausdrücke sind falsch. Korrigieren Sie sie.

◆ Come in, then we can carry on talking while I (1.) *cook* _________ us some tea.

● You have a very nice (2.) *kitchen* _________. I like all this wood.

◆ Thank you.

● Do you (3.) *do much cooking* _________?

◆ No, I don't have time. Brian is the (4.) *cook* _________ in this house. Well, most of the time. At any rate, he gets home first, so he normally (5.) *cooks* _________ our evening meal.

● People always say that English (6.) *kitchen* _________ is not very good. But I don't agree. I've always found that ...

◆ Oh, the water (7.) *is cooking* _________. Excuse me a moment.

A23 A question of how you feel *warm / warm*

Ergänzen Sie *warm* oder *hot*.

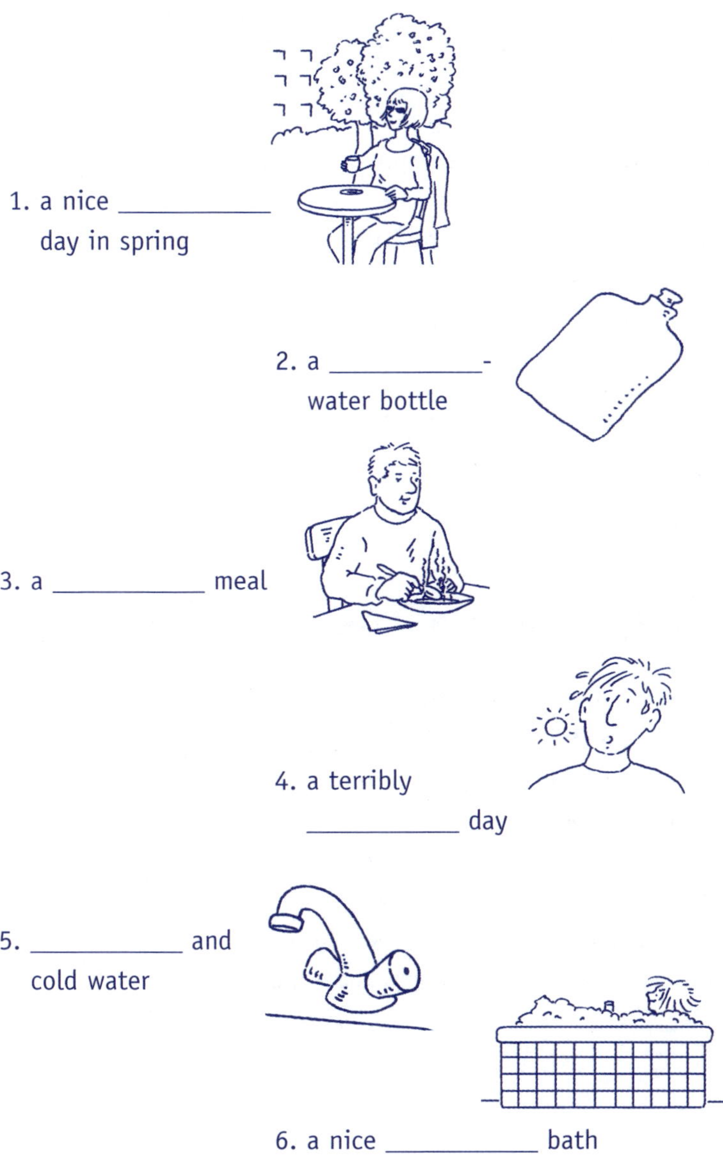

1. a nice ___________ day in spring

2. a ___________-water bottle

3. a ___________ meal

4. a terribly ___________ day

5. ___________ and cold water

6. a nice ___________ bath

A24 A breath of fresh air *frisch / fresh*

Ergänzen Sie.

bright • clean • chilly • fresh • wet

1. I need to get some __________ air.
2. We sat outside till ten in the evening, but then it got quite __________ and so we went inside.
3. After a day's hard work it's good to have a shower and put on some __________ clothes.
4. The place was decorated in nice __________ colours.
5. Careful! __________ paint!

A25 The minimum *null / nil*

Ergänzen Sie.

nil • nought • oh • zero

1. It was a hard-fought match which neither team deserved to lose, so it was right that it finished __________ __________.
2. We had the first frost of the winter last night, the temperature is now just one degree above __________.
3. She broke the world record, but only by point __________ one (0,01) of a second!
4. My mobile number is __________ one five seven, ...
5. In a recession the rate of economic growth drops below __________.

A26 Josh's accident *nächste(r/s), neu / next, new*

Ergänzen Sie passende Wörter.

- ◆ Have you heard the (1.) _________ news?
- ● No, why? What's happened?
- ◆ Josh has crashed his (2.) _________ car.
- ● But he only got it last week.
- ◆ I know. It was the very (3.) _________ model and must have cost him I don't know how much.
- ◆ How did it happen?
- ● Someone stopped him and asked the way to the (4.) _________ bank, so he said, "I'll drive you there, it's only just round the corner." And it was, just round the corner, but they didn't get there because Josh overlooked a red light.
- ◆ (5.) _________ time he'll know better than to show off to strangers.

A27 More on cars *Motor / motor*

Wählen Sie die richtige Lösung, a oder b.

We had a terrible journey back from Scotland. It was raining, but the windscreen wipers weren't working properly. There was something wrong with the electric (a.) engine / (b.) motor (1.). We stopped and got that repaired, but then in the middle of a wild stretch of countryside the car broke down completely. This time, it was something major to do with the (a.) engine / (b.) motor (2.).

1	2

A28 **All the latest** *Technik / technique*

Ergänzen Sie *technique* oder *technology*.

1. In this course you will learn an important new marketing _________.
2. There have been huge advances in medical _________ over the last 50 years.
3. Roberta has a new trainer, and her _________ has improved enormously. She's developing into a first-class player.
4. The company fell behind because it didn't invest in new _________.

A29 **Light and dark** *Schatten / shade, shadow*

Was ist richtig: a oder b?

1. It's too hot in the sun. Let's try and find a table in the (a.) shade / (b.) shadow.
2. As the sun began to go down behind us, our (a.) shades / (b.) shadows on the lawn[1] grew longer and longer.
3. The news of Will's heart attack cast[2] a (a.) shade / (b.) shadow over the whole evening.
4. He's now only a (a.) shade / (b.) shadow of the man he used to be.
5. After lunch, I lay down and slept in the (a.) shade / (b.) shadow of a big chestnut tree[3].

1	2	3	4	5

[1]Rasen [2]warf [3]Kastanienbaum

A30 **And so to bed** *schlafen / sleep*

Was ist richtig: a oder b? Oder sind a und b beide richtig?

1. Sleep researchers have found that we now (a.) are asleep / (b.) sleep over an hour less than fifty years ago.
2. Fifty years ago people were often in bed and (a.) asleep / (b.) sleeping by ten thirty in the evening.
3. It's been a long day and I think it's time for me to go to (a.) bed / (b.) sleep. Goodnight everybody and thanks for a wonderful evening.
4. I'm sorry I disturbed you. I didn't realize you were (a.) asleep / (b.) sleeping.
5. Most nights I switch the light off and (a.) am asleep / (b.) sleep within ten minutes.
6. Sometimes I wake in the middle of the night and have problems (a.) getting back to sleep / (b.) falling asleep again.
7. I'm not one of these people who sleep (a.) in / (b.) late at the weekend. I still get up quite early.
8. The presentation was so boring, the speaker's voice so monotonous that it (a.) brought / (b.) sent me to sleep.

1	2	3	4	5	6	7	8

A31 **Opinion poll results** *Politik / politics, policy*

Ergänzen Sie *politics, policy* oder *policies.*

1. In the opinion poll, over 30% of young people said they weren't interested in _________.
2. In the same poll, over 50% of all respondents said they were dissatisfied with the government's economic _________.
3. As always, the US presidential election seems to be more about personalities. It's not clear what _________ each candidate has on the major issues facing the country.

A32 In the media *Programm / programme, program*

Übersetzen Sie.

1. Sie hatten kein Satellitenfernsehen und es gab nur drei Programme.

   ____

2. Es gibt viele Verbesserungen in der neuen Version des [Computer-] Programms.

   ____

3. Das Festivalprogramm ist nun erschienen.

   ____

4. Welches [TV-]Programm schauen Sie am meisten?

   ____

A33 Not always a house *Haus / house*

Korrigieren Sie – falls nötig!

1. I'm sorry, but Herr Werner is out of the *house* __________.
   Try calling back this afternoon.
2. Ann and Steve have just sold their *house* __________.
3. The hospital always sends a report to your *house doctor* __________.
4. The teacher gives a lot of work to be done at *house* __________.

I'm afraid
he's out
of the office.

A34 What do you mean? *meinen / mean*

Korrigieren Sie – falls nötig.

1. What do you *mean* by ______________ "very expensive"?
2. When I said, "he's too old", I *didn't mean* ______________ you.
3. I *mean* __________ it's a good idea. What's your view?
4. I'm sorry. I *didn't mean* ____________ to hurt you.
5. I agree with you entirely. I *mean* ___________ exactly the same.

A35 Getting it right *Komma / comma*

Ergänzen Sie eine passende Übersetzung von „Komma".

1. The increase was minimal, just nought ______________ seven per cent.
2. In German you always put a __________ before *dass*, but in English you never put one before 'that'.

A36 What do you want? (1) *wollen / want*

Welche Verbform ist richtig?

1. We got to the station just as the train ... leave.
   a. wanted to b. was about to
2. Lots of migrants ... America.
   a. want to b. want to get to
3. Damn! The car ... start.
   a. doesn't want to b. won't
4. There we were, ready to leave, and the car ... start.
   a. didn't want to b. wouldn't

1	2	3	4

A37 What do you want? (2) *wollen / want*

Übersetzen Sie.

1. Wen wollen Sie sprechen?
   ____
2. Ich wollte gerade gehen, als Jim anrief.
   ____
3. Der Besucher will zu Mr Smith.
   ____
4. Ich will ins Bett.
   ____
5. Ich hab's ihr hundert Mal gesagt, aber sie will einfach nicht hören.
   I've told her a hundred times, but ______________________
6. Ich versuchte das Fenster zu öffnen, aber es wollte nicht.
   ____
7. Moment mal! Was wollen Sie damit sagen?! Dass ich ein Dieb bin?!
   Just a moment! ______________________? That I'm a thief?!

A38 **Your money** *Kosten, kosten / cost[s]*

Ergänzen Sie passende Übersetzungen von „kosten/Kosten".

1. The __________ of petrol rose last year by over 15%.
2. Will we save on production __________ by introducing the new technology? That's the key question.
3. The __________ of living in London will be a real shock for them when they move there.
4. It will __________ too much time. We'll have to abandon the idea.
5. Money doesn't seem to be a problem. He wants to go so much that he's prepared to go at his own __________.
6. How much will it __________ to park at the airport?

A39 **Help!** *helfen / help*

Ergänzen Sie die Übersetzung. Verwenden Sie die vorgegebenen Wörter.

It's • do • for • good • is • no • one • only
There's • thing • to • use

1. Es hilft nichts. Wir müssen ganz von vorne anfangen.
   ____________________. We're going to have to start all over again.
2. Honig mit Zitrone hilft gegen Halsschmerzen.
   Honey with lemon ____________________. a sore throat.
3. Da hilft nur eins: alle Banken verstaatlichen.
   ____________________: nationalize all the banks.

A40 Lots of people *Publikum, publik / public*

Ist das *kursiv* gesetzte Wort richtig oder falsch?

1. It's an absolute scandal. This needs to be made *public*.
2. At the end of the play the *public* gave the actors a standing ovation.

A41 It's natural *Natur / nature*

Ergänzen Sie die Übersetzungen.

1. Am Wochenende bin ich gern in der freien Natur.
   At the weekend I like to be out in the ________________.
2. Es liegt in der menschlichen Natur, Fehler zu machen.
   It's h______ ________ to make mistakes.
3. Pflanzen, Tiere, Menschen: wir alle sind Teil der Natur.
   Plants, animals, human beings: we are all part of __________.

A42 Is it OK? *wenn / when*

Ergänzen Sie *when* oder *if*.

1. Is it OK _________ we meet a little bit later?
2. We can discuss everything else _________ we meet.
3. I'll let you know _________ the flight arrives.
4. _________ you need any help, just ask.
5. _________ things continue like this, we'll have to take drastic action.
6. I'll only phone _________ there's a problem.
7. Start without us _________ we're late. Don't wait.
8. _________ we finish, I'll take them on a guided tour.
9. _________ we finish early, I'll fill in time by taking them on a guided tour.

A43 What can you say *Menü, Appetit, grillen / …*

Kreuzen Sie alle korrekten Sätze an.

1.
a. I'll have today's menu, please.
b. I'll have today's special, please.
c. I'll have today's set meal, please.

2.
a. Here you are, sir. Enjoy your meal.
b. Here you are, sir. Bon appétit.
c. Here you are, sir. Good appetite.

3.
a. It's a beautiful evening for a grill.
b. It's a beautiful evening for a barbecue.
c. It's a beautiful evening to grill.
d. It's a beautiful evening to have a grill party.

A44 Plans and activities *Aktion / action*

Welcher Ausdruck passt in die Lücke?

1. Which products are we going to place at the centre of our summer advertising ...?
   a. action b. campaign
2. We already have a provisional plan of ... .
   a. action b. campaign
3. There has been more military ... in Northern Afghanistan.
   a. action b. campaign
4. A number of different charities have launched ... to help the victims of the earthquake.
   a. an action b. a campaign

A45 Criminal activity *rauben / rob*

Kreuzen Sie die richtige Lösung an.

	rob	steal	
1.	○	○	a bank
2.	○	○	jewels from someone's house
3.	○	○	priceless paintings from a museum
4.	○	○	somebody on the underground
5.	○	○	a team of what seemed certain victory
6.	○	○	a star of her diamond ring
7.	○	○	the tomb of an Egyptian king
8.	○	○	stationery from the office
9.	○	○	13 million from an online bank account
10.	○	○	people of their life savings

A46 Not always high *hoch / high*

Übersetzen Sie.

1. Es war kalt und wir hatten hohen Schnee.

2. Santa Claus wohnt im hohen Norden.

3. Es war Hochsommer und das Gras war hoch.

4. Wie hoch war der Betrag, der gestohlen wurde?

5. Sie hat eine hoch bezahlte Stelle bei einer Computerfirma.

6. Die Stadt ist von hohen Bergen umgeben.

7. Hände hoch!

8. Der Zug fuhr mit hoher Geschwindigkeit in den Tunnel hinein.

9. Wir rechnen mit nicht mehr als 30 Personen, wenn es hoch kommt.

10. Immer mehr Menschen erreichen ein hohes Alter.

11. Er hat hohe Schulden.

12. Die Mannschaft hat hoch gewonnen.

A47 It's chaos at home. *lassen / let*

Was passt in die Lücke? Mehrere Lösungen sind möglich.

1. It's chaos at home.
   We ... the whole house ...

   a. are letting ... repaint
   b. are letting ... repainted
   c. are having ... repainted
   d. are making ... repainted

2. I'm a bit short of time.
   ... to explain it to you.

   a. Let Wanda
   b. Get Wanda
   c. Ask Wanda
   d. Make Wanda

3. They ... over half an hour.

   a. kept us waiting
   b. made us wait
   c. let us to wait
   d. made us to wait

4. ...! You know I don't like it.

   a. Let that
   b. Leave that
   c. Let that be
   d. Stop that

5. Can you just ..., please?!

   a. let me
   b. leave me alone
   c. leave me to be
   d. leave me work

6. Can you ... for everyone, please?

   a. let copies make
   b. have copies made
   c. make copies to be made
   d. make it be copied

Und nun übersetzen Sie.

7. Robin und Ann lassen euch grüßen.

   ____

A48 On the road (1) *Straße / street*

Ergänzen Sie *road* oder *street.*

1. a ____________________

2. a ____________________

3. A __________ is what cars, buses etc. use to get from A to B.
4. A __________ is a place where people live, work, go shopping, etc.

A49 On the road (2) *Straße / street*

Kreuzen Sie die richtige Lösung an.

	road	street	
1.	●	●	Excuse me. Is this the ... to Inverness?
2.	●	●	How much crime is there? How safe are the ...s in this part of town?
3.	●	●	The private detective stood on the ... corner reading a newspaper.
4.	●	●	Drivers need to take extra care on the ...s this morning. There is a lot of fog about.
5.	●	●	He was driving far too fast and came off the ... .
6.	●	●	The country ... is best if you want to enjoy the scenery.
7.	●	●	The exhibition centre is on the ... to Walsall.
8.	●	●	The major shopping ...s are to the west of the station.

A50 **Welcome to Wembley ...** *Stadium / stadium*

Was passt in die Lücke?

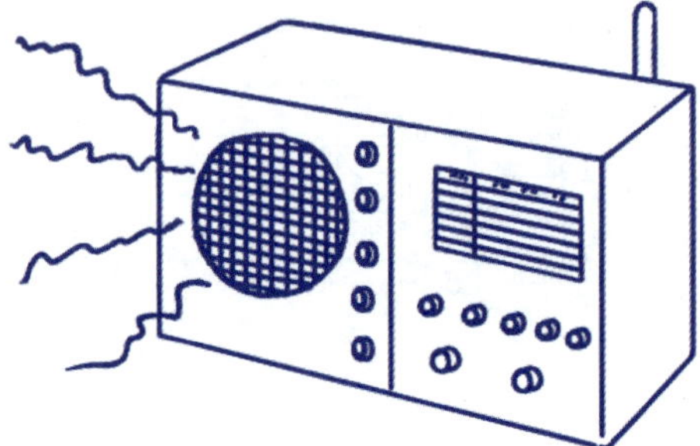

Welcome back to Wembley (1.) ..., where the second half of this important qualifying match is already well under way. At this (2.) ... of the game, ten minutes into the second half, the match is wide open, and either team could win.

1.

a. sports centre
b. sports ground
c. stadion
d. stadium

2.

a. part
b. event
c. segment
d. stage

A51 Make and do (1) *machen / make*

Kreuzen Sie die richtige Lösung an.

	make	do	
1.	○	○	I can't ... this sudoku. Can you help me?
2.	○	○	What am I to ...? I've tried everything.
3.	○	○	Do you have to ... much overtime in your job?
4.	○	○	We need to ... some decisions.
5.	○	○	If I cook, will you ... the washing up?
6.	○	○	I'm afraid I'm going to ... a mistake.
7.	○	○	I'll ... the shopping on my way home.
8.	○	○	Does it ... any difference what I think?
9.	○	○	What do you ... for a living?
10.	○	○	I'd like to ... a Chinese course.
11.	○	○	I used to ... quite a lot of sport.
12.	○	○	I'd like to ... a suggestion if I may.

A52 Make and do (2) *machen / make*

Übersetzen Sie.

1. Wann machen Sie in diesem Jahr Urlaub?

   ____

2. Warte, ich will ein Foto machen.

   ____

3. Es macht nichts.

   ____

4. Sollen wir Pause machen?

   ____

5. Ich mache Diät.

   ____

6. Wann machen Sie Ihre Prüfung?

   ____

7. Mach dir keine Sorgen.

   ____

A53 Make and do (3) *machen / make*

Ergänzen Sie die richtige(n) Verbform(en).

1. The engine ... a funny noise. I think we should stop and see what's wrong.
   ● is doing ● is making
2. In German dogs ... *wau wau,* but in English 'woof woof'.
   ● do ● go ● make
3. On Sunday afternoons we always had to ... a walk. It was awful.
   ● do ● go for ● make
4. I only ... four questions right.
   ● did ● got ● made
5. It's not ideal, but let's ... the best of it.
   ● do ● make
6. I'm ... my best.
   ● doing ● making
7. Let's ... a start, we have a lot to get through.
   ● do ● get ● make
8. Can you ... me a favour?
   ● do ● give ● make
9. Quite a number of employees ... a little sleep during the lunch break.
   ● do ● have ● make
10. You've ... a really good job. Thank you very much indeed.
    ● done ● made
11. At school I used to like ... translations.
    ● doing ● making

B. False friends

Englisch-deutsche Wortpaare mit ähnlicher Form
aber unterschiedlicher Bedeutung

B1 Globalization *Fabrik / fabric*

Kreuzen Sie die richtige(n) Antwort(en) an.

The company I used to work for produces (1.) ... for the furniture industry, for sofas, beds, etc. They used to have (2.) ... in western Europe, but now most of the production is based in Rumania. When the company relocated, many people lost their jobs.

1. a. cloths c. materials
   b. fabrics d. stuffs
2. a. fabrics c. production places
   b. factories d. workplaces

B2 What makes a good film? *Kritik / critic*

Richtig oder falsch? Wenn falsch, wie lautet der richtige Ausdruck?

◆ Did you enjoy the film?
● I did. Films that have a (1.) *happy end* __________ make you feel good.
◆ That doesn't mean they are good films.
● You sound like one of these film (2.) *critics* __________.
Anyway. Have you read the (3.) *critic* __________ of the film in the paper?

B3 Please fill it in. *Formular / formula*

Ergänzen Sie *form* oder *formula*.

1. Can you please fill in this __________?
2. What is your __________ for success?
3. This weekend is the last race in this year's __________ One series.
4. What's the mathematical __________ for calculating the area of a circle?
5. Support in the __________ of cash is also very welcome.

B4 In a café *überhören / overhear*

Was passt in die Lücke? Mehrere Lösungen sind möglich.

As I was sitting in the café waiting for Minako, I (1.) ... two men at the next table talking about a "delivery at midnight", and I thought I heard the word 'cocaine'. I tried to catch what else they were saying. I was listening so intently to their conversation that I (2.) ... my mobile ringing. It was Minako calling to say she'd be late.

1. a. became with
   b. happened to hear
   c. overheard
   d. overcame
2. a. didn't hear
   b. failed to hear
   c. heard over
   d. overheard

B5 Times are changing *Branche, Chef, Personal, ... / ...*

Ergänzen Sie.

1. Banks used to have b _ _ _ _ _ _ _ s in every town.
2. Companies in our b _ _ _ _ _ _ _ s are really feeling the recession.
3. There has been another big t _ _ _ _ _ _ _ _. The second biggest bank in the country has bought up the fourth biggest.
4. We were going so slowly that even people on bikes o _ _ _ _ _ _ _ k us!
5. The company has been forced to cut costs and reduce s _ _ _ _.
6. PIN stands for _ _ _ _ _ _ _ _ _ _ identification number.
7. A firm that organizes funerals[1] is called an _ _ _ _ _ _ _ _ _ _ _ _.
8. Bill Gates must be seen as one of the great ent _ _ pr _ _ eurs of the 20th century.
9. How are you getting on with your new b _ _ s?
10. A _ _ _ _ works in a restaurant and plans and cooks meals.

[1]Beerdigungen

B6 Don't just sit there! *Rückseite / backside*

Was passt in die Lücke? Mehrere Lösungen sind möglich.

Mother	Don't just sit there on your (1.) ...! Get up and do something.
Son	What?
Mother	Well, for a start you can go and get the rest of the shopping out of the car.
Son	Where is it?
Mother	Parked (2.) ... of the building where it always is!

1. a. backside c. bottom
   b. behind d. sit
2. a. at the back side c. on the back side
   b. at the back d. on the back

B7 Definitions *selbstbewusst, sensibel, sympathisch / ...*

Ordnen Sie zu.

pleasant • self-conscious • self-confident
sensible • sensitive • sympathetic

1. Someone who is ______________ is often nervous and worries about what other people think of them.
2. A ______________ person is the opposite of the type of person described in sentence 1. This sort of person feels good about him or herself.
3. A ______________ person is someone who is practical and makes wise decisions.
4. If you are ______________ you have good antennae for how other people feel, you can put yourself in their situation and understand how they feel.
5. If you like another person, you find them nice or ____________.
6. A ______________ person listens carefully to your worries and cares about your problems.

B8 I prefer people like you and me *ordinär / ordinary*

Was passt in die Lücke? Mehrere Lösungen sind möglich.

Mr Bagshot may have lots of money and lots of friends in high places, but I find him distinctly (1.) ... . He's always telling jokes and stories that are in bad taste. I prefer normal, (2.) ... people – people like you and me!

1. a. common c. out of the ordinary
   b. orderly d. vulgar
2. a. ordinal c. ordinary
   b. every day d. usual

B9 What is what? *Keks / cake*

Ergänzen Sie.

1. a ______________________________

2. a ______________________________

B10 **What do you think?** *Meinung / meaning*

Korrigieren Sie.

◆ What do you think of the new proposals that have been put forward by the government?

● I'm sceptical. What's your *meaning* __________?

B11 **Have you got your results?** *Note, Notiz / note, notice*

Ergänzen Sie *note, notice* oder einen anderen passenden Ausdruck.

1. I hear that you've got your exam results. What __________ did you get? – An A in English, and a C in German.
2. I have to write a summary of the meeting, but there's one topic where the __________s I took are not clear.
3. I must make a mental __________ of that so that I don't forget.
4. When he got home he found a __________ on the kitchen table saying she was gone.
5. The best thing to do is to ignore him. Just don't take any __________.
6. There was a big __________ on the gate saying 'Please do not feed the animals'.
7. I carry a little __________book round with me in which I write down all the new words I hear. It's a good way to learn new vocabulary.
8. I can sing OK, but I can't read __________. I have to learn new songs by listening.

B12 Things that arrive *bekommen / become*

Welcher Satz ist richtig?

1.

a. I become the quiche, please.

b. I get the quiche, please.

c. I have the quiche, please.

d. I'll have the quiche, please.

2.

a. Fran has become a baby

b. Fran got a baby.

c. Fran has had a baby.

d. Fran has received a baby.

B13 What the postman brings *Paket / packet*

Übersetzen Sie.

1. Wann holt der Kurier die Pakete ab?

   ____

2. Die Regierung hat ein Maßnahmenpaket bewilligt.
   The government has approved ____________________

3. Ich benutze mehrere Softwarepakete von Microsoft.

   ____

4. Zwei Päckchen Butter und ein Päckchen Tee.

   ____

B14 Different concepts *Konzept / concept*

Ist der *kursiv* gedruckte Ausdruck richtig oder falsch? Wenn falsch, korrigieren Sie ihn.

1. The *concept* __________ of 'democracy' goes back to ancient Greece.
2. I've completed the first *concept* __________ of my dissertation, but it is still very rough and needs more work done on it.
3. The marketing *concept* __________ for the new brand includes a whole range of activities and measures.
4. The question completely *brought him out of his concept* ____________________.

B15 This and that *Mappe, Tablett, Fotograf / map, tablet, ...*

Beschriften Sie die Bilder.

folder • map • photograph • photographer
tablet • tray

1.  ____________ 2. a ____________ 3. a ____________

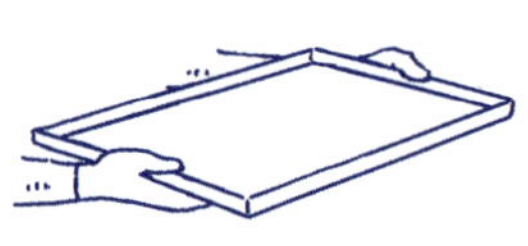

4. a ____________ 5. a ____________ 6. a ____________

B16 Killed by a cup of tea *Mörder, Gift / murder, gift*

Ergänzen Sie.

gift • murder • murderer • poison

Police are investigating the bizarre (1.) __________ of an old lady in an old people's home. It seems that the (2.) __________ killed his or her victim by putting some (3.) __________ into the old lady's early-morning tea. It was her birthday, and she had received a number of cards and (4.) __________.

B17 What's on a piece of paper *Rezept / receipt*

Übersetzen Sie.

1. Ich bezahlte und der Taxifahrer gab mir eine Quittung.

   ____

2. Es schmeckt wunderbar. Du musst mir das Rezept geben.

   ____

3. Das Rezept muss noch von der Ärztin unterschrieben werden.

   ____

4. Was ist Ihr Erfolgsrezept?

   ____

B18 Hard times *Rente / rent*

Was passt in die Lücke? Mehrere Lösungen sind möglich.

1. More and more old people are finding it hard to survive on the state … .

   a. pay
   b. pension
   c. retirement money
   d. old-age allowance

2. She'll be 66 next March and will be … .

   a. going to rent
   b. going into retirement
   c. retiring
   d. going to rest

3. My flat has become too expensive. My landlord[1] put up the … again.

   a. monthly fee
   b. money
   c. rent
   d. tax

B19 Actually, no … *aktuell / actual*

Ergänzen Sie jeweils die passende Entsprechung von „aktuell".

1. ◆ You can't go by that timetable. It's no longer v _ _ _ _.
   ● Sorry?
   ◆ It's no longer u_ to d _ _ _.

2. ◆ Hunault's latest book is set in the present day and is about the winners and losers of globalization.
   ● So it's very t _ _ _ _ _ _ _.

3. ◆ What's in the news?
   ● The same thing as last week and the week before. All the media are full of the c _ _ _ _ _ _ _ crisis in the banking sector.

B20 **Money matters** *sparen, spenden / spare, spend*

Ergänzen Sie (eine passende Form von) *save, spare, spend* oder *donate*.

1. Can you __________ me ten minutes? I'd like to ask you for some advice.
2. It'll __________ time and help to keep the meeting short if you arrange it for quite late in the afternoon.
3. I got €300 out of the bank this morning and I've __________ it all already. I'm not very good at managing my money.
4. When the economic climate cools down, people __________ less to charity.
5. You can __________ a few euros if you book online. It's slightly cheaper.

B21 **An accident** *übersehen, Handy, blinken / oversee, ...*

Korrigieren Sie.

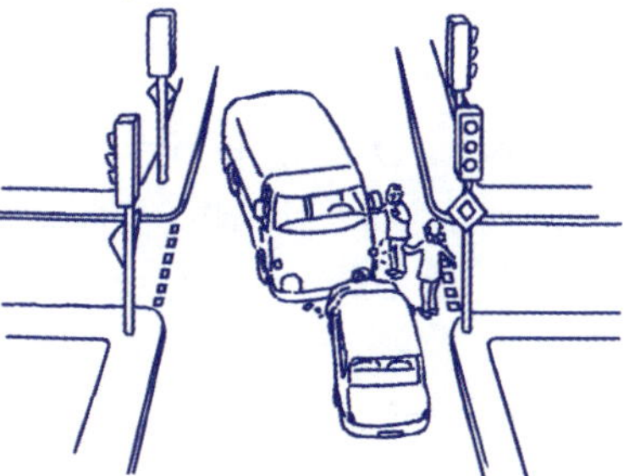

This is how the accident happened. The driver of the delivery van was on his (1.) ~~handy~~ __________ and not paying attention to what was happening on the road. He wanted to turn left, and had (2.) ~~blinked~~ __________ left, but he (3.) ~~oversaw~~ __________ the car coming the other way.

It all happened in the *blink* of an eye, very quickly indeed. There were plenty of other witnesses[1] besides me because I *was overseeing* a group of students who were doing a photography project. It was handy that they all had cameras.

[1]Zeugen

B22 **Children** *brav, Gymnasium, Mobbing / brave, gymnasium, …*

Was passt in die Lücke? Mehrere Lösungen sind möglich.

1.
◆ Our usual babysitter goes to the same school as Tina.
● Which school is that?
◆ The local …

a. gymnasium c. grammar school
b. second school d. higher school

2.
● Is that a good school?
◆ Yes, we're very happy. There don't seem to be any problems with … or anything like that.

a. bullying c. mobbing
b. harassers d. mobbsters

3.
◆ Has everything been OK?
● Yes, the children have been very …, no problem at all. They went to bed when I told them to, did exactly what I asked them to do.
◆ They're not like that with us, I can assure you!

a. brave c. bold
b. good d. well-behaved

B23 **Keeping fit** *Gymnastik, wandern / gymnastics, wander*

Ergänzen Sie *exercises, gymnastics, hiking* oder *wandering*.
Benutzen Sie jedes Wort nur einmal.

1. ____________ is an Olympic discipline. Some of the best athletes are still children.
2. I'm not one of these people who get out of bed in the morning and do their keep-fit ____________.
3. I had an hour to spare, so I spent it ____________ round the old town.
4. Autumn is the best time to go ____________ in the mountains.

B24 The weekend paper *Prospekt, Annonce / prospect, ...*

Ergänzen Sie.

advertisement • announcements • brochures • prospects

The first thing I do when I get the weekend paper is to sort out and throw away all the bits I'm not interested in. These include all the separate advertising (1.) __________ and all the (2.) __________ sections for jobs, housing, cars, etc.
The paper is still then very thick, and my (3.) __________ of getting through all of it very slim. So another thing I don't read is the section with all the birth, marriage and death (4.) __________.

B25 In the air *gründen / ground*

Ergänzen Sie *founded* oder *grounded*.

British Airways was (1.) __________ in 1974, when the two companies BOAC (British Overseas Airways Corporation) and BEA (British European Airways) were merged. BOAC had previously been (2.) __________, when British Airways and Imperial Airways were merged in 1937.
As you can see, today we have thick fog here at the airport, and most of the fleet[1] has been (3.) __________ .

[1]Flotte

B26 Not now, but ... *eventuell / eventually*

Wählen Sie den Ausdruck oder die Ausdrücke mit der gleichen Bedeutung wie *eventually*.

1. The train *eventually* arrived, over 45 minutes late.

   ● sometime ● at last ● finally ● one day

2. *Eventually* all this will belong to you, son.

   ● sometime ● at last ● finally ● one day

B27 Don't wait *eventuell / eventually*

Wählen Sie alle passenden Übersetzungen.

1. Er kommt eventuell nicht. Wir sollen nicht auf ihn warten.
   a. He may not come. We are not to wait for him.
   b. He possibly won't be coming. We are not to wait for him.
   c. It's possible that he won't be coming. We are not to wait for him.
   d. He likely won't be coming. We are not to wait for him.

2. Wir haben eventuell ein Problem.
   a. We can have a problem.
   b. We possibly have a problem.
   c. We may have a problem.
   d. We have a possible problem.

1	2

B28 What you need to make something *Stoff / stuff*

Ergänzen Sie die Übersetzungen.

1. Aus welchem Stoff ist das Zelt?

   What ___________ is the tent made of?

2. Ich habe Stoff gekauft und werde die Vorhänge selber nähen.

   I've bought some ___________ and am going to make the curtains myself.

3. Es gibt verschiedene chemische Stoffe, die diese Eigenschaft haben.

   There are various chemical ___________ that have this property.

4. Wo findet sie den Stoff für ihre Geschichten?

   Where does she find the ___________ for her stories?

B29 Goods *Warenhaus / warehouse*

Was passt in die Lücken?

Goods are produced, stored in a ... (1), then moved to the place where they are sold – for example, big ...s (2), like KDW in Berlin, Macy's in New York, or Selfridges in London.

a. department store
b. shopping store
c. retail house
d. warehouse

B30 A question of religion *Konfession / confession*

Ergänzen Sie.

belief • confession • denomination • denotation

- ◆ What (1.) ________ are you? Protestant or Roman Catholic?
- ● Roman Catholic. At least on paper.
- ◆ So that means you go to (2.) ________?
- ● Sorry?
- ◆ You go to the priest and tell him what you have done wrong.
- ● Well, I should do, or would do if I was a practising Roman Catholic.

B31 Wedding bells *engagiert / engaged*

Sortieren Sie die Buchstaben.

1. Laura and Michael have just got *G A N E G E D* ______________. The wedding is going to take place next March.
2. Laura is a teacher. She's very *T E A D D E D I C* ______________ to her job.
3. Michael is a social worker. He's also very *T E M O M C I T D* ______________ to his work.
4. Both of them are heavily *V O N E V D I L* ______________ in the anti-globalization movement.
5. They are a politically and socially *I V E C A T* ______________ couple.
6. So please don't tell them that I've just been *D E R I H* ______________ by one of the big multi-nationals!

C. Lots of friends

Deutsche Wörter mit mehreren englischen Entsprechungen

C1 **At a party.** *Mann, Frau*

Ergänzen Sie die richtige Übersetzung von „Mann" und „Frau".

C2 Here you are. *bitte*

Was passt zusammen? Ordnen Sie zu.

1. Darf ich mich hierher setzen? – *Bitte schön.*
2. Vielen Dank. – *Bitte schön*.
3. *Bitte schön*, Ihr Schlüssel.
4. Kann ich *bitte* das Salz haben?
5. *Wie bitte*? Ich verstehe leider nicht.

a. Here you are, your key.
b. May I sit here? – Certainly. / Of course. / Please do.
c. Thanks very much. – It's a pleasure. / That's all right. / You're welcome.
d. Sorry? / Pardon? / Excuse me? I'm afraid I don't understand.
e. Can I have the salt please?

C3 In a German restaurant *bitte*

Ergänzen Sie den Dialog mit passenden Ausdrücken aus C2.

◆ Excuse me. Do you mind if I join you?
● Entschuldigung?
◆ May I sit here?
● Yes, (1.) ______________________.
...
◆ Can I see the menu, please?
● *(Gives the menu.)* (2.) ______________________.
◆ Thanks very much.
Hmm. Interesting. But can you explain what this is, 'xzysxwlm'?
● (3.) ______________________?
◆ Sorry, it's my German pronunciation. I can't say it properly.
● Can I see, (4.) ______________________?
◆ Sure. *(Points to something.)* Here.
● Ah, 'Saumagen'. Well, that's something very, er, special, it's ...
◆ Thanks for all your help.
● (5.) ______________________.

C4 A postcard *als*

Ergänzen Sie eine passende Entsprechung für „als".

(1.) ________ we arrived,
it was pouring with rain.
And that's how the holiday
has continued. I don't think
we've had a wetter holiday
(2.) ________ this one!
When people find out that I'm
English, they say, "Well,
(3.) ____________ an
English person you must be used
to this." (4.) __________
if it rained all the time in
England!

C5 Where you go and what you do *besuchen*

Ergänzen Sie eine passende Übersetzung von „besuchen".

attend • go to • visit

1. We're not going away, can't afford a holiday this year. We'll probably take the odd day and go and ____________ friends or relatives.
2. In this country children have to ____________ school until the age of 16.
3. Even if you don't live in the city, you can still enjoy what's on offer culturally, ____________ concerts and things.

C6 **Payment** *(be)zahlen*

Kreuzen Sie die richtige Lösung an.

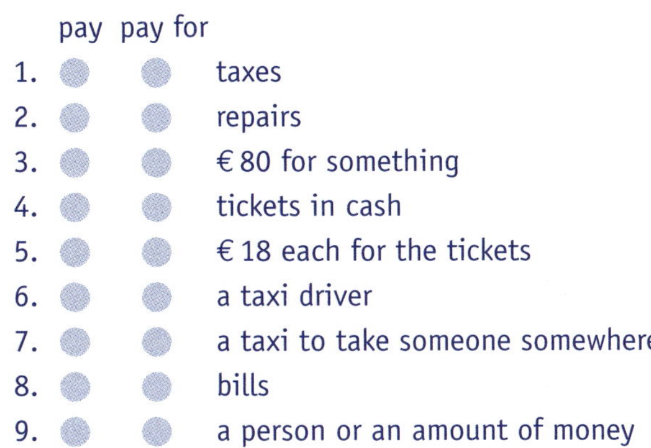

	pay	pay for	
1.	○	○	taxes
2.	○	○	repairs
3.	○	○	€ 80 for something
4.	○	○	tickets in cash
5.	○	○	€ 18 each for the tickets
6.	○	○	a taxi driver
7.	○	○	a taxi to take someone somewhere
8.	○	○	bills
9.	○	○	a person or an amount of money
10.	○	○	a product or service

C7 **My grandmother** *(sich) erinnern, Gedächtnis, Erinnerung*

Ergänzen Sie.

My grandmother says that her (1.) m _ m _ _ y is failing.
Like a lot of older people she can (2.) r _ _ _ _ _ _ _ many things from a long time ago, and some of her (3.) m _ _ _ _ _ _ _ are really vivid. But she has problems with her (4.) s _ _ _ _-term m _ _ _ _ _. She goes into the garden, for example, and then can't (5.) r _ _ _ _ _ _ _ what she went for. And she forgets things like doctor's appointments. She needs someone or something to (6.) r _ _ _ _ _ her.

For her last birthday we grandchildren gave her a mobile phone and showed her how to use the organizer function, so that she gets a (7.) r _ _ _ _ _ _ _ when she needs one. But of course she only gets it if she (8.) r _ _ _ _ _ _ _ _ to switch the mobile on!

C8 A crossword *gesund*

Ergänzen Sie.

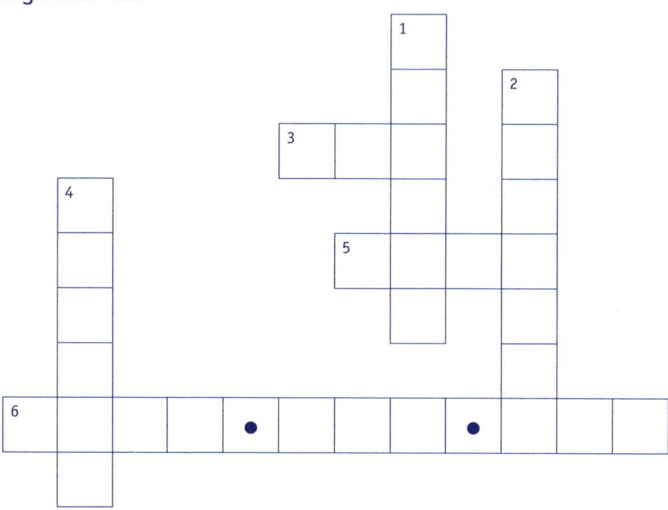

Across

3. My grandmother is still f_ _ and well at the age of 96.
5. I was sorry to hear that you're in hospital. Get w_ _ _ soon!
6. At least there's one thing that the experts seem to agree on – that fruit and vegetables are g_ _ _ f_ _ y_ _.

Down

1. Dave was ill last week, but he's b_ _ _ _ _ again now and back at work.
2. The older you get, the more important it is to adopt a h_ _ _ _ _ _ lifestyle.
4. If you use your c_ _ _ _ _ sense, it's obvious what you should do.

C9 More coming and going *fahren*

Welche Form ist richtig?

1. The traffic got so bad that I gave up ... to work. I now commute by train.
   a. going
   b. driving
   c. travelling
2. Is it difficult to ... a heavy motorbike?
   a. drive b. lead
   c. ride
3. Now that the high-speed line has been completed, trains ... at over 250 km/h and the journey time has been almost halved.
   a. drive
   b. ride
   c. travel
4. How often do the trains ... at this time of day?
   a. ride b. drive
   c. run
5. It's OK, I'm going your way. I'll ... .
   a. drive you home
   b. travel you home
   c. bring you home
6. In the evenings I usually ... .
   a. go with the 6 o'clock train
   b. take the 6 o'clock train
   c. ride the 6 o'clock train
7. It was late so we ... .
   a. went home with a taxi
   b. took a taxi home
   c. drove home with a taxi
8. There was a police radar trap, but I was OK. I was only ... a little over 50 km/h.
   a. doing
   b. driving
   c. riding
9. If it's wet, I don't walk but ... .
   a. go with the bus
   b. take the bus
   c. ride the bus to work
10. How fast does this moped ...?
    a. drive b. go c. do
11. I ... when I was 17.
    a. learned to drive
    b. made my driving
    c. did my driving licence

C10 People who teach *Lehrer*

Ergänzen Sie *teacher* oder *instructor*.

1. a driving ______________________
2. a school ______________________
3. a riding ______________________
4. a swimming ______________________
5. a university __________, or lecturer
6. People who teach skills are called __________s.
7. People who teach a school or academic subject are called __________s.

C11 Not much room *eng*

Ergänzen Sie eine passende Übersetzung von „eng".

close • closely • narrow • tight

1. These trousers are __________. Have they shrunk in the wash, or have I put on weight?
2. We've been __________ friends for over 10 years.
3. Be careful, at the bottom of the hill is a __________ bend.
4. The words *thanks* and *danke* are __________ related.

C12 The right preposition *gegen*

Ergänzen Sie eine passende Entsprechung für „gegen".

1. Es tut mir leid, aber ich kann nichts dagegen tun.
   I'm very sorry, but I can't do anything ________ it.
2. Nehmen Sie etwas gegen Ihren Heuschnupfen?
   Are you taking anything ________ your hay fever?
3. Wir müssten irgendwann gegen 10 ankommen.
   We should arrive sometime ________ 10.
4. Die Mannschaft hat gegen eine viel schwächere verloren.
   The team lost ________ a much weaker one.
5. Es hat viel Widerstand gegen den Plan gegeben.
   There has been a lot of resistance ________ the plan.
6. Er war zu schnell und ist gegen eine Mauer gefahren.
   He was too fast and drove ________ a wall.
7. Die Geiseln wurden gegen Gefangene ausgetauscht.
   The hostages were exchanged ________ prisoners.

C13 A play *spielen*

Wählen Sie die richtige Lösung, a oder b.

I can't (a.) act / (b.) play theatre (1.), but I enjoy going to the theatre. Our local theatre recently (a.) performed / (b.) played (2.) a comedy that (a.) was set / (b.) played (3.) in the 1980s. Somebody I know (a.) acted / (b.) played (4.) the lead. He (a.) acted / (b.) played (5.) a footballer who loves scoring own goals.

1	2	3	4	5

C14 Big, tall, great? *groß*

Ergänzen Sie.

big • great • large • tall

1. Jem's over 1 metre 90 __________.
2. Will it make a __________ difference?
3. I have __________ respect for her.
4. It was a __________ mistake to invite Adrian.
5. They paid a very __________ amount.
6. Personal coaching is __________ business these days.
7. Was Clinton a __________ president?
8. Fiona is my __________ sister. She's two years older.
9. It was a moment of __________ danger.
10. Who lives in that __________ house at the end of the road?
11. She's almost forgotten now, but 20 years ago she was a __________ star.
12. He was a good teacher. He had __________ patience and understanding.

Excuse me. How tall are you?

C15 **Small or little?** *klein*

Ergänzen Sie *small* oder *little*.

1. Which number is __________er: 2.75 or 2?
2. She's just given birth to a __________ boy.
3. They live in a lovely __________ village on the lakeside.
4. The password is 'admin', all in __________ letters.
5. You only need a __________ amount of sugar.
6. Do you have any __________ change, for the parking meter?
7. The room was a bit __________, but it was OK for one night.
8. A __________ car uses less petrol.
9. Our ex-boss was a nasty __________ man.
10. Joey is my __________ brother. I'm a year older than him.

C16 **What was that?** *verstehen*

Was ist richtig: a oder b?

1. Could you speak a bit louder, please. At the back of the room here we can't (a.) hear / (b.) understand what you're saying.
2. The article was about molecules and sub-atomic particles. I'm not a scientist and I couldn't (a.) hear / (b.) understand what it was all about.
3. Can you hold on a minute while I just shut my door. There's a group of visitors being shown round and there's so much noise that I can't (a.) hear / (b.) understand you properly.

1	2	3

C17 A crossword *bleiben*

Ergänzen Sie.

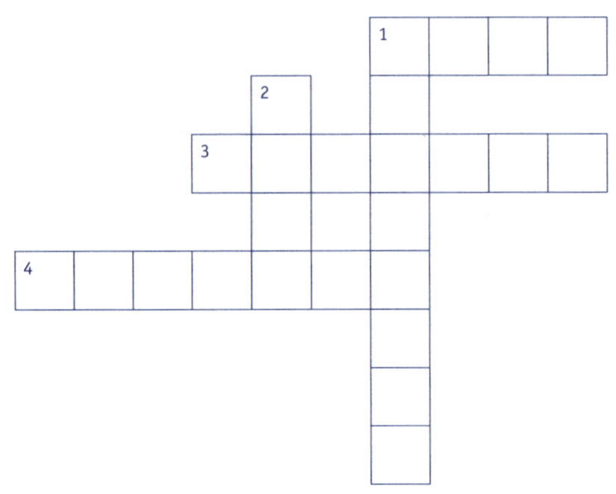

Across

1. How long do you want to _ _ _ _? One night or two?
3. Little _ _ _ _ _ _ _ _ to be done. Most things are now under control.
4. What's the time? This clock seems to have _ _ _ _ _ _ _ _.

Down

1. We all remained _ _ _ _ _ _ _ _ _ until the guest of honour sat down.
2. Please _ _ _ _ quiet, or you'll frighten it away.

C18 A question of speed *schnell*

Ergänzen Sie *fast* oder *quick(ly)*.

1. The car wasn't driving very __________ .
2. I'll just have a __________ look at the sales figures.
3. It's a good __________ road with little traffic.
4. We've got time for a __________ cup of coffee.
5. Wilson ran one of the __________est races of her career.
6. Can you tell me __________ what I'll need to take with me?

C19 **Places** *Platz*

Welcher Ausdruck ist richtig?

1. Can you make ... for one more?
   - place - room
2. In the centre of town there is a big ... .
   - place - square
3. Excuse me, ...? – Sorry. Someone's sitting there.
   - is this place free - is this seat taken
4. The hotel has two tennis ... .
   - courts - places - pitches
5. It also has a golf ... .
   - course - court - place
6. The school sold its ... for redevelopment, to raise money.
   - sport field - sport place - sports ground
7. Janice has got a ... at one of the elite universities.
   - place - study place - studying place
8. Come in and ... .
   - have a seat - take place
9. Down by the river would be a good ... to have our barbecue party.
   - place - space
10. There's ... for the rest of the books in this box here.
    - place - room

C20 Getting from A to B *Reise, Fahrt*

Was passt in die Lücke? Mehrere Lösungen sind möglich.

1.

◆ We weren't expecting you this early.

● Yes, it was a very easy ... today, there was very little traffic on the road.

○ drive ○ journey ○ trip

2.

◆ Do you think you could look after our dog one weekend?

● Sure. You want to go away?

◆ Yes, we'd like to go on a ... to Amsterdam.

○ weekend travel ○ weekend trip ○ weekend journey

3.

● How far are you from the centre of town?

◆ Just a ... .

○ ten-minute bus ride ○ journey of ten minutes with the bus ○ short drive by bus

4.

◆ Would you describe ... as one of your hobbies?

● It would be if I could afford to get away more often!

○ travels ○ travel ○ journeying

5.

◆ Have you been to Bulgaria before?

● No. We've booked a ten-day guided ... so that we can get a feel for the country.

○ journey ○ trip ○ tour

6.

◆ We need to cut down on our outgoings[1].

● Well, one way would be to reduce the number of ... we make.

○ car travels ○ car drives ○ car journeys

[1]Ausgaben

C21 How long (1)? *brauchen*

Drücken Sie den Sachverhalt besser aus – benutzen Sie *take*.

◆ How long ~~do I need~~ from here to Strasbourg?

1. ______________________________

● ~~You need~~ about four hours by car.

2. ______________________________

◆ ~~I needed~~ two whole days to get my presentation ready.

3. ______________________________

● I know. That sort of thing ~~needs~~ a lot of time.

4. ______________________________

C22 How long (2)? *dauern, brauchen*

Übersetzen Sie.

1. Ich brauche deine Hilfe. Es dauert nur ein paar Minuten.

____

2. Du brauchst nicht auf mich zu warten.

____

3. Mit dem Zug braucht man anderthalb Stunden.

____

4. Die Reise dauert anderthalb Stunden.

____

5. Der Film dauert 30 Minuten.

____

6. Sie brauchen nichts mitzubringen, wir haben alles.

____

7. Ich brauche noch zwei Stunden. Für diese Art von Arbeit braucht man lange.

____

C23 Will it hold? *halten*

Was ist richtig: a oder b? Oder sind a und b beide richtig?

1. Will the fine weather (a.) keep / (b.) hold till the weekend?
2. (a.) Hold / (b.) Stop the thief!
3. The crisis (a.) held on / (b.) lasted for well over a year.
4. What's that (a.) you're holding / (b.) you're keeping in your hand? Can I see?
5. We always (a.) held him for trustworthy/ (b.) thought of him as trustworthy.
6. I was so tired, I could hardly (a.) hold / (b.) keep my eyes open.
7. The eggs will (a.) hold / (b.) keep longer in the fridge of course.
8. I need some light. Can you (a.) hold / (b.) keep the torch for me while I try and see what's wrong?
9. Which driver (a.) holds / (b.) keeps the record for the Monza circuit?
10. If you want to be trusted, you have to (a.) hold to / (b.) stick to the rules.
11. I don't trust them. They never (a.) hold / (b.) keep their promise.
12. Just (a.) hold to / (b.) keep to the left and you'll be OK.
13. I mustn't (a.) hold you / (b.) keep you. I expect you have lots to do.
14. To mark the occasion, the vice-president (a.) held / (b.) made a short speech.
15. The friendship didn't (a.) hold / (b.) last long.
16. Can you (a.) hold / (b.) keep your breath for a minute? Try it.

1	2	3	4	5	6	7	8

9	10	11	12	13	14	15	16

C24 How about Wednesday? *passen*

Ergänzen Sie.

fit • match • suit

1. How about Wednesday? Does that _______ you?
2. I always used to think that green didn't _______ me.
3. If the text doesn't _______, you can take this paragraph out.
4. This unit is not quite so wide and should _______ in the corner quite nicely.
5. You can't wear that jacket with those trousers. They don't _______.

C25 What's your son doing? *Studium, studieren*

Was passt in die Lücke? Mehrere Lösungen sind möglich.

1. What's your son doing now? – He ...
   a. is a student c. is at university
   b. studies economics d. studies
2. A lot of top managers in fact never ...
   a. studyed c. were on the university
   b. did a study d. went to university
3. A lot of ... in Britain last not more than three years.
   a. courses c. degree courses
   b. studies d. university courses
4. When are you going to ... ?
   a. begin your study c. start university
   b. begin the studies d. start the university
5. What ... has she chosen?
   a. course c. study
   b. subject d. study course
6. Do many students in this country have jobs ...?
   a. during the study c. when they are at studies
   b. during studies d. when they're at university

1	2	3	4	5	6

C26 By or not by? *bei*

Korrigieren Sie.

1. We didn't stay in a hotel. We stayed ~~by~~ _______ friends.
2. I'm staying ~~by~~ _______ Leonard's place. He has a spare room.
3. ~~By~~ _______ so many problems, it's difficult to know where to start.
4. We live ~~by~~ _______ Hamburg.
5. I work ~~by~~ _______ a firm in the textile industry.
6. She met her partner ~~by~~ _______ a seminar.
7. Let's discuss this in peace and quiet ~~by~~ _______ a glass of wine.
8. People say the view is best ~~by~~ _______ sunset.
9. He died ~~by~~ _______ a car accident.
10. I'm afraid I only have € 20 ~~by~~ _______ me.
11. Guess who I met ~~by~~ _______ the baker's this morning.
12. I stood and watched her ~~by~~ _______ her work.
13. It was not very comfortable ~~by~~ _______ the temperature around zero.

C27 On the job *Arbeit*

Ergänzen Sie *work* oder *job*.

◆ What's your (1.) _________?

● I'm a photographer.

◆ That sounds like interesting (2.) _________.

● That's what most people think, but it's actually quite hard (3.) _________, with a lot of stress if you want to make money at it. It's certainly not my dream (4.) _________.

◆ OK.

● I'm hoping to change my (5.) _________. What I'd really like is a (6.) _________ with animals.

C28 A changed man *(an)erkennen*

Ergänzen Sie *realized* oder *recognized*.

1. He'd lost so much weight that I hardly __________ him.
2. Few people __________ how serious the problem was.
3. I suddenly __________ that I had no money on me.
4. Nobody __________ what had happened till it was too late.
5. Several governments have already __________ the new regime.

C29 **A crossword** *endlich, schließlich*

Ergänzen Sie.

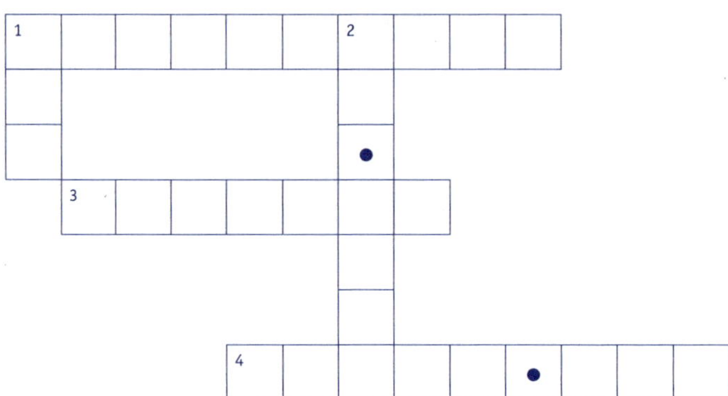

Across

1. It was a long search, but e _ _ _ _ _ _ _ _ _ y we found what we were looking for.
3. It's f _ _ _ _ _ y stopped raining!
4. You can't expect too much of him, a _ _ _ _ a _ _ he's still only 14.

Down

1. I made several offers to help, but he didn't respond, so in the _ _ _ I just left him to it.
2. We've paid off all our debts, a _ l _ _ _!

C30 A question of weight *leicht*

Wählen Sie die richtige Lösung.

1. This bag is so … . It feels as though it's empty.
   ○ easy ○ light ○ slight
2. I'm afraid we seem to have a … problem.
   ○ easy ○ light ○ slight
3. The exam was actually quite … .
   ○ easy ○ light ○ slight
4. There has been … improvement in the economic situation.
   ○ an easy ○ a light ○ a slight
5. … wind was blowing from the northeast.
   ○ An easy ○ A light ○ A slight
6. There was only one really acceptable offer, so … to decide which to accept.
   ○ I found it easy ○ It fell easy ○ It was a slight question

C31 Not from *von*

Korrigieren Sie.

1. It's one of many films ~~from~~ Steven Spielberg.
   ____
2. Oxford is northwest ~~from~~ London.
   ____
3. Six ~~from~~ ten people think the government has handled the crisis well.
   ____
4. Jason is a friend ~~from me~~ from my schooldays.
   ____
5. This magazine article is ~~from~~ someone I know.
   ____
6. The shop is in the arcade to the right ~~from~~ the station.
   ____

C32 More weight *schwer*

Was passt in die Lücke? Mehrere Lösungen sind möglich.

1. How ... is your hand luggage? — a. great b. serious c. heavy
2. I'm ... disappointed. — a. deeply b. heavily c. greatly
3. It's ... to imagine what the world would be like without it. — a. heavy b. hard c. difficult
4. I'm not really ill. It's just a ... cold. — a. heavy b. great c. deep
5. You have to be ... to own property in Monte Carlo. — a. heavily rich b. violently rich c. stinking rich
6. Some of the questions were easy, but a few were really ... . — a. heavy b. serious c. difficult
7. Fortunately, they've not been ... injured. — a. heavily b. seriously c. badly
8. ... fighting continues in the area controlled by the rebels. — a. heavy b. hard c. big
9. People like that deserve to be ... punished. — a. seriously b. deeply c. severely
10. I realize now that it was a ... mistake. — a. heavy b. serious c. big
11. Old people are often ... . — a. heavy in hearing b. hard of hearing c. heavy hearing
12. The storm caused ... damage. — a. grave b. serious c. severe

C33 Bad and worse (1) *schlecht*

Wählen Sie die passende Übersetzung.

1.

◆ Let's see if we can find a suitable time. How about Wednesday?

● *Mittwoch ist schlecht.* Could we make it Thursday instead?

a. Wednesday is bad.

b. Wednesday is difficult.

c. Wednesday is poor.

2.

◆ How long do you think we'll need?

● *Das kann ich schlecht sagen.* Two hours, three hours, something like that.

a. I cannot say that well.

b. I cannot really tell it.

c. I cannot really say.

3.

◆ What shall we tell him – if he asks?

● *Wir können ihm schlecht sagen, dass wir ihm nicht vertrauen.*

a. We can hardly tell him that we don't trust him.

b. We can't well tell him that we don't trust him.

c. We can badly say that we don't trust him.

4.

◆ It's cold in here.

● Yes, I'm sorry. It's this window. *Es schließt schlecht.*

a. It shuts badly.

b. It doesn't shut well.

c. It doesn't shut properly.

1	2	3	4

C34 Bad and worse (2) *schlecht*

Ergänzen Sie. Verwenden Sie jedes Wort nur einmal.

bad • sick • off • poor • poorly

1. Business is not just ________, it's terrible at present.
2. Gone are the days when Chinese products were good value for money but rather ________ quality.
3. I don't like the look or the smell of this fish. I think it's ________.
4. What's the matter, Jack? You don't look very well. – I feel ________.
5. The meeting was ________ attended: only six people came.

C35 All & every *alle(s)*

Übersetzen Sie.

1. Alle denken das Gleiche.

   ____

2. Ich bin bereit alles [egal was] zu tun, um dir zu helfen.

   ____

3. Alle zwei oder drei Tage bekomme ich eine E-Mail.

   ____

4. Mein Motto ist: Alles oder nichts.

   ____

5. Wir brauchen alle eine Pause.

   ____

6. Alle Leute waren begeistert.

   ____

C36 **Dates and deadlines** *bis*

Was ist richtig: a oder b?

1. I'll wait (a.) till / (b.) to six.
2. If they haven't arrived (a.) till / (b.) by then, I'll go without them.
3. You'll have the data (a.) by / (b.) until the end of the week, I promise.
4. There must have been (a.) till / (b.) up to 100 people there.
5. In the holidays they often sleep (a.) till / (b.) to at least 11.
6. (a.) By the time / (b.) Until we'd finished, it was dark.
7. I should get home (a.) till / (b.) by about 7.30, but it might be later.
8. I can count (a.) till / (b.) up to ten in Arabic.
9. Walk along here (a.) till / (b.) as far as the Imperial Hotel.
10. The artist covered the building in silver foil from top (a.) till / (b.) to bottom.

1	2	3	4	5	6	7	8	9	10

C37 **Twins** *gleich*

Ergänzen Sie Angaben (1.) zum Alter, (2.) zur Größe und (3.) zur Kleidung.

David and Peter are twins. As twins, they are of course
(1.) ____________________. But they are also
(2.) ____________________, and they often wear
(3.) ____________________.

C38 A waiter's questions *fertig*

Was fragt der Kellner? Verwenden Sie einmal ready, einmal finished.

C39 A question of ability *können*

Ordnen Sie zu und ergänzen Sie die rechte Spalte.

1. Ich kann kein Spanisch.
2. Du kannst es wirklich gut!
3. Das kann ja jeder.
4. Wir können gut mit einander.
5. Wie konnten Sie nur?!
6. Ich kann einfach nicht mehr.

a. You're really good _______ it.
b. We _______ _______ well together.
c. I don't _______ Spanish.
d. I just can't _______ on.
e. Anyone can _______ that!
f. How _______ you?!

1	2	3	4	5	6

C40 Change *werden*

Welcher Ausdruck ist richtig? Oder sind beide richtig?

1. Bonnie says she wants to ... a journalist when she grows up.
   - be
   - become
2. I'll ... mad if I get any more email enquiries like this.
   - become
   - go
3. It's autumn, and the leaves ... yellow, brown and red.
   - are turning
   - become
4. It ... very difficult to find new markets for our products.
   - is becoming
   - is getting
5. As I ... old, there are many things I no longer take so seriously.
   - go
   - grow
6. They were forecasting rain, but the weather ... better than expected.
   - has got
   - has turned out
7. When I heard Giorgio was coming, I ... very excited.
   - got
   - went
8. My hair ... grey, and it makes me feel old.
   - is going
   - becomes

C41 Oh *(be)merken, sich merken*

Ergänzen Sie. Verwenden Sie jedes Wort nur einmal.

note • notice • realize

1. I didn't ________ you'd already arrived. The message didn't reach me.
2. Please ________ only 8 kg of hand luggage is allowed.
3. I ________d that there was a small crowd of people, but at the time I didn't think anything about it.

C42 **Time** *Zeit*

Korrigieren Sie.

1. I haven't seen Raymond much ~~in the last time~~.

2. ~~In the first time~~, when I was new to the job, there was a lot to learn.

3. I'm going to be travelling quite a lot ~~in the next time~~.

C43 **Once & more** *einmal*

Übersetzen Sie. Verwenden Sie die angegebenen Ausdrücke.

1. Sind Sie schon einmal in Mexiko gewesen? *(ever)*

2 Ich war schon einmal in New York. *(before)*

3. Ich würde gern einmal Irland besuchen. *(sometime)*

4. Hören Sie gut zu, denn ich sage es nur einmal. *(once)*

5. Es war einmal ein König ... *(once upon a time)*

6. Die Stadt war einmal berühmt. *(once)*

C44 **In the past** *früher, frühere(r/s)*

Welcher Ausdruck ist richtig?

1. It's her second marriage. Her ... was called Heinz, too.
   - earlier husband
   - ex-husband
   - husband before
2. They each have a son from ... .
   - an ex-marriage
   - a previous marriage
   - a marriage before
3. We ... in Hamburg.
   - lived earlier
   - former lived
   - used to live
4. I apologize for my lateness. I couldn't make it any ... .
   - more earlier
   - more previously
   - sooner
5. It was ... a nice place to live, but all this new development has spoiled it.
   - earlier
   - once
   - sooner
6. For sale. Only one ... owner.
   - earlier
   - former
   - previous
7. I was born and grew up in the ... East Germany.
   - earlier
   - former
   - previous
8. He says he won't be able to attend 'because of ... engagement'.
   - an earlier
   - a former
   - a previous
9. The place was ... quite famous.
   - earlier
   - once
   - earlier once
10. We ... quite often.
    - used to meet
    - met earlier
    - met previously

C45 A question of position *stehen*

Ergänzen Sie die Übersetzung.

1. Tut mir leid, er steht unter der Dusche.
   Sorry, ______________ a shower.
2. In der Zeitung steht, dass Monkton gewonnen hat.
   In the paper ______________ that Monkton has won.
3. Gelb steht dir.
   Yellow ______________ you.
4. Der Zug war voll und ich musste stehen.
   The train was full and I had to ______________ .
5. Der Rettungsplan steht jetzt.
   The rescue plan ______________ .

C46 While or during? *während*

Wählen Sie die richtige Lösung.

(a.) During / (b.) While (1.) students, James and I had weekend and evening jobs at the same restaurant for several months. He worked in the kitchen, (a.) during / (b.) while (2.) I served out front. We worked there (a.) during / (b.) while (3.) the summer holidays, too. It was hard, I remember, because we didn't have a single day off (a.) while the whole eight weeks / (b.) throughout the whole eight weeks (4.).

1	2	3	4

C47 **Power** *stark*

Welcher Ausdruck passt in die Lücke?

1. There is a ... westerly wind.

   ● heavy ● powerful ● strong

2. He was once a ... smoker.

   ● strong ● heavy ● great

3. It's been raining ... all morning.

   ● strongly ● heavily ● violently

4. Expect another ... frost tonight.

   ● powerful ● hard ● strong

5. Fortunately she's not in ... pain.

   ● great ● heavy ● strong

6. There's ... traffic on all roads out of the capital.

   ● strong ● heavy ● hard

7. The roof has been ... damaged.

   ● strongly ● hard ● badly

8. I'm afraid I have ... reservations[1] about the plan.

   ● strong ● grand ● violent

9. We are ... dependent on what happens in the global economy.

   ● strongly ● heavily ● much

10. She published her memoirs in a ... book.

    ● 600-page long ● 600-page strong ● 600-page heavy

[1]Vorbehalte, Zweifel

C48 A crossword *vor*

Ergänzen Sie.

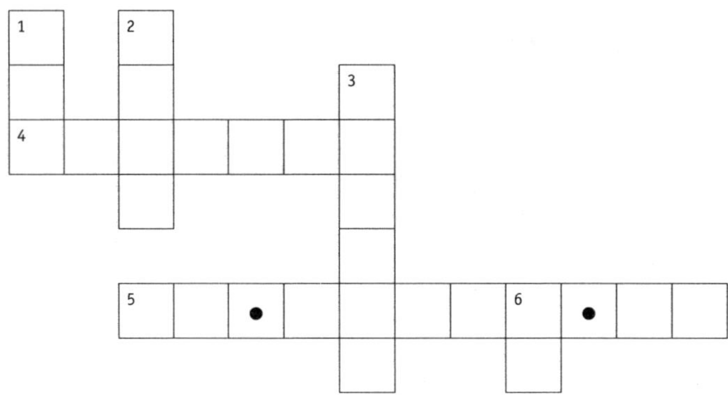

Across

4. I'll meet you o _ _ _ _ _ _ _ the main entrance.
5. You can't park i _ f _ _ _ _ o _ the building, only at the back.

Down

1. I spoke to him only ten minutes _ _ _.
2. He was trembling[1] w _ _ _ fear.
3. I'll try and be there b _ _ _ _ _ the others.
6. It's two minutes _ _ two.

[1]zitterte

C49 **Not busy** *ruhig*

Ergänzen Sie.

calm • quiet • still

1. We live in a _________ street in the suburbs.
2. She always seems to have everything under control and remains _________ in the wildest chaos.
3. The wind was light, the sea was nice and _________.
4. Is something troubling you? You're so _________. You've not said anything all evening.
5. If you won't sit _________, how am I supposed to put the plaster on?

C50 **How?** *wie*

Übersetzen Sie.

1. Wie läuft es? Alles in Ordnung?

   ____

2. Wie war das Wetter?

   ____

3. Wie ist der neue Chef?

   ____

4. Wie sagt man das auf Englisch?

   ____

5. Wie nennt man dieses Ding auf Englisch?

   ____

6. Wie ist die Telefonnummer?

   ____

7. Wie war es, allein zu reisen?

   ____

8. Es ist ein Gebäude wie ein Hotel.

   ____

9. Er ist nicht so alt wie sie.

   ____

C51 With us or against us? *auch*

Welcher Ausdruck passt in die Lücke?

1. Wallis is normally against this sort of idea, but ... he seems to be in favour.
   - also
   - even
   - too
2. I need a break. – ... .
   - I also
   - Me too
   - I as well
3. I like the design. – ... .
   - I also
   - So do I
   - So do I too
4. We won't arrive till quite late. – ... .
   - Neither will we
   - Nor we
   - We also not
5. I'm afraid I haven't understood this. – You're not the only one. I don't understand it ... .
   - too
   - either
   - nor
6. ... it costs more, I think this is the better solution.
   - Also if
   - Even if
   - Even when
7. The roof has been damaged and ... have two windows.
   - also
   - even
   - so

C52 I know *bewusst*

Ergänzen Sie *aware* oder *conscious*.

1. I'm very ______________ that this is not an easy decision for you.
2. As far as I'm ______________, no other company has a comparable product.
3. I didn't ______________ly try to take advantage of the situation.
4. It was not a very ______________ decision on my part.
5. People nowadays are very energy-______________, partly

   because of the cost of energy, partly for environmental reasons.

C53 Permission to drive *Führerschein*

Übersetzen Sie.

1. Die Polizei wollte meinen Führerschein sehen.

   ____

2. Unser Sohn hat gerade angefangen, den Führerschein zu machen.

   ____

3. Unsere Tochter hat bereits den Führerschein.

   ____

C54 Having things with you *tragen*

Ergänzen Sie.

bear • carry • support • wear

1. How formal is this event? What should I ______________?
2. That looks heavy. I'll help you ______________ it.
3. The platform is ______________ed by one central pillar[1].
4. You should ______________ some sort of ID with you at all times.
5. It's a terrible responsibility for her to have to ______________ on her own.
6. Let's hope all this hard work eventually ______________s fruit.
7. I don't normally ______________ a watch at the weekend. My life is so governed by the clock during the week.
8. Who is going to ______________ the costs – us or them?
9. Didn't you use to ______________ glasses?

[1]Säule

C55 Up there *über*

Was passt in die Lücke? Mehrere Lösungen sind möglich.

1. Jackson's office is on the floor ... us.	a. above b. over
2. Andy was in the class ... me at school.	a. above b. over
3. She's always complaining ... the food.	a. about b. on c. over
4. I'm travelling ... Frankfurt because the flight's cheaper.	a. by the way of b. over c. via
5. It can only be a few degrees ... freezing this morning.	a. above b. over c. up of
6. Results this year were well ... average.	a. above b. beyond c. over
7. It took her two years to get ... his death.	a. above b. beyond c. over
8. He's the sort of person who laughs ... his own jokes.	a. above b. at c. over
9. The city is about 600 metres ... sea level.	a. above b. beyond c. over
10. Tears ran ... his face.	a. about b. down c. over
11. Is there any money ...?	a. left b. over c. resting
12. We'll be at home ... Christmas this year.	a. at b. during c. over
13. There's no reason to get annoyed ... it.	a. above b. about c. over
14. Her books are famous ... the borders of Wyoming.	a. above b. beyond c. over
15. They sent a bill ... €60,000.	a. over above b. for over c. over more than

C56 Already and more *schon*

Muss der Ausdruck mit „schon" übersetzt werden – ja oder nein?

1. Es ist *schon* ganz schön schwierig sich zu entscheiden.
2. Wir haben *schon* halb drei.
3. Was macht es *schon* für einen Unterschied?
4. Hat Tony *schon* angerufen?
5. *Schon* bevor er aufstand, wusste ich, was er sagen würde.
6. Ich sehe *schon*, dass wir mehr Zeit benötigen.
7. Sind Sie *schon mal* in Disneyland gewesen?
8. Die ersten Gäste sind *schon* da.
9. Was weiß er mit 18 *schon* vom Leben?
10. *Schon* bald werden wir die ersten Ergebnisse wissen.

Übersetzen Sie die Sätze, in denen „schon" mit übersetzt werden muss.

____

____

____

____

____

____

D. Confusing friends

Englische Wortpaare mit ähnlicher Form aber unterschiedlicher Bedeutung

D1 advice / advise

Ergänzen Sie.

◆ Do you have a moment?
● Sure.
◆ I'd like to ask your (1.) __________.
● What about?
◆ Well, can you (2.) __________ me what to do in a case like this? You see, ...

D2 homework / housework

Ordnen Sie zu.

1. Exercises and tasks given by a teacher	a. housework
2. Cleaning, cooking, etc.	b. homework

D3 interesting / interested

Wählen Sie die richtige Lösung.

◆ There's a photo exhibition next week about the Sahara. Are you (a.) interested / (b.) interesting (1.)? Would you like to go?
● It certainly sounds (a.) interested / (b.) interesting (2.). I've always (a.) been interested in / (b.) been interested for (3.) Africa.

1	2	3

D4 desert / dessert

Übersetzen Sie.

1. Ist die Sahara die größte Wüste der Erde?

   ____

2. Was möchten Sie als Nachspeise?

   ____

D5 aeconomic / economical

Ergänzen Sie.

1. The ___________ situation is improving.
2. The government's ___________ policies have been successful.
3. The new models are much more ___________ and use an average of 15% less energy.
4. It's not a good idea to start a new business in the present ___________ climate.
5. It's much more ___________ to buy in bulk[1].
6. It's a brilliant design, so ___________ on space.

D6 classic / classical

Korrigieren Sie – falls nötig!

1. I don't listen to much *classic* ___________ music.
2. This is a *classic* ___________ case of poor communication.
3. I can't understand people who go to university to study *classic* ___________ Greek.
4. Spielberg has directed a number of *classic* ___________ films.
5. I made the *classic* ___________ mistake.
6. She's just as much at home in *classic* ___________ theatre as in contemporary plays.

[1]in großen Mengen kaufen

D7 beside / besides

Welcher Ausdruck ist richtig?

1. Come and sit ... me.
   ● beside ● besides
2. Do you know anyone else ... the hosts?
   ● beside ● besides
3. I don't have time, and ..., it costs too much.
   ● beside ● besides
4. I do several other sports ... sailing.
   ● beside ● besides
5. ... full time, I also perform as a cabaret artist.
   ● Besides to work ● Besides working
6. My problems seem so insignificant ... yours.
   ● beside ● besides

D8 it's / its

Ergänzen Sie.

1. ___________ so cold in here!
2. The car has some rust, but ___________ engine is OK.
3. The hospital has ___________ own emergency power supply.
4. Somehow the company seems to have lost ___________ way.
5. ___________ called *The Arena*.
6. Sorry, what's ___________ name?

D9 all together / altogether

Ergänzen Sie.

1.
- ◆ Are you paying separately or together?
- ● Well, how much is it ____________?
- ◆ € 146.80.
- ● OK, together.

2.
- ◆ It seems ages since we last met.
- ● It is, in fact I can't remember the last time we were ____________

D10 lay / lie

Ergänzen Sie die passende Verbform.

1. Jacob's tired. He's just gone to ____________ down for a bit.
2. I hate it when Mr Smithers ____________ his hand on my arm.
3. Just think. All this stuff has ____________ here unnoticed for over 50 years.
4. I'm sorry. I ____________ to you, but it was because I wanted to protect you from the truth.
5. This time last week we were ____________ on the beach with not a care in the world.
6. The new carpets are being ____________ today.
7. What's that ____________ on the floor? It looks like a banknote.
8. Snow ____________ on the ground and it was bitterly cold.

	Infinitiv	Vergangenheit	Present Perfect
9.	(to) lay (*legen*)	____________	have/has ____________
10.	(to) lie (*liegen*)	____________	have/has ____________
11.	(to) lie (*lügen*)	____________	have/has ____________

D11 greatly / largely

Kreuzen Sie die richtige Lösung an.

	greatly	largely	
1.	●	●	The forest fires are now ... under control.
2.	●	●	Success is ... a question of who you know.
3.	●	●	Reactions have varied ... .
4.	●	●	Any help would be ... appreciated.

D12 past / passed

Ergänzen Sie.

1. We're on the M3 and have just ___________ exit 12, so we should be with you in about another 20 minutes.
2. We've driven ___________ exit 12.
3. Half an hour ___________ without anything new happening.
4. Has anything happened in the ___________ half hour?
5. It's now ten ___________ four.
6. I thought I just heard someone walk ___________ my door.
7. In the ___________ this place was actually quite famous.
8. But those days have ___________

D13 terrible / terrific

Ordnen Sie zu.

1. We've had a terrific holiday.	a. It's been absolutely fabulous.
2. We've had a terrible holiday.	b. Everything that could go wrong. did go wrong

D14 used to / be/get used to

Welcher Ausdruck passt in die Lücke?

1. I ... for an Italian company before I came here.

   ● used to work ● am used to work ● get used to working

2. When I broke my arm, I suddenly ... with my left hand.

   ● used to write ● was used to write ● had to get used to writing

3. It comes as a shock to most people, but you ... after a while.

   ● use to it ● are used it ● get used to it

4. I ... English in my job. It comes naturally now.

   ● used to use ● am used to using ● am used to use

D15 at last / at least

Ergänzen Sie.

◆ The documentation is complete (1.) ______________.
● How long has it taken to produce it?
◆ I can't remember when we started, but it must be (2.) ______________ six months ago.

D16 raise / rise

Ergänzen Sie die passende Verbform.

1. The price of petrol has ____________ again.
2. They've ____________ prices again.
3. I ____________ my arm to signal that I had a question.
4. Tension ____________ in the room as the discussion intensified.
5. It was mid-winter and the sun ____________ late.
6. We need to ____________ standards.

D17 sometime / sometimes

Was ist richtig: a oder b?

◆ I hope we meet again (a.) sometime / (b.) sometimes (1.).

● Yes, that would be nice.

◆ I (a.) sometime / (b.) sometimes (2.) have to go to Antwerp on business. Maybe we could meet up there?

D18 everyday / every day

Wählen Sie die richtige Lösung.

◆ This sort of thing doesn't happen (a.) every day / (b.) everyday (1.) thank goodness!

● Absolutely! Can you imagine what would happen if this was an (a.) every day / (b.) everyday (2.) occurrence?

D19 historic / historical

Kreuzen Sie die richtige Lösung an.

	historic	historical	
1.	●	●	It was a ... day when peace was declared.
2.	●	●	What you've just told me – is it myth or ... fact?
3.	●	●	People in ... costumes act as guides round the museum.
4.	●	●	Can you explain the ... background to the conflict?

D20 affect / effect

Wählen Sie die richtige Lösung.

◆ What (a.) affect / (b.) effect (1.) are all these changes going to have on us personally, in this department?

● To be honest, I don't think they're going to (a.) affect / (b.) effect (2.) us much at all.

D21 loose / lose

Ergänzen Sie.

1. There was a ___________ connection in the plug, that's why the hair dryer wasn't working.
2. Don't ___________ it, or we shall be in real trouble!
3. Please don't go. It's dangerous and I don't want to ___________ you.
4. It's often cheaper to buy things ___________ rather than packaged.

D22 major / mayor

Wer ist was?

1. ___________________________ 2. ___________________________

D23 in time / on time

Was ist richtig: a oder b?

1. We arrived dead (a.) in / (b.) on time.
2. The train is almost always late, but today, for once, it was (a.) in / (b.) on time.
3. I hope to get there (a.) in / (b.) on time to see the end of the match.

E. All friends together

Gemischte Übungen

E1 In the pub

Korrigieren Sie.

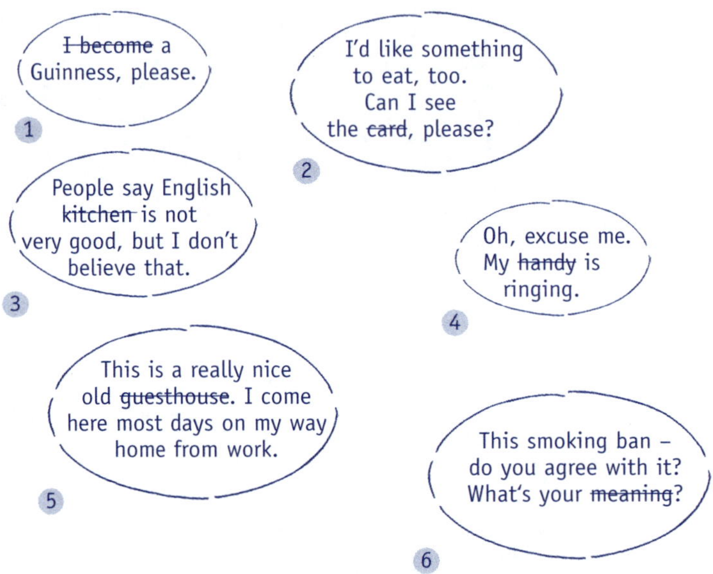

I become a Guinness, please.
1
I'd like something to eat, too. Can I see the card, please?
2
People say English kitchen is not very good, but I don't believe that.
3
Oh, excuse me. My handy is ringing.
4
This is a really nice old guesthouse. I come here most days on my way home from work.
5
This smoking ban – do you agree with it? What's your meaning?
6

E2 An evening at the theatre

Ergänzen Sie. Wählen Sie aus der folgenden Auswahl.

audience • badly visited • interval • pause
piece • play • poorly attended • public spectator

◆ So how was it? Did you enjoy the (1.) __________?

● Yes, I did. But it was only a very small (2.) __________.
And quite a few of those who were there left in the (3.) __________.

◆ I should have come with you. I hate it when the performances are so (4.) __________________.

E3 Television

Korrigieren Sie.

It's difficult to imagine the days when there was no (1.) ~~private~~ ________________ television and there were only two or three state-financed TV (2.) ~~programmes~~ ________________ to choose from. Those were the days when (3.) ~~newsspeakers~~ ________________ never smiled, but read the (4.) ~~newest~~ ________________ news as if they were at a funeral!

E4 Changes at work

Was ist richtig: a oder b?

◆ How long have you been working here?

● (1.) (a.) For / (b.) Since almost ten years. And you?

◆ Only (2.) (a.) for / (b.) since the beginning of the year.

● There have been a lot of changes here (3.) (a.) in the last time / (b.) recently, with a lot of restructuring.
It's been the same throughout the banking (4.) (a.) branch / (b.) business.
The (5.) (a.) economic / (b.) economical climate is quite different from (6.) (a.) a few years ago / (b.) before a few years.

E5 In the canteen

Übersetzen Sie.

◆ Excuse me, there aren't any (1.) *Tabletts* ____________.

● Some more are just coming.

◆ Thanks. And what's on the (2.) *Speiseplan* ____________ today?

● Vegetarian quiche, or chicken, or you can help yourself from the (3.) *Salatbar* ____________.

◆ I'll do that. Salad is (4.) *gesund* ____________.
...
Oh, excuse me. Where's the (5.) *Salatsoße* ____________?

E6 Telephoning

Welcher Ausdruck passt in die Lücke?

1. The phone's ringing. If I ... I'll miss my bus. Can you do it, please?
   ○ answer it ○ go on it
2. What's the ... for France? Is it 0033?
   ○ pre-number ○ code
3. Do you want to ..., or shall I say you're not here?
   ○ accept the conversation ○ take the call
4. When you call back, ... Jane Summertown, then you'll be connected straight to me.
   ○ ask for ○ demand
5. What number do I have to ... for the police in this country?
   ○ choose ○ dial
6. The line went dead so I ... .
   ○ hung up ○ laid the phone down

E7 At school

Korrigieren Sie.

I've just had an invitation to a class ~~meeting~~ ______________ (1.) at my old school, but I don't think I'm going to go. It was a ~~gymnasium~~ ______________ (2.) where all the doctors and lawyers and professional people sent their kids. I never felt that I belonged. I was good ~~in~~ ______________ (3.) most subjects, and I got good ~~notes~~ ______________ (4.) when we ~~wrote~~ ______________ (5.) tests, but I was never really happy there. I wasn't ~~mobbed~~ ______________ (6.) or anything like that, but I was certainly glad when I ~~made~~ ______________ (7.) my final exam, left and ~~started my study~~ ______________ (8.).

E8 Back from holiday

Ergänzen Sie die Übersetzung.

1. Wir haben eine Rundreise durch das ganze Land gemacht.
   We ________ a tour through the whole country.

2. Wir haben nicht in Hotels gewohnt.
   We didn't ________ in hotels.

3. Wir haben in einfachen Pensionen übernachtet.
   We overnighted in simple ________.

4. In Zimmern mit Warm- und Kaltwasser.
   In rooms with ________ and cold water.

5. Die Reise dorthin hat lange gedauert.
   The journey there ________ a long time.

6. Wir haben lange gebraucht.
   ________ ________ ________ a long time.

7. Unsere Pässe wurden ziemlich oft kontrolliert.
   Our passports were ________ quite often.

8. Und wir mussten ständig Formulare ausfüllen.
   And we constantly had to fill in ________.

9. Insgesamt war es eine tolle Reise.
   ________ it was a great trip.

E9 At the weekend

Welcher Ausdruck ist richtig?

1. A lot of people like to ... at the weekend, but that's not my thing.
   - sleep in - sleep out
2. Often I go out for a ... on my motorbike.
   - drive - ride
3. I ... only a car.
   - used to drive - used to driving
4. But ... I sold the car and bought this motorbike.
   - before two years - two years ago
5. I ... my driving test for it a couple of months later.
   - made - took
6. The test wasn't very ... .
   - hard - heavy
7. But I'm not on the ... all the time.
   - road - street
8. I also like to be out and about, in ... .
   - the free nature - the open air
9. I quite often go ... in the mountains, especially in the autumn.
   - hiking - wandering
10. Usually with my camera, because I'm a bit of an amateur ... .
    - photograph - photographer
11. I ... the cinema.
    - am also interested in - also have interest for
12. You name any ... Hollywood film, I've seen it.
    - classic - classical
13. My favourites are ones that ... the first half of the 20th century.
    - are set in - play in

E10 Expressions of time

Korrigieren Sie.

Meeting an old friend

◆ You're looking a bit tired.

● Well, I've been under quite a lot of stress (1.) ~~in the last time~~ _______________. You see, I started a new job (2.) ~~a quarter year~~ _______________ ago.

In the office

◆ What's the (3.) ~~newest~~ _______________ news on the joint venture in China?

● (4.) ~~In this stadium~~ _______________ of the project a lot of things are still unclear.

On the radio

◆ It's three minutes past eleven, and here's Steve Mapleton with up-to-date news and information on the (5.) ~~actual~~ _______________ traffic situation.

In a meeting

◆ I suggest we discuss this later, perhaps (6.) ~~while~~ _______________ lunch.

● Yes, it's going to (7.) ~~cost~~ _______________ too much time to do it now.

At tourist information

◆ There's a shuttle bus, or you can walk.

● How long (8.) ~~do you need~~ _______________ to walk?

◆ Not more (9.) ~~as~~ _______________ fifteen mintes.

E11 People

Übersetzen Sie.

1. Ronaldos Frau ist mir sehr sympathisch.

   ____

2. Anna ist sehr selbstbewusst.

   ____

3. Mark ist mein Sohn aus früherer Ehe.

   ____

4. Ich bin gleich alt wie mein Chef.

   ____

5. Sei vorsichtig. Er ist sehr sensibel.

   ____

6. Bitte lass mich in Ruhe! Ich muss arbeiten.

   ____

7. Mein Reitlehrer ist sehr groß, fast zwei Meter groß.

   ____

8. Sei vernünftig!

   ____

9. Warum sind Sie heute so ruhig?

   ____

10. Wann waren wir das letzte Mal alle zusammen?

    ____

11. Mein Mann ist einer der wenigen Männer, die sich nicht für Fußball interessieren.

    ____

12. Die Kinder waren ganz brav.

    ____

E12 A question of health

Welcher Ausdruck ist richtig?

1. Thank you for calling the Exbridge Health Centre. ... are Monday to Friday, 9 to 12.30, and 3 to 6.30.
   - Consult times
   - Speaking times
   - Surgery hours

2. They say fruit and vegetables are ..., but only of course if they aren't full of pesticides and things.
   - good for you
   - healthy for you
   - good for health

3. The doctor gave me a ... for some pills.
   - recipe
   - prescription
   - receipt

4. They gave me some ... for the first few days after the operation.
   - pain medicine
   - pain tablets
   - painkillers

5. Grandpa can't find his ... .
   - false teeth
   - replacement teeth
   - third teeth

6. You're going to have to take over the presentation. I have ..., I can hardly speak.
   - a really bad sore throat
   - really strong throat pains
   - really bad throat pains

E13 Tricky pairs

Ergänzen Sie.

nearest, next

1. The train is now approaching Aldringham. Aldringham is the __________ station stop.
2. Where's the __________ station to the hotel?

shade, shadow

3. It's too hot in the sun for me, I'm going to have to move into the __________.
4. I thought I saw a __________ on the wall.

back, backside

5. For goodness sake, get up off your __________ and do some work!
6. There are parking spaces at the __________ of the building.

E14 Food & drink

Korrigieren Sie.

1. You can't grow much on a balcony this size, just a few tomatoes, herbs and a couple of ~~salad~~ __________ plants.
2. The fish is served with ~~salt potatoes~~ __________ and a green salad.
3. This curry is ~~sharp~~ __________! How much chili powder did you put in it?
4. The quality of our ~~drink water~~ __________ is actually very good.
5. I need a ~~tablet~~ __________ to carry all these glasses.
6. ~~Good appetite~~ __________ everyone!
7. I'm trying to lose weight and cut down on any food that ~~makes fat~~ ______________.
8. We're planning to ~~grill~~ __________ this evening in the back yard. Why don't you join us?
9. I think it's true that you feel better if you have one ~~warm~~ __________ meal a day.
10. What shall I do with the ~~rests~~ __________ from lunch? Feed them to the dog?
11. We don't eat much bread. If we buy a big ~~bread~~ __________ we often end up throwing half of it away because it's gone stale.
12. Ann has emailed the ~~receipt~~ __________ for that Moroccan dish she served last weekend.
13. You could have put a bit less vinegar in the salad ~~sauce~~ __________. It's a bit sour.
14. What's on the ~~card~~ __________ today? – It's Friday, so it's fish!
15. A lunch ~~pause~~ __________, what's that? I never have time.
16. We stopped at this ~~guesthouse~~ __________ called *Zum weißen Lamm* and had a fantastic German meal.

E15 At work

Übersetzen Sie die deutschen Wörter und ergänzen Sie den Text.

My company has just been taken over, but most of the *(Personal)* 1. ______________ have kept their jobs. A couple of the older ones *(sind in Rente gegangen)* 2. ____________________________.
Business is good and a lot of us *(machen Überstunden)* 3. ______________________ on a regular basis. Our new (Chef) 4. ______________, or rather the new owner of the company, is an *(Unternehmer)* 5. ______________ with business interests worldwide. He only *(trifft)* 6. ______________ the big decisions and leaves the day-to-day running of his companies to local managers.

E16 Business matters

Welcher Ausdruck passt in die Lücke?

1. The ... risk on this project is great, but so too are the rewards.
   a. economic b. economical c. economous
2. Our bank account looks healthy, we are ... .
   a. in plus b. in the red c. in the black
3. The Cayman Islands is one of these off-shore ... .
   a. tax oases b. tax havens c. tax paradises
4. It's a non-profit organization. They ... any surplus they make to charity.
   a. donate b. spend c. transfer
5. Who is going to ... all the extra research?
   a. pay b. pay for c. balance
6. I don't like ... financial risks.
   a. going into b. making c. taking
7. We must prevent this happening ... .
   a. at every price b. on any price c. at all costs

1	2	3	4	5	6	7

Lösungen

2

A. True friends?

A1 1. c / 2. e / 3. b / 4. a / 5. d / 6. take 7. bring
▶ herbringen = bring; hin-, wegbringen = take

A2 1. brought 2. got 3. took 4. take 5. bring 6. put
▶ siehe A1

A3 1. b / 2. c / 3. d / 4. c / 5. c / 6. c / 7. d / 8. b / 9. d / 10. b
▶ herkommen = come; hinkommen = get; hingehören = go; kommen lassen = send for

A4 1. map 2. menu 3. tickets 4. card 5. ticket
▶ Landkarte = map; Speisekarte = menu; Eintritts-, Fahrkarte = ticket; Karte zum Schreiben = card

A5 1. to walk 2. last 3. go to school 4. isn't working 5. is your flight / does your plane go / does your flight go 6. run 7. That's impossible
▶ gehen (allgemein) = go; zu Fuß gehen = walk; verkehren = run, go; funktionieren = work; (an)dauern = last

A6 1. a / 2. b / 3. a / 4. b / 5. b
▶ aus dem Gedächtnis verlieren = forget; liegen lassen + Ortsbestimmung = leave

A7 1. a wine glass 2. a glass of wine 3. a jar of olives 4. a jar of honey
▶ Glas (Material, Trinkgefäß, Getränk) = glass; Glas (Aufbewahrungsgefäß mit Deckel) = jar

A8 1. salad 2. gravy 3. dressing 4. sauce 5. lettuce
▶ Salat (als Gericht/Beilage) = salad; Salat (als Pflanze/Blätter) = lettuce; Bratensoße = gravy; Salatsoße = dressing; Schokoladensoße = chocolate sauce

A9 1. sharp 2. hot/spicy
▶ scharf (Messer, Frost) = sharp; scharf (Essen) = spicy/hot

A10 1. guest 2. host 3. guest 4. customers 5. guest 6. visitor 7. passenger 8. inn 9. guesthouse

A11 1. korrekt 2. studying/revising 3. korrekt
▶ lernen (generell) = learn; für die Schule lernen, wiederholen = study/revise

A12 1. false 2. wrong 3. false 4. wrong 5. false 6. wrong 7. wrong 8. wrong 9. wrong 10. false
▶ unwahr, unecht = false; fehlerhaft, nicht korrekt = wrong

A13 1. have/take a coffee break 2. There was a short pause 3. The play was very long and there were two intervals/intermissions. 4. On some days I have so much to do that I don't take/have a lunch break. 5. Listen and repeat in the pause. 6. Break is after the second lesson.
▶ kurze Unterbrechung = pause; längere Unterbrechung, Erholungspause = break; Pause bei Konzerten o.a. = interval / intermission

A14 1. b / 2. a, b / 3. a / 4. a / 5. a / 6. a / 7. a

▶ bei Sachen mit überdurchschnittlichem Durchmesser = thick; bei Personen = fat; bei Geld o.a. (üppig) = big fat; bei Fehlern = big; bei Freunden (eng, vertraut) = close

A15 1. Does that cost extra?
2. I'll pay for the wine separately.
3. I bought the wine specially for you.
4. He did it on purpose, I'm sure.

▶ zusätzlich = extra; gesondert = separately; speziell = specially; absichtlich = on purpose

A16 1. (for) a long time 2. For twenty years 3. length 4. length 5. a long time

▶ long i.d.R. nur in Fragen und verneinten Sätzen, sonst a long time

A17 1. b / 2. a

▶ Preis, den man zahlt = price; Preis, den man gewinnt = prize

A18 1. Have you heard / Did you hear
2. listening 3. listened to 4. hear
5. listen 6. Listen, hear

▶ hören (akustisch wahrnehmen) = hear; hören (Radio, Musik) = listen to; zuhören, sich anhören, auf jmdn./etw. hören = listen to

A19 1. tell 2. tell 3. say 4. Say 5. tell 6. Tell

▶ angesprochene Person wird nicht genannt = say; sie wird genannt = tell. Ausnahmen: tell a story (eine Geschichte erzählen), tell the truth (die Wahrheit sagen), tell lies (lügen).

A20 1. Can you tell me what it costs / will cost? 2. I always tell the truth. 3. She said Happy birthday, but it wasn't my birthday. 4. She's a very quiet person. She doesn't say much. 5. What did he tell you / say to you? 6. What did he say? 7. He said he couldn't tell us anything. 8. The match was boring. – You can say that again!

▶ siehe A19

A21 1. control 2. check 3. control
4. control 5. checked 6. checked
7. checks

▶ unter Kontrolle haben, steuern = control; kontrollieren (überprüfen, ob etw. in Ordnung ist, z.B. Fahrkarten, Sicherheit) = check

A22 1. make 6. cuisine/food
7. is boiling

▶ Essen zubereiten im Allgemeinen = cook; Tee, Kaffee, Suppe zubereiten = make; sieden = boil

A23 1. warm 2. hot 3. hot 4. hot
5. hot 6. hot/warm

▶ angenehm warm = warm; unangenehm warm = hot; warm (bei Wasser, Essen) = hot

A24 1. fresh 2. chilly 3. clean
4. bright 5. Wet

A25 1. nil nil 2. zero 3. nought/zero
4. oh/zero 5. zero

▶ beim Sport = nil; bei Temperaturangaben = zero; in Dezimalzahlen = nought, zero; in Telefon- und Kontonummern = oh, zero

A26 1. latest 2. new 3. latest
4. nearest 5. Next
▶ nächste(r/s) (räumlich am nächsten) = nearest; nächste(r/s) (zeitlich/räumlich nächstfolgend) = next; neueste(r/s) (aktuellste[r/s]) = latest

A27 1. b / 2. a
▶ Motor eines kleineren Geräts = motor; Motor (bei Auto, Bus usw.) = engine

A28 1. technique 2. technology
3. technique 4. technology
▶ Methode, Arbeitsweise = technique; Wissenschaft, Technologie = technology

A29 1. shade 2. shadows 3. shadow
4. shadow 5. shade
▶ schattiger Platz = shade; Schattenumriss = shadow

A30 1. b / 2. a / 3. a / 4. a,b / 5. a / 6. a / 7. a, b / 8. b
▶ schlafen (bei Schlafgewohnheiten, -dauer, - qualität, -weise) = sleep; schlafen (im Zustand des Schlafens sein) = be asleep; ausschlafen, lange schlafen = sleep in/late

A31 1. politics 2. policy/policies
3. policy/policies
▶ Politik (politisches Leben) = politics; Politik (Handlungsweise in einem bestimmten Bereich) = policy

A32 1. They didn't have satellite TV and there were only three channels.
2. There are a lot of improvements in the new version of the program. 3. The festival programme has now appeared. 4. Which channel do you watch most?
▶ Plan = programme (GB) / program (AE); Computerprogramm = program; Fernsehkanal = channel

A33 1. office/building 2. korrekt 3. GP (= general practitioner) 4. home
▶ Wohnhaus = house; Gebäude = building; Firmenräume = office

A34 1. korrekt 2. korrekt 3. think
4. korrekt 5. think
▶ sagen wollen = mean; glauben = think

A35 1. point (0.7%) 2. comma
▶ Zeichensetzung im Text = comma; in Dezimalzahlen = point

A36 1. b / 2. b / 3. b / 4. b
▶ wollen (generell) = want; im Begriff sein, etwas zu tun = to be about to do something; nicht wollen (wenn etwas Erwünschtes nicht eintritt/eintrat) = won't/wouldn't

A37 1. Who(m) do you want to speak to/with? 2. I was just about to leave when Jim called/phoned.
3. The visitor wants to see Mr Smith.
4. I want to go to bed.
5. she just won't listen 6. I tried to open the window, but it wouldn't. 7. What are you trying to say?!
▶ siehe A36

A38 1. cost 2. costs 3. cost 4. take 5. expense 6. cost

A39 1. It's no use. 2. is good for 3. There's only one thing to do
▶ behilflich sein = help; helfen gegen (bei Arzneimitteln usw.) = be good for; nichts helfen (aussichtslos sein) = be no use/good

A40 1. richtig 2. falsch (richtig: audience)
▶ publik = public; Publikum = audience

A41 1. open air / countryside 2. human nature 3. nature
▶ natürliche Welt der Pflanzen, Tiere usw. = nature; Wesen = nature; die freie Natur = the open air / the countryside

A42 1. if 2. when 3. when 4. If 5. If 6. if 7. if 8. When 9. If
▶ unter der Bedingung, dass ... = if; bei gleichzeitig oder unmittelbar vorzeitig ablaufenden Handlungen = when

A43 1. b, c / 2. a, b / 3. b

A44 1. b / 2. a / 3. a / 4. b
▶ Tat, Handlung = action; Werbe-, Spende-, Militäraktion = campaign

A45 1. rob 2. steal 3. steal 4. rob 5. rob 6. rob 7. rob 8. steal 9. steal 10. rob
▶ einer Person/Bank etw. nehmen = rob; etw. rauben = steal

A46 1. It was cold and we had deep snow. 2. Santa Claus lives in the far north. 3. It was high summer and the grass was long. 4. How large was the amount that was stolen? 5. She has a highly paid job with a computer company. 6. The town is surrounded by high mountains. 7. Hands up! 8. The train went into the tunnel at high speed. 9. We're not expecting more than 30 people at the most. 10. More and more people are living to a great age. 11. He has heavy debts. 12. The team won by a long way / by a wide margin.

A47 1. c / 2. b, c / 3. a, b / 4. d / 5. b / 6. b / 7. Robin and Ann send their best wishes.

A48 1. street 2. road 3. road 4. street

A49 1. road 2. streets 3. street 4. roads 5. road 6. road 7. road 8. streets

A50 1. d / 2. d
▶ Stadion = stadium; in diesem Stadium = at this stage

A51 1. do 2. do 3. do 4. make 5. do 6. make 7. do 8. make 9. do 10. do 11. do 12. make
▶ herstellen, erzeugen, schaffen usw. = make; erledigen, sich beschäftigen mit = do; machen (in festen Wendungen) = have, take, go ...

A52 1. When are you having a holiday / going on holiday this year?
2. Wait, I want to take a photo.
3. It doesn't matter. 4. Shall we take/have a break? 5. I'm on a diet.
6. When are you taking your exam?
7. Don't worry.
▶ Siehe A51

A53 1. is making 2. go 3. go for
4. got 5. make 6. doing
7. make 8. do 9. have 10. done
11. doing / making
▶ Siehe A51

B. False friends

B1 1. b, c / 2. b
▶ Fabrik = factory; fabric = Stoff

B2 1. happy ending 2. korrekt
3. review
▶ Happy End = happy ending; Kritik = review; critic = Kritiker/in, Rezensent/in

B3 1. form 2. formula 3. Formula
4. formula 5. form
▶ Formular = form; formula = Formel

B4 1. b, c / 2. a, b
▶ überhören = don't hear, fail to hear; overhear = (zufällig) mithören

B5 1. branches 2. business 3. takeover
4. overtook 5. staff 6. personal
7. undertaker 8. entrepreneurs
9. boss 10. chef
▶ Branche = business; branch = Zweigstelle; Chef = boss; chef = Koch, Küchenchef; Personal = staff; personal = persönlich; Übernahme = takeover; overtake = überholen; Unternehmer = entrepreneur; undertaker = Bestattungsunternehmen

B6 1. a, b, c / 2. b
▶ Rückseite = back; backside = Hintern

B7 1. self-conscious 2. self-confident
3. sensible 4. sensitive 5. pleasant
6. sympathetic
▶ selbstbewusst = self-confident; self-conscious = gehemmt, unsicher; sensibel = sensitive; sensible = vernünftig; sympathisch = pleasant; sympathetic = mitfühlend

B8 1. a, d / 2. c
▶ ordinär = common, vulgar; ordinary = durchschnittlich, normal

B9 1. cake 2. biscuit / cookie
▶ Keks = biscuit (BE) / cookie (AE); cake = Kuchen

B10 opinion
▶ Meinung = opinion; meaning = Bedeutung

B11 1. marks/grades 2. notes 3. note
4. note 5. notice 6. notice
7. note 8. music
▶ Note = mark/grade; note = Notiz, Zettel; Notiz = note; notice = Anschlag

B12 1. d / 2. c
▶ bekommen = get/have/receive; become = werden

B13 1. When is the courier going to pick up / collect the parcels? 2. ... a package of measures 3. I use several Microsoft software packages.
4. Two packets of butter and a packet of tea.
▶ Paket = parcel, package; packet = Päckchen

B14 1. korrekt 2. draft 3. plan
4. threw him
▶ Konzept = plan/draft; concept = Begriff

B15 1. a map 2. a tablet 3. a folder
4. a tray 5. a photograph
6. a photographer
▶ Mappe = folder; map = Landkarte; Tablett = tray; tablet = Tablette; Fotograf = photographer; photograph = Foto

B16 1. murder 2. murderer 3. poison 4. gifts
▶ Mörder = murderer; murder = Mord; Gift = poison; gift = Geschenk

B17 1. I paid and the taxi driver gave me a receipt. 2. It tastes wonderful. You must give me the recipe. 3. The prescription still has to be signed by the doctor. 4. What's your recipe for success?
▶ Rezept (beim Arzt) = prescription; Rezept (beim Kochen oder als Erfolgsrezept) = recipe; receipt = Quittung

B18 1. b / 2. b, c / 3. c
▶ Rente = pension; rent = Miete

B19 1. valid, up to date 2. topical
3. current
▶ gültig = valid; von momentanem Interesse = topical; gegenwärtig = current; actual(ly) = tatsächlich

B20 1. spare 2. save 3. spent
4. donate 5. save
▶ sparen = save; spare = entbehren; spenden = donate; spend = (Geld) ausgeben; (Zeit) verbringen

B21 1. mobile (phone) / cell phone
2. indicated 3. overlooked
▶ übersehen = overlook; oversee = beaufsichtigen; Handy = mobile (phone) (BE) / cell phone (AE); handy = praktisch, griffbereit; blinken = indicate; blink = zwinkern

B22 1. c / 2. a / 3. b, d
▶ Gymnasium = grammar school; gymnasium = Turn-, Sporthalle; Mobbing = bullying; mob = belagern; brav = good; brave = mutig;

B23 1. Gymnastics 2. exercises
3. wandering 4. hiking
▶ Gymnastik (Wettkampfdisziplin) = gymnastics; Gymnastik (private Freiübungen) = exercises; wandern = hike; wander = ziellos streifen, bummeln

B24 1. brochures 2. advertisement
3. prospects 4. announcements
▶ Prospekt = brochure; prospect = Aussicht; Annonce = advertisement; announcement = Bekanntgabe, Ankündigung

B25 1. founded 2. founded 3. grounded
▶ gründen = found; ground = Startverbot erhalten (bei Flugzeugen)

B26 1. at last, finally 2. sometime, one day
▶ eventually = schließlich, endlich

B27 1. a, b, c / 2. b, c, d
▶ eventuell = may ..., ... possibly ..., (it's) possible ...

B28 1. material/fabric 2. material / fabric 3. substances 4. material
▶ Stoff (Gewebe) = material/fabric; Stoff (natürlicher Bestandteil) = substance; Stoff (Handlung) = material; stuff = Zeug

B29 1. d / 2. a
▶ Warenhaus = department store; warehouse = Lager(haus)

B30 1. denomination 2. confession
▶ Konfession = denomination; confession = Beichte

B31 1. engaged 2. dedicated 3. committed 4. involved 5. active 6. hired
▶ engagiert = involved, dedicated, committed; engaged = verlobt

C. Lots of friends

C1 1. husband 2. man 3. woman 4. wife 5. My goodness / Oh boy!
▶ Frau / Mann (weiblicher / männlicher Mensch) = man / woman; Ehefrau / -mann = wife / husband

C2 1. b / 2. c / 3. a / 4. e / 5. d
▶ in Bitten, Fragen = please; Reaktion auf Dank = not at all / that's OK / it's a pleasure ...; Reaktion auf Entschuldigung = it's/that's all right / never mind; Zustimmung zu einer Bitte = certainly / of course / please do; wie bitte? = sorry? excuse me? pardon?; beim Überreichen = here you are.

C3 1. Certainly. / Of course. / Please do. 2. Here you are. 3. Sorry? / Pardon? / Excuse me? 4. please 5. It's a pleasure. / That's all right. / You're welcome.
▶ siehe C2

C4 1. When 2. than 3. as 4. As
▶ zeitlich = when; bei Komparativen = than; „genau wie" = as; als (ob) = as (if); in der Eigenschaft als ... = as

C5 1. visit 2. attend / go to 3. go to
▶ besuchen (als Gast, Tourist usw.) = visit; besuchen (Schule, Kirche usw.) = attend/go to; besuchen (kulturelle Veranstaltungen) = go to

C6 1. pay 2. pay for 3. pay 4. pay for 5. pay 6. pay 7. pay for 8. pay 9. pay 10. pay for
▶ bei Produkten und Dienstleistungen = pay for; bei Personen, Beträgen, Rechnungen = pay

C7 1. memory 2. remember
3. memories 4. short-term memory
5. remember 6. remind 7. reminder
8. remembers

▶ sich erinnern = remember; jmdn. erinnern = remind somebody; Erinnerung (im Gedächtnis) = memory; Erinnerung (Gedächtnisstütze) = reminder; Gedächtnis = memory

C8 Across: 3. fit 5. well 6. good for you
Down: 1. better 2. healthy
4. common

▶ in guter körperlicher Verfassung = healthy / fit; genesen = better; gesundheitsfördernd = good for you

C9 1. b / 2. c / 3. c / 4. c / 5. a / 6. b / 7. b / 8. a. / 9. b / 10. b / 11. a

▶ fahren (ganz allgemein) = go; bei Auto = drive; bei Fahrrad und Motorrad = ride; mit Geschwindigkeitsangabe = do / travel at; im Sinne von „verkehren" = run; fahren mit Verkehrsmitteln = take

C10 1. instructor 2. teacher
3. instructor 4. instructor
5. teacher 6. instructors
7. teachers

▶ Lehrer für Kopfarbeit = teacher; Lehrer für praktische Fertigkeiten = instructor

C11 1. tight 2. close 3. narrow
4. closely

▶ schmal = narrow; eng anliegend, stramm = tight; nahe, vertraut = close; als Adverb = closely

C12 1. about 2. for 3. around/about
4. to 5. to 6. into 7. for

▶ etw. dagegen tun = do something about; als Schutz gegen etw. = for; zeitlich = around / about; bei Widerstand o.a. = to; bei Austausch = for

C13 1. a / 2. a / 3. a / 4. b / 5. b

▶ als Schauspieler auftreten = act; aufführen = perform; sich abspielen = to be set; (eine Rolle) spielen = play

C14 1. tall 2. big/great 3. great 4. big/great 5. large 6. big 7. great
8. big 9. great 10. big/large
11. big/great 12. great

▶ bei Sachen = big; bei Menschen = tall; im Sinne von kräftig, älter = big; beträchlich = big, great (bei Nomen ohne Plural nur great möglich); berühmt, bedeutend = great; umsatzstark, erfolgreich = big; bei Mengen, Dimensionen = large

C15 1. smaller 2. little 3. little
4. small 5. small 6. small 7. small
8. small 9. little 10. little

▶ als neutraler Ausdruck = small; emotional gefärbt (niedlich / schrecklich klein) = little; jünger = little

C16 1. hear 2. understand 3. hear

▶ begreifen = understand; akustisch wahrnehmen = hear

C17 Across: 1. stay 3. remains
4. stopped
Down: 1. standing 2. keep

▶ im gleichen Zustand bleiben = stay, keep; am gleichen Ort bleiben = stay; übrig bleiben = remain; stehenbleiben (nicht mehr gehen) = stop

C18 1. fast 2. quick 3. fast 4. quick 5. fast 6. quickly

▶ schnell (von der Bewegung her) = fast; schnell (nur kurze Zeit beanspruchend) = quick

C19 1. room 2. square 3. is this seat taken 4. courts 5. course 6. sports ground 7. place 8. have a seat 9. place 10. room

▶ Ort, Stelle, Studienplatz = place; ausreichend Raum = room, space; in einer Stadt = square; beim Tennis = court; beim Golf = course; Sitzplatz = seat

C20 1. drive / journey / trip 2. weekend trip 3. ten-minute bus ride 4. travel 5. tour 6. car journeys

▶ Reise generell (meist Vergnügungsreise mit Aufenthalt am Zielort) = trip; als Autofahrt = drive; längere Fahrt ohne Aufenthalt = journey; das Reisen = travel; Rundreise = tour

C21 1. How long does it take from here to Strasbourg? 2. It takes about four hours by car. 3. It took me two whole days to get my presentation ready. 4. I know. That sort of thing takes a lot of time.

▶ brauchen (Zeit) = take

C22 1. I need your help. It will only take a few minutes. 2. You don't need to / You needn't wait for me. 3. By train it takes one and a half hours. 4. The journey takes one and a half hours. 5. The film lasts 30 minutes. 6. You don't need to / You needn't bring anything with you, we have everything. 7. I need another two hours. This sort of job/work takes a long time.

▶ etw./jmdn. benötigen = need; brauchen nicht zu ... = don't need to / needn't; brauchen (Zeit) = take/last

C23 1. b / 2. b / 3. b / 4. a / 5. b / 6. b / 7. b / 8. a / 9. a / 10. b / 11. b / 12. b / 13. b / 14. b / 15. b / 16. a

▶ mit Hand / Körperteil halten = hold; in einem Zustand belassen = keep; jmdn. festhalten = stop; bei Versprechen = keep; bei Rede = make, give; jmdn. für etw. ansehen = think of someone as something; sich halten an = stick to; (an)dauern = last

C24 1. suit 2. suit 3. fit 4. fit 5. match

▶ passen (Größe, Dimensionen) = fit; gut stehen = suit; passen (zu etw. anderem) = match; recht sein = suit

C25 1. a, c / 2. d / 3. a, c, d / 4. c / 5. a, b / 6. d

▶ studieren = be a student, be at / go to university; Studium = subject, (university/degree) course

C26 1. with 2. at 3. With 4. near
5. for/with 6. at/on 7. over 8. at
9. in 10. on/with 11. at 12. at
13. with

▶ bei jdm zu Hause = with someone / at someone's house; in der Nähe von = near; bei Firma = for; bei Bedingungen = at

C27 1. job 2. work 3. work 4. job
5. job 6. job

▶ Arbeit (allgemein oder als Arbeitsort) = work; einzelne, bestimmte Arbeit, Anstellung = job
Beachten Sie: work kann nicht mit dem unbestimmten Artikel stehen.

C28 1. recognized 2. realized/recognized
3. realized 4. realized
5. recognized

▶ mit den Sinnen wiedererkennen = recognize; geistig entdecken = realize; politisch = recognize

C29 Across: 1. eventually 3. finally
4. after all
Down: 1. end 2. at last

▶ als Folge, am Schluss = eventually, in the end; später als erwartet bzw. gewünscht = finally; schließlich doch, wenn man es richtig betrachtet = after all; endlich nach langem Ersehnen = at last

C30 1. light 2. slight 3. easy
4. a slight 5. A light 6. I found it easy

▶ einfach = easy; geringfügig = slight; von geringem Gewicht = light

C31 1. by 2. of 3. out of 4. of mine
5. by 6. of

▶ bei Urhebern = by

C32 1. c / 2. a, c / 3. b, c / 4. a /
5. c / 6. c / 7. b, c / 8. a / 9. c /
10. b, c / 11. b / 12. b, c

▶ schwer (von Gewicht) = heavy; schwierig = difficult, hard; ernsthaft = serious

C33 1. b / 2. c / 3. a / 4. c

C34 1. bad 2. poor 3. off 4. sick
5. poorly

▶ negativ = bad; sich schlecht (krank) fühlen = feel sick; bei Qualität = poor; bei Lebensmitteln = off

C35 1. Everybody / Everyone thinks the same. 2. I'm prepared/willing to do anything to help you. 3. Every two or three days I get an email.
4. My motto is: All or nothing.
5. We all need a break. 6. Everybody / Everyone was enthusiastic.

C36 1. a / 2. b / 3. a / 4. b / 5. a /
6. a / 7. b / 8. b / 9. b / 10. b

▶ bis (+ zeitlicher Endpunkt) = till/until; bis spätestens = by; bei Mengen-/Zahlenangaben = up to; räumlich = as far as / to

C37 1. the same age 2. the same size 3. the same clothes

▶ gleich + bestimmtes Adjektiv = the same + Nomen

C38 1. Have you finished? 2. Are you ready for dessert?

▶ bereit = ready; erledigt, abgeschossen = finished

C39 1. c, speak 2. a, at 3. e, do 4. b, get on 5. f, could 6. d, go/carry

C40 1. be / become 2. go 3. are turning 4. is becoming / is getting 5. grow 6. has turned out 7. got 8. is going

▶ Berufspläne = be / become; Zustandsveränderung = get / become; Negativveränderung = go; allmähliche Veränderung = grow; Farbveränderung = turn / go

C41 1. realize 2. note 3. noticed

▶ sich geistig bewusst werden = realize; mit den Sinnen wahrnehmen = notice; sich merken = note, remember

C42 1. recently/lately 2. At the beginning 3. in the next (few) weeks/months

C43 1. Have you ever been to Mexico? 2. I've been to New York before. 3. I would like to visit Ireland sometime. 4. Listen carefully because I'm only going to say it once. 5. Once upon a time there was a king 6. The town was once famous.

C44 1. ex-husband 2. a previous marriage 3. used to live 4. sooner 5. once 6. previous 7. former 8. a previous 9. once 10. used to meet

▶ vorhergehend = previous; ehemalig = former / ex; früher (eher) = earlier/ sooner; früher einmal = once; früher habe/bin ich immer ... = I used to ...

C45 1. he's having 2. it says 3. suits 4. stand 5. is complete/finished

C46 1. b / 2. b / 3. a / 4. b

▶ während (Konjunktion) = while; während (Präposition vor Nomen) = during

C47 1. strong 2. heavy 3. heavily 4. hard 5. great 6. heavy 7. badly 8. strong 9. heavily 10. 600-page long

▶ bei Regen, Rauchen, Verkehr = heavy

C48 Across: 4. outside 5. in front of
Down: 1. ago 2. with 3. before 6. to

▶ räumlich = in front of/outside; zeitlich (Gegenteil von „nach") = before; zeitlich (im Sinne von „her") = ago; bei Uhrzeit = to

C49 1. quiet 2. calm 3. calm 4. quiet 5. still

▶ leise, unauffällig, schweigsam = quiet; ruhig, gelassen, reglos = calm / still (Sitzen)

C50 1. How are things? Everything OK? 2. What was the weather like? 3. What's the new boss like? 4. How do you say that in English? 5. What's this thing called in English? 6. What's the phone number? 7. What was it like travelling alone? 8. It's a building like a hotel. 9. He's not as old as her.

C51 1. even 2. Me too 3. So do I 4. Neither will we 5. either 6. Even if 7. so

C52 1. aware / conscious 2. aware 3. consciously 4. conscious 5. conscious

▶ um etw. wissend = aware / conscious (bei „as far as …" nur aware möglich, vor Nomen nur conscious möglich); wissentlich = conscious(ly); …-bewusst = …-conscious

C53 1. The police wanted to see my driving licence (BE) / driver's license (AE). 2. Our son has just started taking driving lessons.
3. Our daughter has already passed her (driving) test. / Our daughter already has a driving licence / driver's license.

C54 1. wear 2. carry 3. supported 4. carry 5. bear 6. bears 7. wear 8. bear 9. wear

▶ befördern = carry; am Körper anhaben = wear; im übertragenen Sinne = bear

C55 1. a / 2. a / 3. a / 4. c / 5. a / 6. b / 7. c / 8. b / 9. a / 10. b / 11. a / 12. a, b, c / 13. b, c / 14. b / 15. b

▶ räumlich = above/over; betreffend = about; auf dem Wege = via; bei Zahlenangaben = over

C56 1. nein 2. ja 3. nein 4. ja 5. ja 6. nein 7. ja 8. ja 9. nein 10. ja

2. It's already half past two. 4. Has Tony phoned yet? 5. Even before he got/stood up, I knew what he would say. 7. Have you ever been to Disneyland? / Have you been to Disneyland before? 8. The first guests are already here / have already arrived. 10. Very soon we shall/will hear the first results.

D. Confusing friends

D1 1. advice 2. advise

▶ advice = Rat(schlag) (Nomen); advise = (be)raten (Verb)

D2 1. b / 2. a

▶ homework = Hausaufgabe(n); housework = Haushaltsarbeit(en)

D3 1. a / 2. b / 3. a

▶ interesting = interessant; interested = interessiert

D4 1. Is the Sahara the largest desert in the world? 2. What would you like for dessert?

▶ desert = Wüste; dessert = Dessert

D5 1. economic 2. economic 3. economical 4. economic 5. economical 6. economical

▶ economic = die Wirtschaft betreffend; economical = sparsam

D6 1. classical 2. korrekt 3. classical 4. korrekt 5. korrekt 6. classical

▶ classic = angesehen, typisch, von bleibendem Wert; classical = klassisch (in Bezug auf Musik, die Antike)

D7 1. beside 2. besides 3. besides 4. besides 5. Besides working 6. beside

▶ beside = (örtlich) neben; besides = neben (= außer), außerdem

D8 1. It's 2. its 3. its 4. its 5. It's 6. its

▶ it's = es ist (= it is); its = sein, ihr

D9 1. altogether 2. all together

▶ altogether = insgesamt; all together = alle zusammen

D10 1. lie 2. lays 3. lain 4. lied 5. lying 6. laid 7. lying 8. lay 9. laid, laid 10. lay, lain 11. lied, lied

D11 1. largely 2. largely 3. greatly 4. greatly

▶ largely = größtenteils; greatly = sehr

D12 1. passed 2. past 3. passed 4. past 5. past 6. past 7. past 8. passed

▶ passed = Form des Verbs pass (vergehen, überholen, vorbeigehen an); past = Präposition / Adverb (an ... vorbei, vorbei)

D13 1. a / 2. b

▶ terrible = furchtbar; terrific = gewaltig, toll

D14 1. used to work 2. had to get used to writing 3. get used to it 4. am used to using

▶ used to (+ Verb in Grundform) = früher + Verb in der Vergangenheit; be used to (+ -ing-Form) = es gewohnt sein, zu ...; get used to = sich gewöhnen an

D15 1. at last 2. at least

D16 1. risen 2. raised 3. raised 4. rose 5. rose 6. raise

▶ raise, raised, raised = an-, auf-, hochheben; rise, rose, risen = steigen, an-, auf-, hochsteigen, sich erheben

D17 1. a / 2. b

▶ sometime = irgendwann; sometimes = manchmal

D18 1. a / 2. b

▶ every day = jeden Tag; everyday = alltäglich

D19 1. historic 2. historical 3. historical 4. historical

▶ historic = historisch (= bedeutsam); historical = geschichtlich, aus der Geschichte

D20 1. b / 2. a

▶ affect = beeinflussen, betreffen (Verb); effect = Auswirkung (Nomen)

D21 1. loose 2. lose 3. lose 4. loose

▶ loose = lose; lose = verlieren

D22 1. mayor 2. major

▶ major = Major; mayor = Bürgermeister

D23 1. b / 2. b / 3. a

▶ in time = rechtzeitig; on time = pünktlich

E. All friends together

E1 1. I'll have 2. menu 3. cuisine / food 4. mobile (phone) (BE) / cell phone (AE) 5. inn/pub 6. opinion

E2 1. play/piece 2. audience 3. interval 4. poorly attended

E3 1. commercial 2. channels 3. newsreaders 4. latest

E4 1. a / 2. b / 3. b / 4. b / 5. a / 6. a

E5 1. trays 2. menu 3. salad bar 4. good for you 5. salad dressing

E6 1. answer it 2. code 3. take the call 4. ask for 5. dial 6. hung up

E7 1. reunion 2. grammar school 3. at 4. marks/grades 5. did/took 6. bullied 7. took/passed 8. went to/started university

E8 1. did / went on 2. stay 3. guesthouses 4. hot 5. took 6. It took us 7. checked 8. forms 9. Altogether

E9 1. sleep in 2. ride 3. used to drive 4. two years ago 5. took 6. hard 7. road 8. the open air 9. hiking 10. photographer 11. am also interested in 12. classic 13. are set in

E10 1. lately/recently 2. three months 3. latest 4. At this stage 5. current 6. during/over 7. take 8. does it take 9. than

E11 1. I like Ronaldo's wife a lot. / Ronaldo's wife is very nice. 2. Anna is very self-confident. 3. Mark is my son from my/a previous marriage. 4. I'm the same age as my boss. 5. Be careful. He's very sensitive. 6. Please leave me alone / in peace. I have to (do some) work. 7. My riding instructor is very tall, almost/nearly two metres tall. 8. Be sensible! 9. Why are you so quiet today? 10. When was the last time we were all together? 11. My husband is one of the few men who are not interested in football. 12. The children were very good.

E12 1. Surgery hours 2. good for you 3. prescription 4. painkillers 5. false teeth 6. a really bad sore throat

E13 1. next 2. nearest 3. shade 4. shadow 5. backside 6. back

E14 1. lettuce 2. boiled potatoes 3. hot/spicy 4. drinking water 5. tray 6. Bon appétit / Enjoy it 7. makes me/you fat 8. have a barbecue 9. hot 10. leftovers 11. loaf 12. recipe 13. dressing 14. menu 15. break 16. inn

E15 1. staff 2. have gone into retirement / have retired 3. do / are doing overtime 4. boss 5. entrepreneur 6. takes/makes

E16 1. a / 2. c / 3. b / 4. a / 5. b / 6. c / 7. c

3 Phrases for Everyday Communication

Inhalt Teil 3

Übungen

A. Sich begegnen und vorstellen

1. Hello, I'm Francis Docherty.
2. My name is Handley.
3. How was your flight?
4. Long time, no see.
5. How are you?
6. Nice to meet you.
7. And this is ...
8. Is there anybody here that you know?
9. Excuse me. Are you Ms O'Leary?
10. I have an appointment.
11. At a conference.
12. I didn't expect to see you here.

Check-up

A1 Hello, I'm Francis Docherty.

Was passt zusammen?

1. Hello, I'm Francis Docherty.
2. I'm sorry. What was your name again?
3. Excuse me. Are you by any chance Daniela Becker?
4. May I have your name, please?
5. Good morning. Can you tell me if Mr Watson is here?
6. You must be Helen.
7. Do you know where I can find her?

a. No, sorry. I'm not.
b. I don't think he is at the moment.
c. Over there, she's the woman in the blue jacket.
d. Mellor, Antonia Mellor.
e. Yes, that's right. And you must be David.
f. Sure. It's Elizabeth Joyce.
g. Pleased to meet you.

1	2	3	4	5	6	7
g						

A2 My name is Handley.

Ergänzen Sie die Dialoge mit passenden Wörtern.

◆ Good evening. My (1.) ___name___ is Handley, Jeb Handley.
● Hello, Mr Handley. (2.) N__________ to (3.) __________ you.
(4.) I'__________ Gerlinde Funkenthal.
◆ (5.) P__________ to meet you, ...
Sorry. (6.) __________ was your name (7.) __________?
● Gerlinde, Gerlinde Funkenthal.
◆ Ah, Gerlinde.
◆ (8.) __________ morning. I'm Philip Keynes.
I'm here to (9.) __________ Ms Schlegel.
● I'm Tina Schlegel. (10.) __________ do you (11.) __________?
(12.) __________ you like to come this way?

A3 How was your flight?

Ergänzen Sie.

a good trip • go all right • OK • ~~your flight~~

1. How was ____*your flight*____?
2. Did you have ________________?
3. Did everything ________________?
4. Was the journey ________________?

any help • take one of those for you
with your bags • you a hand

5. Can I help you ________________?
6. Do you need ________________?
7. Shall I give ________________?
8. Let me ________________.

after all this time • see you again • to be here • to Munich

9. Welcome ________________.
10. It's good ________________.
11. It's great to ________________.
12. It's nice to meet face to face ________________.

A4 Long time, no see.

Ordnen Sie die Satzteile.

◆ (1.) ~~Jack. / no see / Hello, / Long time~~

Hello, Jack. Long time, no see.

● (2.) seems / it / ages. / Yes,

____

◆ (3.) Vancouver. / last / The / was / in / time

____

● (4.) ago. / years / be / four / That / must

____

◆ (5.) could / be. / well / It

____

● (6.) things? / How / are

____

◆ (7.) thanks. / And / Fine, / you?

____

A5 How are you?

Ordnen Sie ein.

a. How are you?
b. Not so bad.
c. So how's it going?
d. Good.
e. Could be better.
f. Yeah, fine.
g. How are things?
h. Pretty good.
i. How are you doing?
j. Great!
k. A bit so-so.
l. Fine, thanks.

1. „Wie geht's?"	a,
2. „Es geht mir (ziemlich) gut."	b,
3. „Es geht mir nicht so gut."	e,

A6 Nice to meet you.

Welcher Satz ist falsch oder unpassend?

1. Sie lernen jemanden das erste Mal kennen und begrüßen ihn.
   a. I'm pleased to meet you.
   b. ~~König, good da~~y.
   c. Nice to meet you.
2. Sie sind sich nicht sicher, ob Sie sich schon mal kennengelernt haben.
   a. I don't think we've met, have we?
   b. Sorry, but have we met before?
   c. We don't know us, do we?
3. Sie wollen sich vorstellen.
   a. Can I introduce myself?
   b. I'm Jens Klein.
   c. May I introduce me?
4. Sie wollen jemanden dritten vorstellen.
   a. Let me introduce you to my colleague.
   b. I'd like you to meet my colleague.
   c. That is my colleague, Bernd Müller. Bernd, that is Mr Simons.
5. Sie wollen den Namen erfragen.
   a. Can I have your name, please?
   b. How is your name, please?
   c. Sorry, what was your name?

A7 And this is ...

Übersetzen Sie.

1. Das ist mein Mann Johannes. ______________________
2. Ich freue mich, Sie kennenzulernen. ______________________
3. Ich habe viel von Ihnen gehört. ______________________
4. Sandra erzählt oft von Ihnen.______________________

A8 Is there anybody here that you know?

Ergänzen Sie.

an old friend of mine • introduce you to some people
this is • ~~that you know~~

1. Is there anybody here *that you know*?
2. Let me ______________________.
3. ______________________ Andrea from Germany
4. She's ______________________.

for names • haven't we • if you remember • was familiar

5. We've met before, ______________________?
6. I have a terrible memory ______________________.
7. I knew your face ______________________.
8. We met at a party a couple of years ago ______________________.

I just couldn't • I knew • I'm sorry • it's lovely

9. ______________________ to see you again.
10. ______________________ I didn't recognize you.
11. ______________________ I'd seen you before somewhere.
12. ______________________ remember where.

anyway • can I • good, thanks • not so bad

13. ______________________ how are you?
14. ______________________. And you?
15. Oh, ______________________, thanks.
16. ______________________ get you a drink?

A9 Excuse me. Are you Ms O'Leary?

Bringen Sie a.–g. in die richtige Reihenfolge, um das Gespräch zu vervollständigen.

◆ Excuse me.
Are you Ms O'Leary?
● Yes, that's right.
◆ (1.) b
● (2.) …
…

Karin Meyer
a. He sends his apologies[1]. He had a deadline to meet and had to finish something off.
b. ~~I'm Karin Meyer, from Datazoom.~~
c. It's a pleasure.
d. Yes, that's right. Nice to meet you, too.

Ms O'Leary
e. And thank you for picking me up.
f. Oh hello. Sorry, I was expecting Thomas.
g. Oh, OK. Well nice to meet you – Karin, was it?

1	2	3	4	5	6	7
b						

[1] Er lässt sich entschuldigen

A10 I have an appointment.

Ergänzen Sie.

as soon as she can • Certainly • could you tell me
~~Do you speak English?~~ • how can I help you?
you would mind waiting • I have an appointment
is expecting you • she's still in a meeting • take a seat

◆ Guten Morgen.
● Guten Morgen. (1.) *Do you speak English?*
◆ Yes, of course. (2.) ____________________
● My name's Jackson. (3.) I ____________________ with Frau Gebhardt.
◆ Ah yes, Mr Jackson. Frau Gebhardt (4.) ____________________. Just a moment, please.
● Sure.
◆ Isabelle? ... Mr Jackson ist da. ... Gut, sag' ich ihm.
...
I'm sorry but (5.) ____________________.
She asks if (6.) ____________________ just a moment.
She'll be down (7.) ____________________.
● That's OK.
◆ Would you like to (8.) ____________________.
Can I get you something to drink?
● No, I'm fine thank you.
Er, (9.) ____________________ where the toilets are?
◆ (10.) ____________________. Just down here on the right.
● Thank you.

A11 At a conference.

Ergänzen Sie passende Wörter.

Good afternoon (1) ___ladies___ and (2.) ______________.

I'd like to (3.) ______________ you to this presentation.

It's a great (4.) ______________ for me to be here today.

If you have any (5.) ______________, I'll be (6.) ______________

to answer them as we go along.

On (7.) ______________ of Baker International I (8.)

______________ you all a successful and rewarding conference.

A12 I didn't expect to see you here.

Sortieren Sie die Buchstaben und ergänzen Sie.

◆ Hello, Ron. I didn't (1.) CEXPTE ___expect___ to see you here.

● (2.) SEXECU ____________ me?

◆ I said I didn't think I'd meet you here.
This is really quite a (3.) SERUPSIR ____________.

● I'm (4.) RADAFI ____________ there's a (5.) DREAMINGSUNNTDIS ____________.
I think you've (6.) STINMAKE ____________ me for someone else.

◆ Oh. You're not Ron Huggins?

● No, sorry.

◆ Oh, my (7.) SPOOLIGEA ____________. You look just like him!

Check-up

Übersetzen Sie.

1. Wie war noch mal Ihr Name?

   ____

2. Sind Sie zufällig Barbara Giles?

   ____

3. Nett, Sie kennen zu lernen.

   ____

4. Wie war Ihr Flug?

   ____

5. Willkommen in Deutschland.

   ____

6. Lange nicht gesehen.

   ____

7. Wie geht's?

   ____

8. Sind wir uns schon mal begegnet?

   ____

9. Ich würde Sie gern meiner Kollegin vorstellen.

   ____

10. Nehmen Sie bitte Platz.

    ____

B. Sich verabschieden

1. Bye!
2. See you again soon.
3. Thank you for all you have done for me.
4. Say hello to Joanne for me.
5. We'll keep in touch.
6. Goodness, is that the time?
7. Will you excuse me, please?

Check-up

B1 Bye!

Ordnen Sie ein.

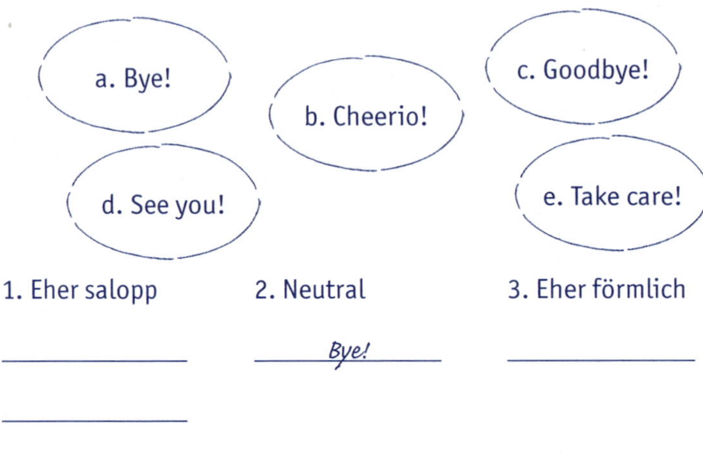
a. Bye!
b. Cheerio!
c. Goodbye!
d. See you!
e. Take care!

1. Eher salopp	2. Neutral	3. Eher förmlich
____________	Bye!	____________
____________		
____________		

B2 See you again soon.

Ordnen Sie zu.

1. I'll see you again
2. I'll look forward to seeing you at Easter then,
3. I'll see you then in a
4. Bye for now then. I'll see you after
5. See you later
6. Till next
7. See you this
8. We'll meet again tomorrow

a. couple of weeks, I suppose.
b. Christmas, sometime in the New Year.
c. evening at the restaurant then.
d. morning, and continue our discussions then.
e. if not before.
f. on.
g. soon.
h. week then.

1	2	3	4	5	6	7	8
g							

B3 Thank you for all you have done for me.

Ergänzen Sie.

Have a good flight
have a safe journey home
~~if everything is on time~~
if I feel like it
plenty to read and listen to
thanks again for everything
you get there
you've arrived safely

- ◆ I'll leave you to it then now.
- ● Thank you for all you've done for me.
- ◆ No problem. What time will you be home?
- ● About midnight (1.) *if everything is on time*.
- ◆ It's going to be a long day for you.
- ● I can sleep (2.) ________________.
  And I've got (3.) ________________.
- ◆ Well, (4.) ________________.
  And text me when (5.) ________________
  so that I know, (6.) ________________.
- ● I will, and (7.) ________________
- ◆ It was a pleasure. (8.) ________________!
- ● Thanks. Bye.
- ◆ Bye!

B4 Say hello to Joanne for me.

Ordnen Sie die Satzteile.

1. ~~for / to / Joanne / hello / Say / me, / please.~~
   Say hello to Joanne for me, please.
2. Michael. / best / my / to / Give / wishes.
   ____
3. and / Ann / love / Give / children. / the / my / to
   ____
4. give / Please / wife. / to / regards / my / your
   ____
5. again. / It's / great / to / you / see / been
   ____
6. you / meet / was / It / nice / to
   ____
7. meeting / pleasure / been / a / has / you. / It
   ____

B5 We'll keep in touch.

Ergänzen Sie.

~~in touch~~ • to get in touch next time you're over
to see you again soon • to seeing you again soon
when you come over again

1. We'll keep/stay *in touch*.
2. I look forward ______________________________.
3. I hope ______________________________.
4. Let me know ______________________________.
5. Don't forget ______________________________.

B6 Goodness, is that the time?

Wer sagt was? Sortieren Sie.

a. ~~Goodness, is that the time?~~
b. Do you really have to leave?
c. I don't want to keep you.
d. I'm afraid I have to go soon.
e. I'm sorry, but I really must be going.
f. Is it that late already?
g. Won't you have another drink before you go?
h. That's a pity.
i. It's time I started making my way.
j. You don't have to go just yet, do you?

1. Der Gast, der gehen will:	*a,*
2. Der Gastgeber:	

B7 Will you excuse me, please?

Ergänzen Sie passende Ausdrücke.

◆ Will you (1.) *excuse* me, please?
I'm (2.) ________ I have to leave now. I have another meeting.

● Of (2.) ________. No problem.

◆ Frau Walther will look (3.) _____ you and (4.) ________ a taxi for you when you're ready to leave, and so on.

● Thanks.

◆ I hope we've (5.) ___________ everything.

● I can't think of anything else at the moment.

◆ Well, if there's anything we've (6.) _________ just (7.) _____ me an email or (8.) _____ me a call. We've had a very (9.) __________ meeting.

● Yes, I feel that too.
Well, (10.) _________ then, and have a good (11.) _________ home.

Check-up

Übersetzen Sie.

1. Bis später.

   ____

2. Pass auf dich auf.

   ____

3. Guten Flug!

   ____

4. Kommen Sie sicher nach Hause.

   ____

5. Nochmals danke für alles.

   ____

6. Grüßen Sie Tom von mir.

   ____

7. Wir bleiben in Verbindung.

   ____

8. Ich freue mich darauf, Sie bald wiederzusehen.

   ____

9. Ich hoffe, Sie bald wiederzusehen.

   ____

10. Es wird langsam Zeit, dass ich mich auf den Weg mache.

    ____

C. Small Talk machen

1. Where are you from?
2. Do you come from Germany?
3. Are you here on vacation?
4. Is this your first time here?
5. You must give me your address.
6. Oh right.
7. That's interesting.
8. I was born in Stuttgart.
9. I live near Freiburg.
10. Where do you live exactly?
11. What do you do for a living?
12. Small talk topics.
13. Do you have any plans for the summer?
14. What do you do in your spare time?
15. ... is really not my thing.
16. What's the weather like?
17. It's been absolutely glorious.
18. Do you have any children?
19. A patchwork family.
20. Business or pleasure?
21. Do you have time for a drink?
22. What line are you in?
23. Your German is really very good.
24. How's the family?

Check-up

C1 Where are you from?

Was passt zusammen?

1. Where are you from?
2. What part of the country is that?
3. Where is that near?
4. Is that a big place?
5. How big is that?
6. Do you know Regensburg?

a. The east. It's between Berlin and Dresden.
b. It's not far from Dortmund.
c. Not really, more medium-sized, I suppose.
d. A place near Frankfurt.
e. Not very well. I've been there once.
f. I don't know what the population is, 30,000 perhaps.

1	2	3	4	5	6
d					

C2 Do you come from Germany?

Ergänzen Sie den Dialog mit passenden Wörtern.

◆ Do you (1.) ___*come*___ from Germany?
● Yes, that's right.
◆ What (2.) ____________?
● The west, not (3.) ____________ from Cologne.
Do you know Germany at all?
◆ Not very well, I'm afraid.
So is this your first visit (4.) ____________ the States?
● No. We've been several times (5.) ____________.
◆ Oh right. And where are you (6.) ____________ this time?
● Montana. My wife has (7.) ____________ there.
Do you know Montana at all?
◆ I'm afraid not. I'm from the east (8.) ____________.

C3 Are you here on vacation?

Bringen Sie a.–j. in die richtige Reihenfolge, um das Gespräch zu vervollständigen.

◆ So are you on vacation?
● Yes, that's right.
◆ (1.) b
● (2.) ...
...

American
a. How long do you have this time?
b. ~~And where are you going?~~
c. California's great. Is this your first trip to the States?
d. Oh business, business. My name's Hank, by the way.
e. Yes. I've been on a trip to France and Spain.

German
f. And I'm Wolfgang.
g. Three weeks. What about you? Are you on your way home?
h. California and the west coast.
i. My second. I was in Florida for a week last year.
j. Work or pleasure?

1	2	3	4	5	6	7	8	9	10
b									

C4 Is this your first time here?

Wählen Sie die richtige Lösung, a oder b.

◆	So is this your first time here?	
●	Yes, it is. In the past (1.) ... Spain.	a. we've usually been to
		b. we were usually in
◆	Are you enjoying (2.) ...?	a. you
		b. yourselves
●	Yes, thanks. We're having (3.)	a. a great time
		b. much fun
◆	Which hotel (4.) ...?	a. are you staying at
		b. do you live in
●	The Metro.	
◆	(5.) ...?	a. How's it?
		b. What's it like?
●	It's OK, a bit (6.)	a. loud
		b. noisy

1	2	3	4	5	6
a					

C5 You must give me your address.

Was passt zusammen?

1. You must give me
2. I'll give you
3. My surname is Caridia,
4. Hannah – it's spelled like Anna,
5. Is that your home number
6. And my email is
7. My mobile number is
8. If you're ever in London

a. my card.
b. but with an 'h' at each end.
c. you must get in touch.
d. your address.
e. it's a Greek name.
f. or your office?
g. markus dot becker at x minus online dot d e.
h. zero one double two, five two seven eight double nine three.

1	2	3	4	5	6	7	8
d							

C6 Oh right.

Was passt zusammen?

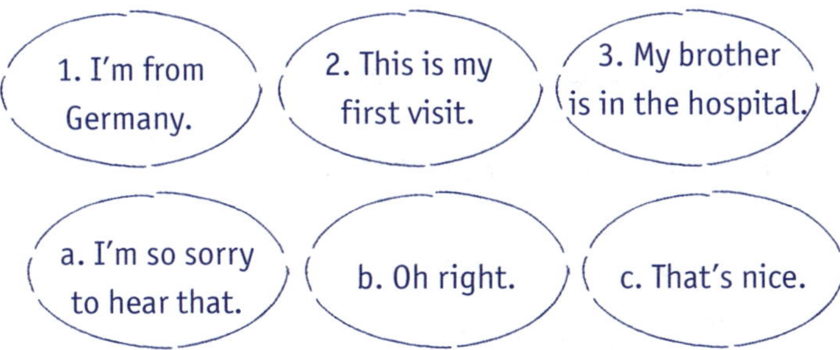

1. I'm from Germany.
2. This is my first visit.
3. My brother is in the hospital.
a. I'm so sorry to hear that.
b. Oh right.
c. That's nice.

C7 That's interesting.

Sortieren Sie.

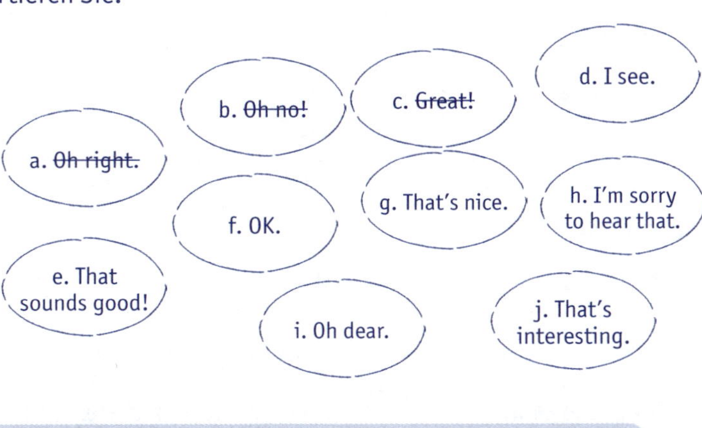

a. ~~Oh right.~~

e. That sounds good!

1. Neutral reagieren, Interesse zeigen:	a,
2. Auf gute Nachricht reagieren:	c,
3. Auf schlechte Nachricht reagieren:	b,

C8 I was born in Stuttgart.

Bringen Sie a.–k. in die richtige zeitliche Reihenfolge – von der Geburt bis zur Gegenwart.

a. But we moved to Munich when I was four.
b. I trained as a nurse.
c. That's where I met my husband.
d. ~~I was born in Stuttgart.~~
e. We came back to Germany three years ago.
f. I went to school in Bavaria.
g. He was a doctor in the hospital there.
h. So we're thinking of going back to New Zealand.
i. After I qualified I spent two years in New Zealand.
j. I left school at eighteen.
k. But my husband doesn't really like it here.

1	2	3	4	5	6	7	8	9	10	11
d										

C9 I live near Ulm.

Korrigieren Sie.

1. ~~I live in the near of Ulm~~.	I live *near* Ulm.
2. ~~I am born in the east~~.	I ______ born in the east.
3. ~~I went to the school in Magdeburg~~.	I went ______ school in Magdeburg.
4. ~~I trained as graphic designer.~~	I trained as ______ graphic designer.
5. ~~My partner is teacher.~~	My partner is ______ teacher.
6. ~~I was never in England.~~	I have never ______ ______ England.
7. ~~I don't know England good~~	I don't know England ______.

C10 Where do you live exactly?

Ergänzen Sie.

about • by • from • ~~in~~ • near • of • to

So where do you live exactly?

1. *In* northern Germany.
2. West ______ Hannover.
3. Close ______ the Dutch border.
4. Not far ______ Dresden.
5. ______ the sea.
6. ______ Salzburg.
7. ______ 60 kilometres south of Berlin.

C11 What do you do for a living.

Ergänzen Sie.

~~after~~ • ~~at~~ • at • at • between • for • for • in in • out of • with • with

What do you do (for a living)?

1. I'm *at* home looking *after* the kids.
2. I have a part-time job ______ the weekend and ______ the evenings.
3. I'm ______ jobs ______ the moment, actually.
4. I was ______ a job ______ about 18 months.
5. I work ______ a local company.
6. I'm ______ an organization ______ the tourist industry.

C12 Small talk topics.

Wenn man jemanden zum allerersten Mal kennenlernt, sind einige Gesprächsthemen und Fragen tabu. Was kann man sagen bzw. fragen, was sollte man lieber vermeiden?

1. It's a bit warm today, isn't it?
2. Are you divorced?
3. Can I get you a drink?
4. Do you speak German?
5. Have you been on holiday this summer?
6. How much do you earn?
7. So how's your blood pressure these days?
8. Is this your first time here?
9. What line (of business) are you in?
10. What's the weather like with you at the moment?

Angemessene Aussagen: *1,*

C13 Do you have any plans for the summer?

Ordnen Sie die Satzteile.

1. ~~any / the / So / plans / summer? / you / do / have / for~~
   So do you have any plans for the summer?
2. decided. / haven't / We // home. / stay / may / We / at
   ____
3. usually / We / don't / in / summer. / away / the / go
   ____
4. September. / two / May / I'm / take / to / in / planning /or / weeks
   ____
5. Easter. / off / at / had / I / days / ten
   ____

C14 What do you do in your spare time?

Ergänzen Sie *do*, *go*, oder *play*.

1.	*go* and see friends	9.	_______ skiing
2.	_______ computer games	10.	_______ tennis
3.	_______ cycling	11.	_______ to the gym
4.	_______ do-it-yourself	12.	_______ walking
5.	_______ gardening	13.	_______ to exhibitions
6.	_______ with the kids	14.	_______ jobs round the house
7.	_______ on the internet	15.	_______ and see a movie
8.	_______ out for a drink	16.	_______ out to eat

C15 ... is really not my thing.

Sortieren Sie.

a. ... ~~is/are really not my thing~~.
b. I hate ...
c. I like ...
d. I'm interested in ...
e. I'm not into ... at all.
f. I'm quite keen on ...
g. I'm really into ...
h. ... doesn't/don't interest me.

1. Das interessiert mich:
2. Das interessiert mich nicht: *a,*

Zusatzaufgabe: Und nun machen Sie drei Aussagen über sich.

____

____

____

C16 What's the weather like?

Ergänzen Sie.

as • bit • like • quite • so • rain • time • what's

◆ (1.) *What's* the weather (2.) __________ with you?

● Not (3.) __________ good (4.) __________ here.
A (5.) __________ cold for the (6.) __________ of year.
And we've had (7.) __________ a lot of (8.) __________.

brought • change • hope • lucky • stays • terrible

◆ It's nice to see the sun for a (9.) __________.

We've had a (10.) __________ summer.

● We've been quite (11.) __________.

◆ You've obviously (12.) __________ the good weather with you!

Let's (13.) __________ it (14.) __________ like this for a bit!

C17 It's been absolutely glorious.

Was passt zusammen (Bild und Satzteile)?

1. We've had snow,
2. It's quite thundery,
3. ~~It's been absolutely glorious,~~
4. It's so foggy,
5. We've had rain all day,

a. it's been absolutely tipping it down[1].

b. the kids are delighted of course, but I find it a real pain.

c. ~~wall-to-wall sunshine all day~~.

d. warm and sultry[2], very sticky.

e. you can't see more than a few metres.

[1] es hat regelrecht geschüttet

[2] schwül

Bild	A	B	C	D	E
Satz	*3 + c*				

C18 Do you have any children?

Welche Antwort passt nicht?

1. Do you have any children?
   a. Yes, three, two girls and a boy.
   b. I have two grown-up sons from my first marriage.
   c. There are two grandchildren, a boy and a girl.
   d. No, it's just me and my partner.

2. And this is ...?
   a. Jack, my husband.
   b. yes, we're together.
   c. my partner, Florence.
   d. my ex-husband, Jerome's dad.

C19 A patchwork family.

Ergänzen Sie.

baby • broke up • daughter • divorced • ~~ex-husband~~
ex-wife • get on • granddaughter • husband
married • mother • related • re-married
separated • son • son-in-law • step-daughter • wife

Hi, there. This is a photo of the patchwork family, or the patchwork families that I am somehow a member of. Where shall I start? I'll start with me. I'm Sandy. Can you see me?
I was first married to Ron. So Ron is my (1.) *ex-husband*.
We have one (2.) ______________, Rebecca. She's (3.) ______________ to Ricky, so he's my and Ron's (4.) ______________. Rebecca and Ricky have a (5.) ______________ daughter, Lucy.
So Lucy is Ron and my (6.) ______________. So far so good?
After Ron and I (7.) ______________ and got (8.) ______________, Ron soon (9.) ______________. His second (10.) ______________ is Tricia. Actually she was the reason the marriage (11.) ______________, but she and I are OK with each other now.
Ron and Tricia have a 16-year-old (12.) ______________, that's Gordon. See him? I'm not (13.) ______________ to him, but I like him and we (14.) ______________ well with each other.
On the other side, you can see Alexis and Regina. Alexis and Regina are married. Regina is Joel, my (15.) ______________'s (16.) ______________ – he was married to her before he married me. Got it? They have a daughter, Monica. So she's my (17.) ______________ (because I'm married to Joel, and she's Joel's daughter, got it?). Joel and I don't have any children together. That makes things a bit easier.
Right, we're nearly there now. There's just one person left now, Sonia. Sonia is Alexis' daughter from his first marriage.
I can't remember Sonia's (18.) ______________'s name, Alexis' ex. I've never actually met her. She lives in Canada now. And is no doubt married to someone else now, who was probably married before and ...

C20 Business or pleasure?

Ergänzen Sie den Dialog mit passenden Wörtern.

◆ Is this (1.) *business* ____ or pleasure?

● Sorry?

◆ Are you (2.) __________ a business trip or is this a private (3.) __________?

● Oh, private. My niece[1] is (4.) __________ married to a Scotsman.

◆ Oh really. In Scotland?

● Yes, in Aberdeen. Do you know Aberdeen at (5.) __________?

◆ Not very (6.) __________. I've (7.) __________ there once, I think.
I (8.) __________ there once with my parents when I was a (9.) __________. I don't (10.) __________ much about it.

C21 Do you have time for a drink?

Bringen Sie a.–g. in die richtige Reihenfolge, um das Gespräch zu vervollständigen.

◆ Do you have time for a drink? When's your flight?
● (1.) f
◆ (2.) ...
...

◆ Andy	● Joel
a. 21.10. Let's go somewhere and catch up[2] a bit.	d. Good idea. I could do with a bit of exercise after all that sitting.
b. Do you feel like a walk? It's not too far.	e. Fine. I could do with a bite to eat, too.
c. Well, there's a little bistro I know that's quite handy for the airport. Is that OK for you?	f. ~~Not till 20.40. Yours~~?
	g. That sounds good. Shall we get a taxi?

1	2	3	4	5	6	7
g						

[2]uns austauschen

C22 What line are you in?

Ergänzen Sie.

~~are you in~~ • do you do • have you ever heard
to work for • work for

1. What line ___*are you in*___?
2. Who do you ________________?
3. What ________________?
4. Is that a good company ________________?
5. ________________ of Blix, the entertainment group?

an engineer • a year out • plastics • the administrative side

6. I'm in ________________.
7. I'm taking ________________.
8. I'm on ________________.
9. I'm ________________.

C23 Your German is really very good.

Sortieren Sie.

a. ~~Your German is really very good~~.
b. I can get along in Spanish.
c. I can understand OK, but my spoken Italian is not too good.
d. I couldn't speak Russian to save my life!
e. I speak some Mandarin, enough to get by on.
f. I was never any good at languages.
g. My French is really very rusty.
h. You're absolutely fluent.

1. Gute Sprachkenntnisse: *a,*
2. Mittlere Sprachkenntnisse:
3. Schlechte Sprachkenntnisse:

C24 How's the family?

Ergänzen Sie.

and the rest of the family • back in the spring
~~both still at college~~ • can imagine • for the best
getting by, you know • getting paid • I'm sorry to hear that
he's doing • step on the ladder • very hard for Ann

◆ So how's the family?
● Fine, thanks.

◆ You have two sons, right?
● A son and a daughter.

◆ Right, right. (1.) *Both still at college*?
● No, Jochen has finished. (2.) ____________ an internship[1] with a company in Augsburg.

◆ That sounds good.
● He's not (3.) ____________ at all. But it's the first (4.) ____________.

◆ (5.) ____________? How's Andrea?
● She's OK, (6.) ____________. What about you?

◆ Well, Ann's mother died (7.) ____________.
● Oh, (8.) ____________

◆ It was really (9.) ____________. She had Alzheimer's.
● That must have been (10.) ____________.

◆ It was, for all of us actually.
● I (11.) ____________.

[1]Praktikum

Check-up

Übersetzen Sie.

1. Wo sind Sie her?

   ____

2. Kennen Sie Deutschland überhaupt?

   ____

3. Ist dies Ihr erster Besuch in Deutschland?

   ____

4. Ich heiße übrigens Martin.

   ____

5. Ach so. Das ist ja interessant.

   ____

6. Es tut mir leid, das zu hören.

   ____

7. Ich bin in Berlin geboren.

   ____

8. Ich lebe in der Nähe von Aachen.

   ____

9. Was machen Sie beruflich?

   ____

10. Ich gebe Ihnen meine Adresse.

    ____

11. Wie ist das Wetter bei Ihnen?

    ____

12. Es ist gewittrig.

    ____

13. Ich habe zwei erwachsene Söhne aus erster Ehe.

___

14. Das ist mein Stiefsohn.

___

15. Ich interessiere mich nicht für Fußball.

___

16. Do-it-yourself ist nicht mein Ding.

___

17. Geschäftlich oder privat?

___

18. Ich könnte etwas Bewegung gebrauchen.

___

19. Wie geht's der Familie?

___

20. Die erste Stufe auf der [Karriere-]Leiter.

___

D. Nachfragen und sich verständigen

1. Could you repeat that, please?
2. Excuse me, do you speak English?
3. We say 'faul' in German.
4. Could you write it down for me?
5. It's the thing ...
6. A for Alpha.
7. Can you spell that, please?
8. I can't understand a word.
9. Can you all hear me?
10. It's the thing ... (2)

Check-up

D1 Could you repeat that, please?

Welche Übersetzung ist richtig bzw. passend? Oder passen beide?

1. Könnten Sie das bitte wiederholen?
   a. Could you say that again, please?
   b. Could you repeat that, please?
2. Wie bitte?
   a. Pardon? b. Sorry?
3. Könnten Sie langsamer sprechen?
   a. Could you speak more slowly?
   b. Could you talk slowlier?
4. Tut mir leid, das habe ich nicht verstanden.
   a. Sorry, I didn't catch that.
   b. Sorry. I didn't understand.
5. Entschuldigung. Was haben Sie gesagt?
   a. Sorry, what did you say?
   b. Sorry, what have you said?
6. Was bedeutet *remove*?
   a. What does *remove* mean?
   b. What means *remove*?
7. Können Sie mir folgen?
   a. Are you with me? b. Do you follow me?
8. Wie heißt das auf Englisch?
   a. How is that called in English?
   b. What is that called in English?
9. Wie spricht man das aus?
   a. How do you pronounce that?
   b. How do you speak that?
10. Wie buchstabiert man das?
    a. How do you spell that? b. How is that spelled?

1	2	3	4	5	6	7	8	9	10
a+b									

D2 Excuse me, do you speak English?

Ergänzen Sie.

Is that right • I think I've got that now
~~Excuse me~~ • Just a little • Now I understand
Sorry, I don't understand
Sorry, what was the word again • What's that in German

◆ (1.) ___*Excuse me*___, do you speak English?
● (2.) ____________________.
◆ I'm looking for a chemist.
● (3.) ____________________.
◆ A shop where I can buy medicine – aspirin.
● Ah! (4.) ____________________.
(5.) ____________________________________?
◆ Chemist. You can also say 'pharmacy'.
(6.) ___________________________?
● Apotheke.
◆ Apetaker? (7.) ____________________?
● Apotheke.
◆ Ah, OK. (8.) _________________________.
So is there one near here, an Apotaker?
● Yes, in this street, 200 or 300 metres along on this side.
◆ Thank you. You've been a great help.

D3 We say 'faul' in German.

Was passt zusammen?

1. We say 'faul' in German. What's the English equivalent?
2. How do you pronounce this word, H E I G H T?
3. How do you spell that please?
4. In 'I've read it' – how do you say 'read'?
5. Is that with one L or two?
6. Is that all small letters?

a. The first is a capital.
b. It rhymes with 'red'.
c. Like 'high', but with a t on the end.
d. Someone who doesn't do much is 'lazy'.
e. K N I F E.
f. With a double L.

1	2	3	4	5	6
d					

D4 Could you write it down for me?

Ergänzen Sie die Sätze mit passenden Wörtern.

1. Could you write it *down* for me?
2. It helps if I see it in ____________.
3. I need to see it ____________ down.
4. Sorry, I don't know the English ____________.
5. What's the ____________ in German, do you know?
6. I've ____________ how to say it in English.
7. Can you ____________ me an example?
8. Can you say it a ____________ way?
9. What's another way of ____________ that?

D5 It's the thing ...

Ordnen Sie zu.

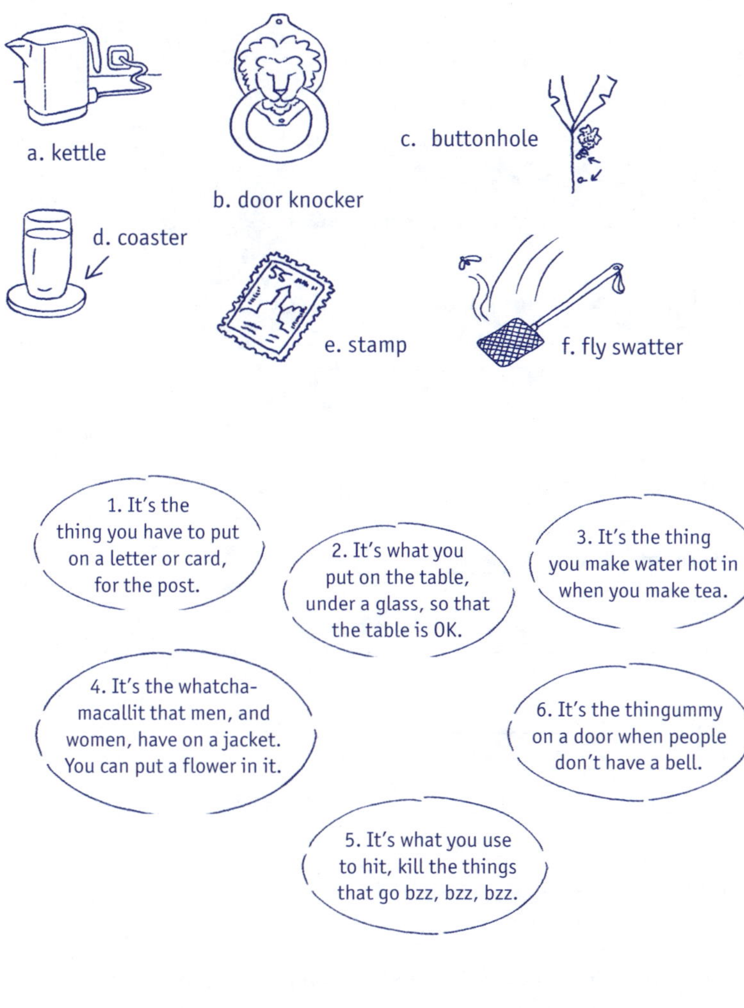
a. kettle
b. door knocker
c. buttonhole
d. coaster
e. stamp
f. fly swatter
1. It's the thing you have to put on a letter or card, for the post.
2. It's what you put on the table, under a glass, so that the table is OK.
3. It's the thing you make water hot in when you make tea.
4. It's the whatcha-macallit that men, and women, have on a jacket. You can put a flower in it.
6. It's the thingummy on a door when people don't have a bell.
5. It's what you use to hit, kill the things that go bzz, bzz, bzz.

1	2	3	4	5	6
e					

D6 A for Alpha.

Buchstabieren Sie die Städtenamen mithilfe der Tabelle.

A for Alpha	J for Juliett	S for Sierra
B for Bravo	K for Kilo	T for Tango
C for Charlie	L for Lima	U for Uniform
D for Delta	M for Mike	V for Victor
E for Echo	N for November	W for Whisky
F for Foxtrot	O for Oscar	X for X-ray
G for Golf	P for Papa	Y for Yankee
H for Hotel	Q for Quebec	Z for Zulu
I for India	R for Romeo	

1. Seattle: *sierra, echo, alpha, tango, tango, Lima, echo*
2. Amsterdam: ____________________
3. Nairobi: ____________________
4. Frankfurt: ____________________
5. Edinburgh: ____________________
6. Beijing: ____________________

Zusatzaufgabe: Wie buchstabieren Sie Ihren Nachnamen nach dem internationalen Alphabet?

____

____

D7 Can you spell that, please?

Ergänzen Sie.

Can you spell that, please?
Yes, B A G E L.

B • F • I • ~~A~~ • Q

1. A rhymes with J and K.
2. __ rhymes with Y.
3. __ rhymes with U and W.
4. __ rhymes with C, D, E, G, P, T and V.
5. __ rhymes with L, M, N and S.

C • I • ~~O~~ • Q • R • T • X • Y

6. The letter O sounds like the word 'oh'.
7. The letter __ sounds like the word 'are'.
8. The letter __ sounds like the word 'tea'.
9. The letter __ sounds like the word 'why'.
10. The letter __ sounds like the word 'eye'.
11. The letter __ sounds like the word 'see'.
12. The letter __ sounds like the word 'ex'.
13. The letter __ sounds like the word 'queue'.

Sprechen Sie laut vor.

14. Sorry, did you say a or h?
15. Sorry, did you say e or i?
16. Sorry, did you say v or w?
17. Sorry, did you say g or j?
18. Sorry, did you say i or y?
19. Sorry, did you say a or r?

D8 I can't understand a word.

Was passt zusammen?

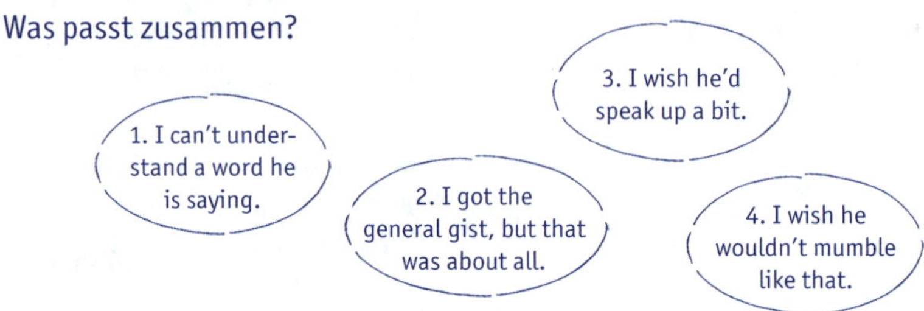

1. I can't understand a word he is saying.
2. I got the general gist, but that was about all.
3. I wish he'd speak up a bit.
4. I wish he wouldn't mumble like that.

a. Der Sprecher versteht nur Bahnhof.

b. Der Sprecher findet, dass der Redner zu leise ist.

c. Der Sprecher findet, dass der Redner nuschelt.

d. Der Sprecher hat grob verstanden, viel mehr aber auch nicht.

1	2	3	4

D9 Can you all hear me?

Ergänzen Sie den Dialog mit passenden Ausdrücken.

Speaker: Can you all hear me (1.) *at the back of the room*?
Voice: Fine, thanks.
Voice: Loud and (2.) ______.
Speaker: And can everybody see the picture on the (3.) s_____n alright?
Voice: It's not very clear. It's not dark enough in here.
Speaker: OK. Can we (4.) ______ the curtains, or let down the (5.) ________, please?
Voice: The picture's also too small. I can't read the script.
Speaker: I'll try and move the projector back a bit. Is that (6.) ____ better?
Voice: Yes, it's OK now.
Speaker: Right, and what about the player here. If I play the DVD, can you all hear it OK at the back of the room?
Voice: Not really.
Speaker: I'll (7.) _____ the volume (8.) __ a bit, then.

D10 It's the thing ... (2)

Bilden Sie Sätze und ordnen Sie diese den Zeichnungen zu.

It's	~~the basket thing~~	where you put in your card and get money
	the thing at the bank	that you have on your car, there are four of them
	the round thing	when it's very hot
	what you (have to) do	~~you put your shopping in at the supermarket~~
	what you need / use	with the key when you open the door
		when you go to a new place to live
		when you cut something
		when something's broken

1. It's the basket thing you put your shopping in at the supermarket.
2. ______________________________
3. ______________________________

Check-up

Übersetzen Sie.

1. Könnten Sie das bitte wiederholen?
____
2. Was bedeutet ‚replacement'?
____
3. Wie spricht man dieses Wort aus?
____
4. Tut mir leid, ich verstehe nicht.
____
5. Können Sie es mir aufschreiben?
____
6. Ich kenne das englische Wort nicht.
____
7. Können Sie es anders ausdrücken?
____
8. Wie heißt das auf Deutsch?
____
9. Könnten Sie bitte langsamer sprechen?
____
10. Sie waren eine große Hilfe.
____

E. Höfliche Ausdrucksformen

E1 Please do.

Welche Reaktionen sind möglich? Es können auch alle vier möglich sein.

1. ◆ Yes?
   ● ... ask a question?
   a. Can I b. May I c. Could I d. Will I

2. ◆ Can I ask a question?
   ● Yes, … .
   a. please do b. sure c. go ahead d. of course

3. ◆ I'll show you the way.
   ● That's very kind of you, … .
   a. thanks b. best thanks c. hearty thanks d. thanks a lot

4. ◆ Thank you for all your help.
   ● … .
   a. No problem b. Please c. That's OK d. You're welcome

5. ◆ I think you're in my seat.
   ● Oh, am I? … .
   a. I'm sorry b. My apologies c. I'm afraid d. Excuse me

6. ◆ May I smoke here?
   ● ...
   a. I'm afraid it's not allowed b. I'm sorry, but you can't
   c. Unfortunately not d. No, it's forbidden

7. ◆ I've made a mistake. I'm sorry.
   ● … .
   a. Never mind b. Nothing matters c. It's OK
   d. Don't worry

1	2	3	4	5	6	7
a, b, c						

E2 Excuse me, I have a request.

Was passt zusammen?

1. Excuse me, I have
2. May I
3. Excuse me. Is this
4. Could you
5. Do you mind if
6. Is it OK
7. Would you mind
8. I'd like
9. Please

a. put this on the table for me?
b. I sit here?
c. just check my emails?
d. a request.
e. to make a reservation.
f. moving your car?
g. seat taken?
h. don't do that again.
i. to park here?

1	2	3	4	5	6	7	8	9
d								

E3 Could you help me?

Ergänzen Sie.

Can you tell me • ~~Excuse me~~ • I'll try • I wonder
You're welcome • You've been a great help

◆ (1.) Excuse me.
● Yes?
◆ (2.) ________________ if you could help me.
● (3.) ________________ .
◆ (4.) ________________ where the Hotel Orion is?
● The Hotel Orion. Ah yes. You go down here, and then …
◆ Thanks very much. (5.) ________________.
● (6.) ________________.

E4 Thanks.

Sortieren Sie ein.

a lot • indeed • many • a million • very much

(1.) ____________ thanks.

Thanks (2.) ____________.

(3.) ____________.

Thank you (4.) ____________ (5.) ____________.

6. Welche Wendung ist am wenigsten förmlich? ________________

7. Welche Wendung ist am intensivsten? ________________

8. Wie lautet die richtige Ergänzung nach *thanks* und *thank you?*

   a. Thanks / Thank you for helping me.

   b. Thanks / Thank you that you've helped me.

E5 May I ask just one more question?

Ergänzen Sie.

anyway • ahead • could • course • ~~may~~ • might • sorry

- ◆ (1.) *May* I ask just one more question.
- ● Of (2.) _________. Go (3.) _________.
- ◆ (4.) _________ you tell me where I (5.) _________ get a memory card?
- ● A memory card? For a camera?
  I think you'd have to go into town for that. (6.) _________.
- ◆ Oh, OK. Thanks (7.) _________.

E6 What's the matter?

Ordnen Sie die Satzteile.

◆ Oh no!

● What's the matter?

◆ I've spilt[1] some coffee.
(1.) ~~sorry. / I'm~~
I'm sorry.

● Don't worry.

◆ But it's all over the table. (2.) awfully / sorry. / I'm

____

● It doesn't matter.

◆ (3.) I'm / terribly / sorry. / so

____

● It's not the end of the world.

◆ (4.) know / happened. / it / have / could / don't / I / how

____

● It could happen to anyone.

◆ (5.) apologize. / I / must / really

____

(6.) know / don't / stupid / so / how / have / I / I / been / could

____

● Anthea, stop! It's only a cup of coffee, for goodness sake!

E7 Saying sorry.

Sortieren Sie ein.

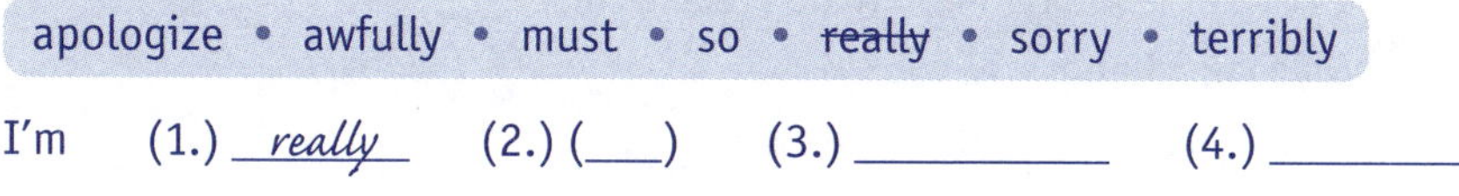

I'm (1.) _really_ (2.) (___) (3.) ________ (4.) ________.
____

I really do (5.) ____ (6.) ________.

E8 It's my fault.

Ergänzen Sie.

1. ◆ I've forgotten to bring the film you lent me.
   ● Never ____ . Bring it next week.
2. ◆ It's my fault that this has happened.
   ● It ______________________________ anyone.
3. ◆ It's my mistake entirely. I'm sorry.
   ● _________________ about it, really.
4. ◆ I have only myself to blame.
   ● True, but ________________________ world, is it?

E9 Who is to blame?

Ergänzen Sie die passende Übersetzung aus E8.

1. Es ist ganz allein mein Fehler.

   ____

2. Ich habe mir das nur selbst zuzuschreiben.

   ____

3. Ich bin schuld.

   ____

E10 Can you give me a hand please?

Sortieren Sie von 1 (= am wenigsten höflich) bis 5 (= am höflichsten).

a. ~~Can you give me a hand please?~~
b. I wonder if you'd mind giving me a hand?
c. Give me a hand, will you?
d. Could you give me a hand please?

1	2	3	4
	a		

E11 Would you mind ...?

Formulieren Sie Sätze mit *Would you mind?*

1. ~~Could you not say anything to Mr Franks about this, please?~~
   Would you mind not saying anything to Mr Franks about this please?
2. Could you keep it to yourself, please.
   Would you mind
3. Please don't smoke here.
   Would you mind
4. Could you repeat that?
5. Could you drive not quite so fast?
6. Could you park a little further down, please.
7. Could you make copies for everyone, please?

E12 Would you mind ...? (2)

Formulieren Sie Sätze mit *Would you mind?*
Beachten Sie die Vergangenheitsform im if-Teil des Satzes.

1. ~~Can we meet a bit later?~~
   Would you mind if we met a bit later?
2. Could I bring a friend?
   Would you mind if
3. Could I just use the phone for a minute?
4. Is it OK if I ask Alan to do that?
5. Is it OK if we change the agenda round a bit?

Check-up

Übersetzen Sie.

1. Kann ich eine Frage stellen? – Bitte.

   Can I ask a question? – ____________

2. Vielen herzlichen Dank.

   ____

3. Machen Sie sich keine Sorgen.

   ____

4. Ich habe die Fotos vergessen. – Macht nichts.

   I've forgotten the photos. – ____________

5. Ich habe eine Bitte.

   ____

6. Würde es Ihnen etwas ausmachen, Ihr Auto umzusetzen?

   ____

7. Es ist ganz allein mein Fehler.

   ____

8. Ob Sie mir wohl helfen könnten?

   ____

9. Danke trotzdem.

   ____

10. Ich muss mich wirklich entschuldigen.

    ____

F. Komplimente und Nettigkeiten

1. You're looking great.
2. What beautiful flowers!
3. You have a very nice apartment.
4. What an interesting story!
5. It's been such a wonderful evening.
6. You've done a really good job.
7. You look so wonderfully relaxed.

Check-up

F1 You're looking great.

Was passt zusammen?

1. You're looking great, really good.
2. That's a nice dress.
3. This is delicious.
4. How do you manage to keep so fit?
5. If I had a son like him,
6. I like this sofa.
7. What beautiful wine glasses!

a. It tastes really good.
b. I'd be really proud of him.
c. It's really comfortable.
d. Where did you buy them?
e. The colour really suits you.
f. I wish I could!
g. I don't think I've seen you looking so well.

1	2	3	4	5	6	7
g						

F2 What beautiful flowers!

Ergänzen Sie *What a/an* oder *What*.

1. ___*What*___ beautiful flowers!
2. ______________ lovely view!
3. ______________ nice flat you have!
4. ______________ enchanting garden!
5. ______________ enchanting children!
6. ______________ wonderful weather we're having!
7. ______________ friendly neighbours you have!
8. ______________ stylish furniture!

F3 You have a very nice apartment.

Bringen Sie a.–i. in die richtige Reihenfolge, um das Gespräch zu vervollständigen.

◆ You have a very nice apartment.
● (1.) ___h___
◆ (2.) ___d___
(3.) ______
● (4.) ______
(5.) ___g___
◆ (6.) ______
Is that the Olympic stadium I can see?
● Yes, that's right.
(7.) ____________________ you can see the mountains.
◆ (8.) ______
● (9.) ______
When it's raining, you can't see them at all!

◆ Guest

a. And the view is magnificent!
b. You feel as if you can reach out and touch them!
c. It has a really nice atmosphere.
d. ~~I like this room especially.~~

● Host

e. But only on a day like today!
f. And if you come over here a bit
g. ~~We like to sit here in the evenings~~.
h. T~~hank you. We like it too~~.
i. It's our favourite room too.

F4 What an interesting story!

Ergänzen Sie die fehlenden Buchstaben *a, e, i, o, u* und *y*.

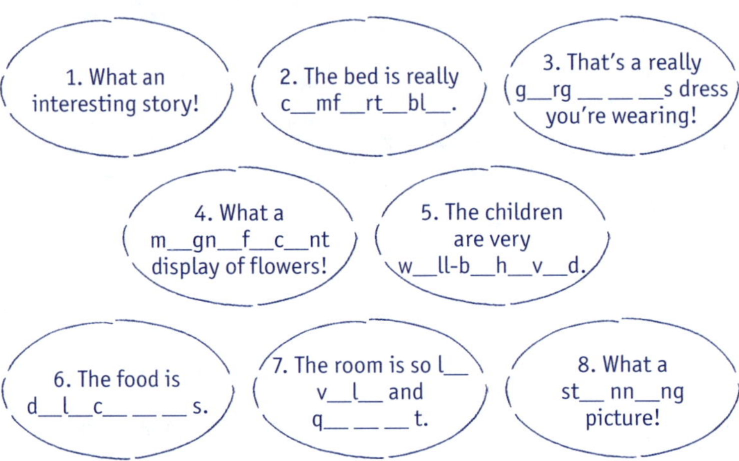

1. What an interesting story!
2. The bed is really c__mf__rt__bl__.
3. That's a really g__rg__ __ __s dress you're wearing!
4. What a m__gn__f__c__nt display of flowers!
5. The children are very w__ll-b__h__v__d.
6. The food is d__l__c__ __ __s.
7. The room is so l__ v__l__ and q__ __ __t.
8. What a st__nn__ng picture!

F5 It's been such a wonderful evening.

Korrigieren Sie – falls nötig.

1. ~~It's been so a wonderful evening~~.
   It's been such a wonderful evening.
2. You look so relaxed!
   ____
3. I've never seen you so relaxed.
   ____
4. We've had a so marvellous time.
   ____
5. The children are so well-behaved.
   ____
6. I've never seen so enormous tomatoes.
   ____
7. I've rarely heard so an interesting life-story.
   ____

F6 You've done a really good job.

Ergänzen Sie eine Form von *do* oder von *make.*

You've (1.) *done* a really good job today. We've (2.) ______ a very favourable impression. It (3.) ______ a big difference that you were able to come and I didn't have to (4.) ______ everything on my own. The speech you (5.) ______ this morning was one of the best I've heard you (6.) ______. You really (7.) ______ your best, and we have (8.) ______ great progress today.

F7 You look so wonderfully relaxed.

Setzen Sie die Wörter in Klammern in der richtigen Form ein.

1. You look so (~~wonderful, relaxed~~) *wonderfully relaxed*.
2. You seem very (happy) ____________________.
3. This must have been (terrible, expensive) ____________________. You really shouldn't have gone to such expense!
4. What an (incredible, original) ____________________ present!
5. You've made really (fantastic, clever) ____________________ use of the space in this room.
6. This is (undoubted) ____________________ the best wine I've drunk for a long time.
7. It sounds (real, exciting) ____________________.
8. It's (delicious, cool) ____________________ in here.

Check-up

Übersetzen Sie.

1. Sie sehen großartig aus.

____

2. Die Farbe steht Ihnen.

____

3. Es ist köstlich.

____

4. Der Raum hat eine wirkliche schöne Atmosphäre.

____

5. Die Aussicht ist herrlich!

____

6. Was für schöne Gläser!

____

7. Was für ein wunderbares Wetter!

____

8. Sie wirken so entspannt.

____

9. Wie schaffen Sie es [nur], so fit zu bleiben?

____

10. Es klingt wirklich aufregend.

____

G. Freudige und traurige Anlässe

G1 Happy birthday!

Ergänzen Sie den passenden Glückwunsch.

1. Happy birthday

2. ______________________

3. ______________________

4. ______________________

5. ______________________

G2 Congratulations!

Zu welchem Anlass passen diese Glückwünsche?

1. Neue Arbeitsstelle
2. Bestandener Führerschein
3. Bevorstehende Prüfung
4. Geburt
5. Hochzeitstag

a. Congratulations on passing your driving test!

b. ~~Good luck with your new job!~~

c. Congratulations on your wedding anniversary!

d. Congratulations on the birth of your baby!

e. Good luck with your exam!

1	2	3	4	5
b				

G3 What have you done to yourself?

Ergänzen Sie.

Get well soon! • How did that happen? • ~~I've broken my arm.~~
I've got the flu. • I won't keep you • Oh dear.
That must be very painful. • What have you done to your hand?
What's the matter?

◆ What have you done to yourself?
● (1.) *I've broken my arm.*

◆ (2.) __________ I'm sorry to hear that.
(3.) ______________________________
● I fell over on some ice.

◆ How long will you have to wear the plaster?

● Joan? Your voice is very soft.
(4.) ______________________________
◆ I'm in bed. (5.) ______________________________

● Oh, I'm sorry.
(6.) ______________________________ then.
(7.) ______________________________

◆ (8.) ______________________________.
● I burned it.

◆ Oh no! (9.) ______________________________
How did it happen?
● I was carrying some wood to a camp fire and tripped[1] and fell.
◆ Oh no!

[1]stolperte

G4 You sound as if you have a cold.

Was passt zusammen?

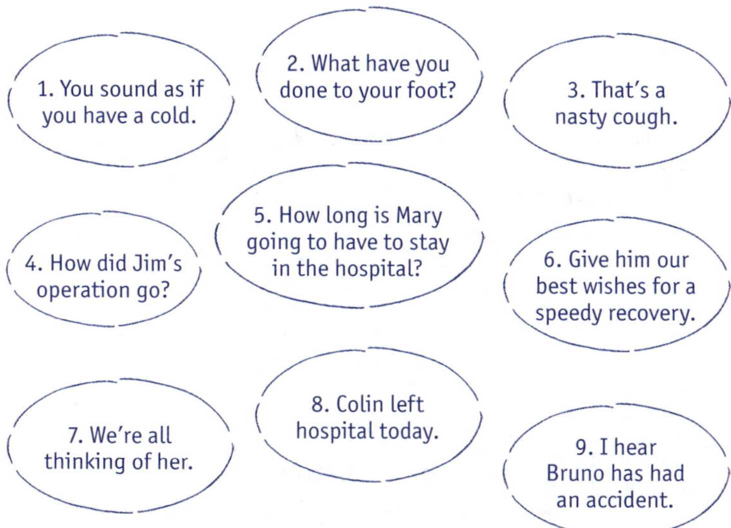

1. You sound as if you have a cold.
2. What have you done to your foot?
3. That's a nasty cough.
4. How did Jim's operation go?
5. How long is Mary going to have to stay in the hospital?
6. Give him our best wishes for a speedy recovery.
7. We're all thinking of her.
8. Colin left hospital today.
9. I hear Bruno has had an accident.

a. Yes, I don't know where I picked that up.
b. Yes, but it wasn't his fault. It was the other driver.
c. Fine, no complications, all OK. He should be out in a couple of days.
d. I fell over and sprained[1] it.
e. Thank you. That's very kind of you.
f. I will.
g. ~~Yes, but it's getting better.~~
h. The doctors aren't sure. Certainly another few days.
i. That's great news!

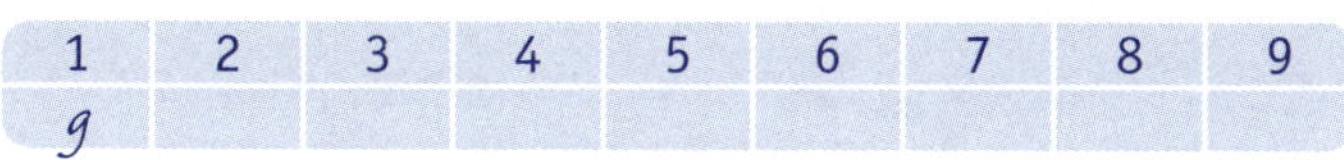

1	2	3	4	5	6	7	8	9
g								

[1]verstauchte

G5 We send our best wishes.

Was passt jeweils zum gleichen Anlass?

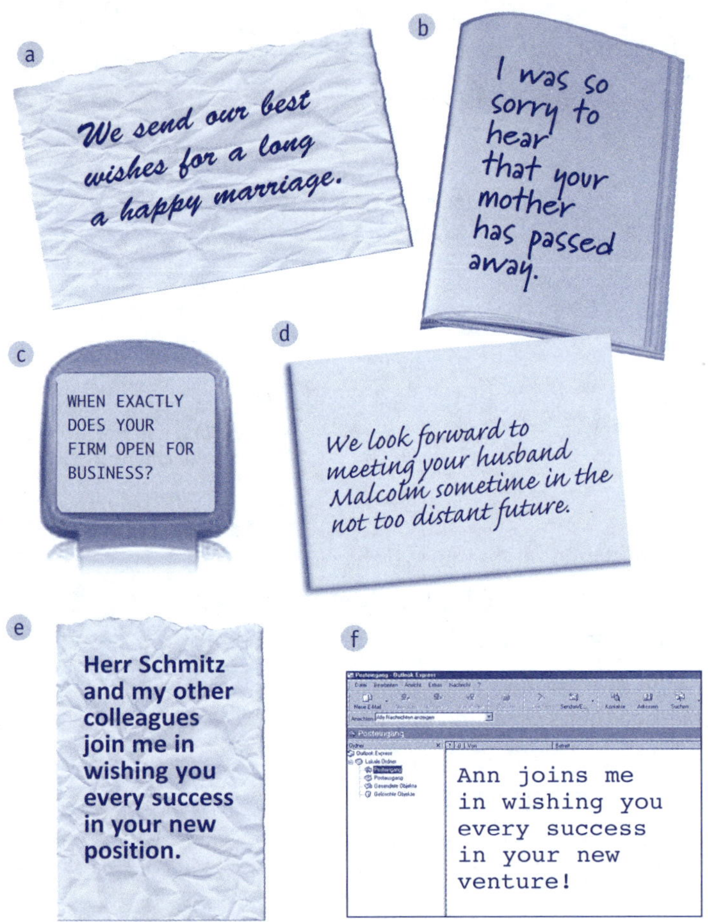

a
We send our best wishes for a long a happy marriage.
b
I was so sorry to hear that your mother has passed away.
c
WHEN EXACTLY DOES YOUR FIRM OPEN FOR BUSINESS?
d
We look forward to meeting your husband Malcolm sometime in the not too distant future.
e
Herr Schmitz and my other colleagues join me in wishing you every success in your new position.
f
Ann joins me in wishing you every success in your new venture!

g

I should like to offer my sincere condolences.

h

I would like to offer my very best wishes on your promotion to Director Overseas.

1. Hochzeit a + ___
2. Neue Firma ___ + ___
3. Todesfall ___ + ___
4. Beförderung ___ + ___

Check-up

Übersetzen Sie.

1. Fröhliche Weihnachten!

   ____

2. Gutes Neues Jahr!

   ____

3. Viel Glück bei Ihrer Prüfung!

   ____

4. Herzlichen Glückwunsch!

   ____

5. Werde bald wieder gesund!

   ____

6. Was ist los?

   ____

7. Mein herzliches Beileid.

   ____

8. Wir wünschen ihm eine baldige Genesung.

   ____

9. Wir denken an Euch.

   ____

10. Das sind ja tolle Nachrichten!

    ____

H. Vorschläge und Empfehlungen

1. What shall we do this evening?
2. What can you recommend?
3. How about a break?
4. I suggest waiting.
5. How/What about ...?
6. At the Tourist Information Centre.

Check-up

H1 What shall we do this evening?

Ergänzen Sie.

do you really want to • we could go • ~~what shall we do~~
what would you like • why don't we phone

Brad (1.) *What shall we do* this evening?
(2.) ________________ to do?

Angel (3.) ________ to a movie.

Brad Again? (4.) __________________?
We went on the weekend.
(5.) ____________ up Jim and Marie and ask them round for a drink. We haven't seen them for ages.

let's • I don't feel like it
if that's what you want to do • if you like • I suggest
it would do us both good • you can

Angel You can meet up with Jim (6.) ____________,
but I don't want them both round here.
(7.) ____________________ to get some exercise.
(8.) _____ get our running things on and go round the park.

Brad (9.) ________ if you like, but (10.) ________________.

Angel OK. Well, (11.) ___________ that I go running and you see if you can meet Jim. –
(12.) _________________________.

H2 What can you recommend?

Ordnen Sie die Satzteile.

Waiter: Are you ready to order?

Guest: (1.) ~~recommend / you / can / what~~

What can you recommend?

Waiter: The halibut is fresh off the boat.

Guest: (2.) afraid / I / I'm / fish / really / don't / like

____

Waiter: (3.) about / then / how / steak / a

____________________________________?

Guest: (4.) fancy / evening / this / don't / I / really / steak

____

Do you have anything really Scottish?

Waiter: (5.) haggis / well, / could / you / try

____

(6.) recommend / really / can / it / I

____

Guest: (7.) vegetarian quiche / the / I'll / maybe / have / just

____

________________________?

Waiter: Of course, sir.

(8.) see / like / to / list / wine / the / you / would

____

________________________?

H3 How about a break?

Welcher der beiden Sätze ist jeweils höflicher?

1. a. How about a break?
   b. May I suggest that we take a break?
2. a. We could walk there, if that's OK with you. It's not far.
   b. Why don't we just walk it? It's not far.
3. a. I'll show you some of the pictures, shall I?
   b. Would you like to see some of the pictures?
4. a. Let's get some advice from Jemma.
   b. Shall we ask Jemma for some advice? Would that be an idea?
5. a. You must take your valuables[1] with you.
   b. I would strongly recommend that you take your valuables with you.

1	2	3	4	5

[1]Wertsachen

H4 I suggest waiting.

Korrigieren Sie die Sätze wie im Beispiel.

1. ~~I suggest to wait till the rain stops~~.

   *I suggest **waiting** till the rain stops*.

   *I suggest **that** we wait till the rain stops*.

2. ~~What do you suggest to do tomorrow~~?

   ____

   ____

3. ~~The hotel suggests to park only on a secure car park.~~

   ____

   ____

4. ~~I suggest to leave the car here and to walk the rest of the way.~~

   ____

   ____

5. ~~How did they suggest to send it?~~

   ____

   ____

H5 How/What about ...?

Formulieren Sie die Sätze um.

1. We could invite Anna too.

   How about inviting Anna too ?

2. You can come with us.

   What about ________________________?

3. Why don't we go to the cinema?

   What about ________________________?

4. Would you like to go away for the weekend?

   How about ________________________?

5. I suggest that we take them to the beach.

   What about ________________________?

6. Why don't we hire a car?

   How about ________________________?

H6 At the Tourist Information Centre.

Ergänzen Sie den Dialog mit passenden Wörtern.

◆ How can I help you?

● We're here in the area for three days, and I (1.) ________________ if you could (2.) ________ us some suggestions (3.) ______ what we could see and do?

◆ Have you seen anything at all yet?

● No, not yet.

◆ Well, you could start (4.) ___ doing one of the guided walks maybe.
They take you round all the interesting parts of the old city centre, the cathedral, the quayside, and so (5.) ___.

● Yes, I suppose we could do that for a (6.) _________.

◆ That will give you a general overview of the place.
Then it really (7.) ___________ on what you're into.
There's a very interesting Centre for the History of the Cinema and Popular Culture, for example. Or if you're more (8.) _____ mystery, there's a night-time Ghosts and Legends tour.
I think the (9.) ______ thing might be (10.) ___ you just have a look through these brochures here. I'll be pleased to answer any questions.

● OK, thanks. If we want to get out of town, are there places you can (11.) _____________?

◆ Well, we're very close to Dartmoor of course. And then there's the Jurassic Coast, which is a World Heritage site.

● That (12.) _________ interesting. Where exactly is that?

Check-up

Übersetzen Sie.

1. Was sollen wir heute Abend machen?

   ____

2. Warum rufen wir nicht Tina an?

   ____

3. Wir wär's, wenn wir Anna einladen würden?

   ____

4. Lasst uns ausgehen.

   ____

5. Was können Sie empfehlen?

   ____

6. Ich schlage vor zu warten.

   ____

7. Es täte uns beiden gut, uns ein bisschen zu bewegen.

   ____

8. Du kannst, wenn du magst, aber mir ist nicht danach.

   ____

9. Ich kann es wirklich empfehlen.

   ____

10. Es hängt davon ab, worauf Sie stehen.

    ____

I. Widersprechen und sich beschweren

1. I'm sorry to have to say this.
2. Different opinions.
3. At a hotel.
4. There are no towels.
5. I would love to be able to help you.
6. I'm appalled!
7. I fully understand.

Check-up

I1 I'm sorry to have to say this.

Was passt zusammen?

1. I'm sorry to have to
2. I'm afraid that I see it
3. What's your opinion
4. What exactly do you mean
5. I'm afraid I have a complaint
6. I'm very sorry, but that's
7. If you ask me,
8. If you don't mind

a. to make.
b. by that? Could you explain?
c. rather differently.
d. say this, but I don't agree.
e. I'm afraid I don't think this is a very good idea.
f. my saying so, I think that would not be very wise.
g. on this? How do you feel?
h. quite out of the question.

1	2	3	4	5	6	7	8
d							

I2 Different opinions.

Jeweils eine Wendung ist falsch. Streichen Sie sie durch.

1. Sie fragen jemanden nach seiner Meinung.
   a. What do you think?
   b. What's your meaning?
   c. What's your view on this?
   d. Do you have an opinion about this?

2. Sie sagen Ihre Meinung.
   a. In my opinion …
   b. It seems to me that …
   c. I tend to think that …
   d. My meaning is that …

I3 At a hotel.

Ordnen Sie die Satzteile.

◆ (1.) ~~Jack Thompson / in / this / room / 364 / is~~

This is Jack Thompson in room 364.

● (2.) Mr Thompson / you / I / help / can / how

____

◆ (3.) slight / there's / a / I'm / afraid / problem

____

● (4.) sorry, / I'm / sir // is / it / what

____

◆ (5.) freezing / the / is / cold / room

____

(6.) with / do / to / something / it / be / must / air-conditioning / the

____

● (7.) up / someone / right / send / I'll

____

◆ Thank you.

I4 There are no towels.

Ergänzen Sie

1. There are *no towels*.
2. ______________ is blocked.
3. ______________ won't open.
4. ______________ in the bathroom is broken.
5. There's ______________.

I5 I would love to be able to help you.

Ergänzen Sie.

In other circumstances[1] • I haven't offended[2] you
I have to • It's very difficult • ~~I would love to be able~~
I hope you will understand

1. *I would love to be able* to help you, but I'm afraid I can't.
2. I hope __________.
3. It's very kind of you to offer, but I'm afraid __________ say no.
4. __________ for me to say this.
5. __________, but what you are asking is just not possible.
6. __________ there would be no question.

I6 I'm appalled!

Briten und Amerikaner bringen eine Beschwerde oder Kritik meist „verpackt", d.h. höflich und zurückhaltend vor. Welche dieser Formulierungen sind angemessen?

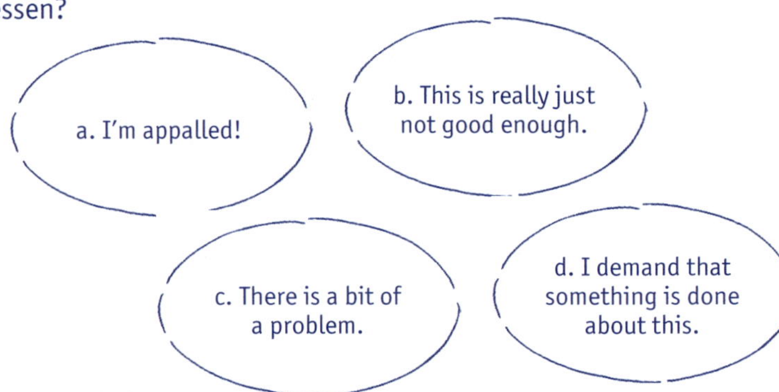

a. I'm appalled!
b. This is really just not good enough.
c. There is a bit of a problem.
d. I demand that something is done about this.

[1]unter anderen Umständen [2]beleidigt

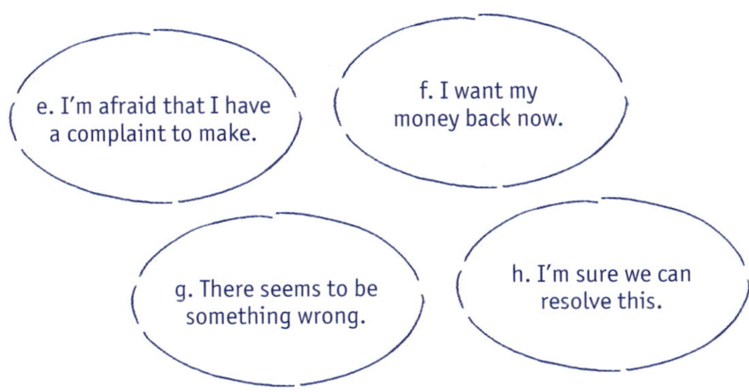

e. I'm afraid that I have a complaint to make.
f. I want my money back now.
g. There seems to be something wrong.
h. I'm sure we can resolve this.

Angemessene Formulierungen ______________________________

I7 I fully understand.

Was passt zusammen?

1. If I were in your shoes I would do exactly the same.

2. Forget it.

3. No harm done.

4. Please don't misunderstand me.

5. I fully understand.

6. Let's draw a line under it.

7. There's no harm in asking.

a. Ich habe volles Verständnis.
b. Versteh mich bitte nicht falsch.
c. Fragen kostet nichts.
d. Schwamm drüber.
e. Nichts passiert.
f. ~~An Ihrer Stelle würde ich nichts anderes tun~~.
g. Ziehen wir einen Strich darunter.

1	2	3	4	5	6	7
f						

Check-up

Übersetzen Sie.

1. Ich bin leider anderer Meinung.

____

2. Was verstehen Sie genau unter ‚bald'?

____

3. Wie ist Ihre Meinung?

____

4. Ich habe eine Beschwerde vorzubringen.

____

5. Es tut mir leid, dies sagen zu müssen, aber …

____

6. Wenn Sie mich fragen, glaube ich nicht, dass das eine gute Idee wäre.

____

7. Das kommt leider gar nicht in Frage.

____

8. Wenn ich das so sagen darf, ist es jetzt zu spät.

____

9. Ich hoffe, ich habe Sie nicht beleidigt.

____

10. Unter anderen Umständen wäre das kein Problem.

____

J. Meinungen und Gefühle

1. Do you really think so?
2. I have my doubts.
3. How important is this to you?
4. I'm not really bothered.
5. Don't worry.
6. Disappointment, sadness, happiness
7. Regrets
8. Likes and dislikes

Check-up

J1 Do you really think so?

Ordnen Sie ein.

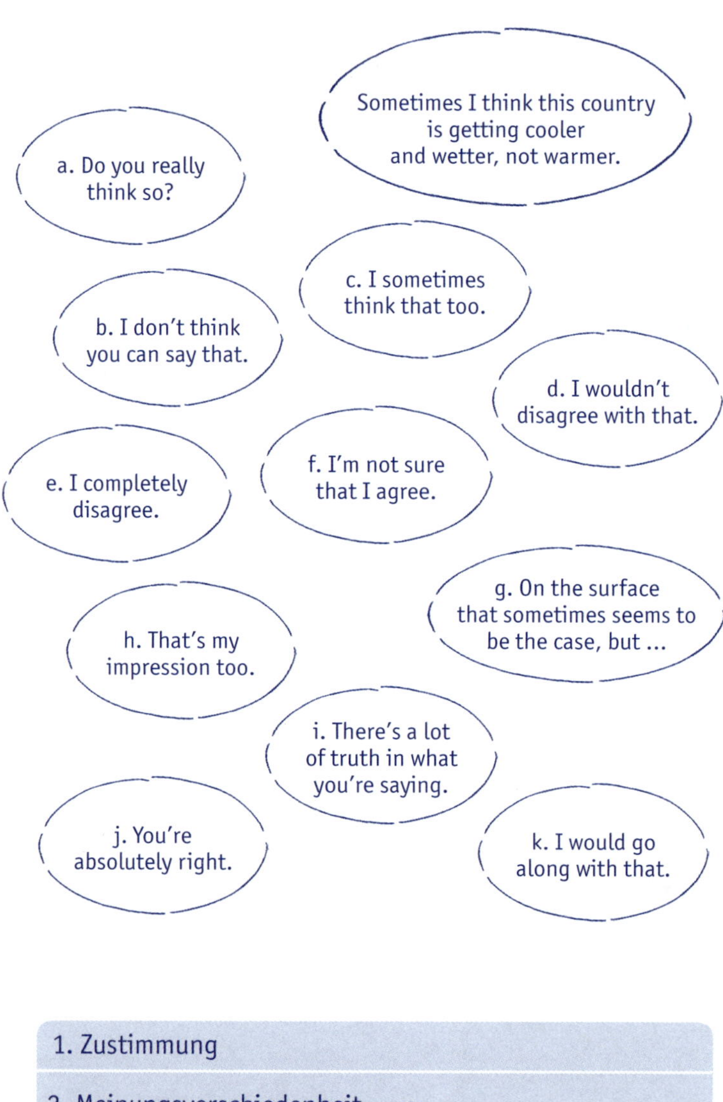

Sometimes I think this country is getting cooler and wetter, not warmer.
a. Do you really think so?
b. I don't think you can say that.
c. I sometimes think that too.
d. I wouldn't disagree with that.
e. I completely disagree.
f. I'm not sure that I agree.
g. On the surface that sometimes seems to be the case, but ...
h. That's my impression too.
i. There's a lot of truth in what you're saying.
j. You're absolutely right.
k. I would go along with that.

1. Zustimmung
2. Meinungsverschiedenheit a,

J2 I have my doubts.

Ergänzen Sie.

~~I doubt very much whether~~ • I have my doubts about
I'm not sure • I'm rather sceptical

1. *I doubt very much whether* we'll get there on time now.
2. ________________ that postponing the decision is a good idea.
3. ________________ Will's ability to take on this mammoth task.
4. I have to admit that ________________.

made up my mind • one way or the other
on the other • undecided

5. As yet, I'm ________________.
6. I haven't ________________.
7. I'm not sure ________________.
8. On the one hand it gives us more time, but ________________ it means we won't have a decision before next year.

bound to be • without a shadow
certain • totally and utterly

9. I'm ________________ that this is the right thing to do.
10. There are ________________ people who disagree.
11. I'm ________________ convinced.
12. You did the right thing ________________ of doubt.
13. Welche Redewendung drückt am stärksten Zweifel aus?

    ____

14. Welche Redewendung drückt am stärksten Überzeugung aus?

    ____

J3 How important is this to you?

Ordnen Sie zu.

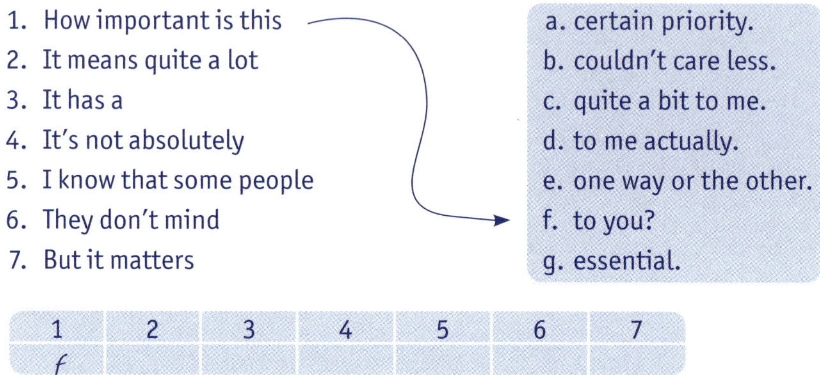

1. How important is this
2. It means quite a lot
3. It has a
4. It's not absolutely
5. I know that some people
6. They don't mind
7. But it matters

a. certain priority.
b. couldn't care less.
c. quite a bit to me.
d. to me actually.
e. one way or the other.
f. to you?
g. essential.

1	2	3	4	5	6	7
f						

J4 I'm not really bothered.

Ergänzen Sie passende Wörter.

◆ I'm quite hungry. What about you?
● I'm not really (1.) *bothered*. But if you're having something, I'll join you.
◆ I'll see what's in the freezer.
● OK. I'm happy to have (2.) what_ _ _ _ there is.
◆ There's a salami pizza, and a spring roll, but that seems to be it. What do you want?
● I'm (3.) e_ _ _. It doesn't (4.) m _ _ _ _ _ to me what I have.
◆ Are you sure?
● Yes, it's all the (5.) s _ _ _ to me.
◆ OK, I'll have the pizza.
● I thought you'd say that.
◆ Why is that what you fancy?
● No, no. I really don't (6.) m _ _ _.
◆ Then I'll have the spring roll.

J5 Don't worry.

Sortieren Sie die Buchstaben
und ergänzen Sie.

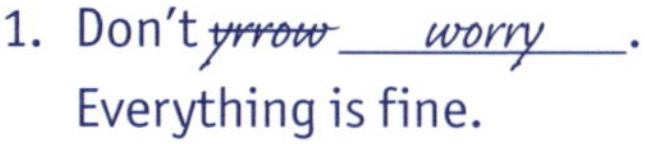

1. Don't ~~*yrrow*~~ *worry*.
   Everything is fine.

2. I find this development really quite *marlagin* __________.

3. I'm *nerdenocc* __________ about Jack. He's working far too much.

4. I'm very *veedlier* __________ to hear that everying went well.

5. It's a great *githew* __________ off my *nimd* __________
   that John has finally found a job.

6. Maybe it will *ets* __________ your mind at *sert* __________
   if I tell you that nobody got a higher grade than C.

7. The political situation in Georgia became a major *sauce*
   __________ for *rencnoc* __________.

8. The situation is really not serious. I wouldn't *sole* __________
   any *leeps* __________ over it if I were you.

9. There's really *gothnin* __________ to worry *boatu* __________.

10. They were an hour late, and I was starting to get really
    siouxna __________.

11. Where have you been? I've been worried *ciks* __________.

12. I tell you: this whole business has really been causing me
    pelleses __________ nights.

13. I don't like the *kolo* __________ of the weather forecast.
    We seem to be in for a very heavy storm.

J6 Disappointment, sadness, happiness

Welcher Satz passt nicht zu den anderen?

1. a. I'm really disappointed.
   b. The event has been a real letdown.
   c. This news is a great disappointment to all of us.
   d. I'm really very encouraged by this development.
   e. The project has not lived up to our expectations.
   f. This new media centre is not all it's cracked up to be[1].

2. a. Keith is feeling very sorry for himself.
   b. The situation has really been getting me down.
   c. I left with a heavy heart.
   d. It's all so sad.
   e. What the participants said really cheered me up.
   f. The area where they live is a pretty dismal and dreary[2] place.

3. a. I feel on top of the world.
   b We're all in a very good mood.
   c. I'm delighted, thrilled, absolutely over the moon.
   d. It's been a real bombshell.
   e. Your news really lifted my spirits, perked me up[3] no end.
   f. You've made my day.

1	2	3

J7 Regrets

Ergänzen Sie.

bitterly • do the same again • live to • regret • sorry • ~~wish~~

1. I _wish_ I hadn't agreed to go to the party.
2. If you don't tell me who did this, you'll ________________ regret it!

[1]nicht so gut wie erwartet [2]düster und farblos [3]hat mich aufgemuntert

3. We were ________________ that we had to leave first thing the next morning.
4. This is a great opportunity. You won't ________________ your decision.
5. I don't regret what I did. If I could turn the clock back, I'd ________________.
6. I ________________ regret using a 'consultant' who went on to steal my business idea.

J8 Likes and dislikes

Ergänzen Sie passende Wörter.

white wine	fish	bananas	Italian food	meat	desserts
+ –	+	– –	+ +	–	+ +

1. I quite *like* white wine, but if you give me the choice, I always p _ _ _ _ _ red. Do you have a p _ _ _ _ _ _ _ _ _ for one or the other?
2. I know the smell of fish t _ _ _ _ some people off. But I'm f _ _ _ of it.
3. I can't s _ _ _ _ bananas. I _ _ _ _ them! I d _ _ _ _ _ the smell, the taste, everything!
4. I really _ _ _ _ Italian food. I a _ _ _ _ it.
5. I don't c _ _ _ for meat. I eat it sometimes, but I'm not really much of a meat p _ _ _ _ _ .
6. I have a s _ _ _ _ tooth. I never miss out on dessert. I have a w _ _ _ _ _ _ _ for chocolate. On a menu I'll _ _ for anything that's got chocolate in it.

Zusatzaufgabe: Und nun machen Sie drei Aussagen über sich.

____

____

Check-up

Übersetzen Sie.

1. Ich bin ganz anderer Meinung.

____

2. Ich glaube nicht, dass man das [so] sagen kann.

____

3. Ich muss zugeben, dass ich ziemlich skeptisch bin.

____

4. Ich bin unentschlossen.

____

5. Ich bin voll und ganz überzeugt.

____

6. Manchen Leuten ist es völlig egal.

____ less.

7. Ich bin [fast] krank vor Sorge gewesen.

____

8. Wir sind alle guter Laune.

____

9. Ich fühle mich überglücklich.

____ world.

10. Ich bereue es bitter.

____

K. Geschichten und Witze erzählen

1. Have you heard the joke about ...?
2. Have I ever told you ...?
3. Tell us another one.
4. Did you hear what happened to us ...?
5. He didn't really say that, did he?
6. Question tags.
7. Did you see this?
8. Do you believe in ghosts?

Check-up

K1 Have you heard the joke about ...?

Was passt zusammen?

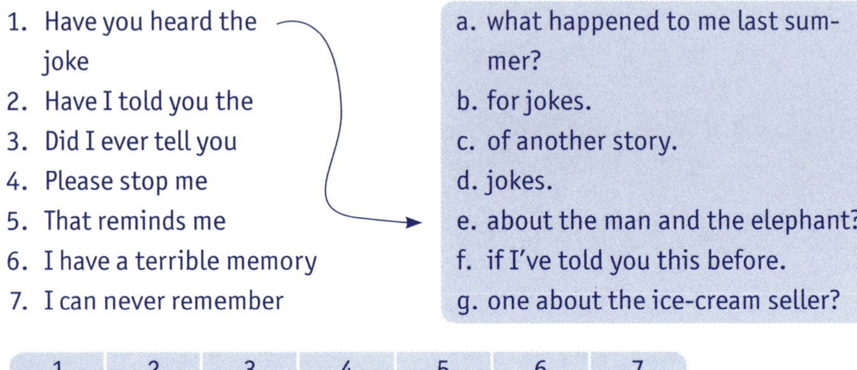

1. Have you heard the joke
2. Have I told you the
3. Did I ever tell you
4. Please stop me
5. That reminds me
6. I have a terrible memory
7. I can never remember

a. what happened to me last summer?
b. for jokes.
c. of another story.
d. jokes.
e. about the man and the elephant?
f. if I've told you this before.
g. one about the ice-cream seller?

1	2	3	4	5	6	7
e						

K2 Have I ever told you ...?

Bringen Sie in die richtige Reihenfolge.

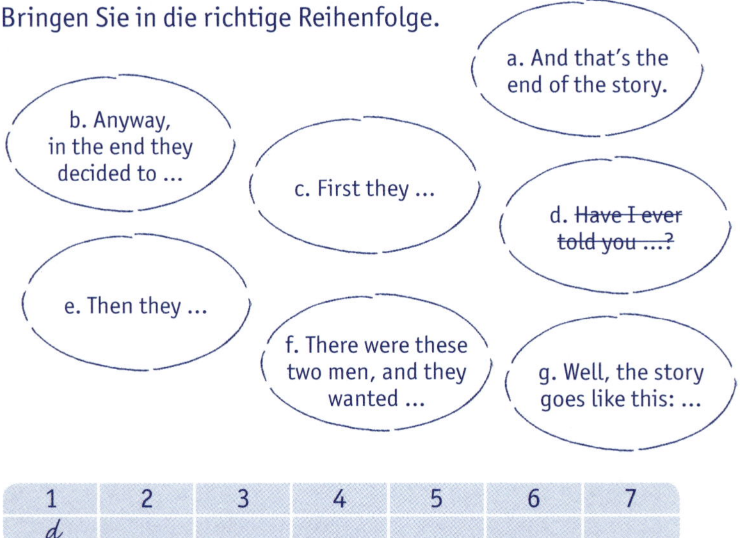
a. And that's the end of the story.
b. Anyway, in the end they decided to ...
c. First they ...
d. ~~Have I ever told you ...?~~
e. Then they ...
f. There were these two men, and they wanted ...
g. Well, the story goes like this: ...

1	2	3	4	5	6	7
d						

K3 Tell us another one.

Ergänzen Sie.

Do you get it? • Do you know the one about
Have you got it now? • I don't think so
I'm a bit slow sometimes • ~~Tell us another one~~.
That's a good one! • Well, there's this

◆ (1.) *Tell us another one* .

● (2.) ________________________ the couple in bed?

◆ No, (3.) ________________________

● (4.) ________________________ couple asleep in bed.
And suddenly the wife wakes up and says, 'My husband's coming!' And when the husband hears this, he jumps out of bed and hides in the wardrobe[1].
...
(5.) ________________________

◆ No, sorry. (6.) ________________________

● The wife thinks she's in bed with someone else and the husband thinks ... (7.) ________________________

◆ Oh yes! (8.) ________________________

[1]Kleiderschrank

K4 Did you hear what happened to us ...?

Ordnen Sie die Sätze, damit sich eine Geschichte ergibt.

a. 'I'll send someone along,' the receptionist said.
b. 'I do too,' I said. 'But you go first.' So she went.
c. 'There's a snake in the bath,' she said.
d. She'd only just closed the door, when I heard a shout, and she came running back out again.
e. ~~And then Sandra said she needed to go to the bathroom~~.
f. We waited and waited, and finally someone came.
g. We unlocked the door, went in, and put our suitcases down on the bed.
h. ~~At first I didn't believe her. I thought she was pulling my leg~~.
i. But she was deadly serious. 'There is really, go and look.'
j. But when he went into the bathroom, there was nothing there.
k. ~~Did you hear what happened to us last year in Kenya~~?
l. So I went and looked, and there was one.
m. ~~We arrived and checked in, got our key and went to our room~~.
n. ~~We didn't know what to do, so we called reception~~.
o. We had a reservation in this safari lodge.

1	2	3	4	5	6	7	8	9	10	11	12	13	14	15
k		m		e				h			n			

K5 He didn't really say that, did he?

Was passt zusammen?

1. He didn't really say that,
2. Is that really
3. I don't
4. That's so
5. Do you think
6. Come on, it was
7. You're pulling
8. You'll

a. believe it!
b. only a joke.
c. never believe this.
d. that's funny? I don't.
e. true?
f. my leg!
g. did he?
h. funny.

1	2	3	4	5	6	7	8
g							

K6 Question tags.

Ergänzen Sie die Sätze mit einer Rückfrage wie im Beispiel.

1. You don't really believe that, *do you*?
2. That didn't really happen, ________?
3. It's not really true, ________?
4. They didn't really do that, ________?
5. You're pulling my leg, ________?
6. I felt such a fool, ________, Anna?
7. I bet you've never been in a situation like that before, ________?

K7 Did you see this?

Ergänzen Sie.

and the guy ate it?! • apologize for any inconvenience
apparently • ~~did you see this~~ • eventually
he can have cardboard • himself • somewhere • the best bit is
was having one of his off days • wait for it • what?!

◆ (1.) *Did you see this*?

● What?

◆ A posh restaurant has been closed down because it served a cardboard coaster[1] as meat.

● (2.) ____________________

◆ Yes, (3.) ____________________ it's a place up north (4.) ____________, and one evening a customer came in as usual and ordered a meal. So the waiter passed the order to the kitchen, and (5.) ____________________ the food came and he took it to the man at the table.

● So?

◆ (6.) ____________________. The customer took one bite and said, 'This meat tastes like cardboard.' So the waiter said 'I'm sorry, sir', and took the food back into the kitchen and told his boss that there was a customer complaining. The boss (7.) ____________________ and went straight up the wall[2]. He started shouting around and said, 'So, it tastes like cardboard, does it, my best Scottish beef? Well, if he wants cardboard, (8.) ____________________!' And he grabbed a coaster, soaked it in gravy, then covered it in egg yolk and fried it. The waiter apparently refused to serve this, so the boss did it (9.) ____________________. He marched into the restaurant, placed the plate on the table and said, 'I (10.) ____________________ sir, it's my mission that no customer should leave this restaurant dissatisfied', and he put the plate with the cardboard meat on the table.

[1]Untersetzer [2]ging an die Decke

- (11.) ____________________?
- Yes. (12.) ____________________ that when the waiter went past a few minutes later, the customer stopped him and said, 'This is much better. But the vegetables are a bit cold.'

K8 Do you believe in ghosts?

Ergänzen Sie mit passenden Ausdrücken.

- Do you believe (1.) *in* ghosts?
- No, I don't. There are no such things (2.) ____________ ghosts.
- Well, what do you think of this then?
Last week I was driving to Wales to see some friends that
I hadn't see for a long time. It was late, about half past ten, and a clear,
(3.) ____________ night. There wasn't much
(4.) ____________ on the road, and I was (5.) ____________ there, just
a (6.) ____________ of miles to go.
(7.) ____________, I was driving through this wood when
(8.) ____________ I saw this headless rider on a white horse come
straight out of the wood and across the road in front
of me. I slammed on the brakes[1] and the car skidded[2] to a halt.
I got out, but there was nothing to be heard and nothing
(9.) ____________. I stood there rubbing my eyes. I thought
I must have (10.) ____________ it all. But there were my brake marks on
the road. I had seen something.
- How many pubs had you stopped at?
- None actually. I know what you're (11.) ____________ at, but (12.) ____________ till you hear this: When I got to my friends' place and told them what happened, they said ...

[1]trat in die Bremse [2]schleuderte

Check-up

Übersetzen Sie.

1. Hast du [den Witz] verstanden?

2. Ich kann mir Witze nie merken.

3. Kennen Sie den Witz mit dem Elefanten?

4. Das erinnert mich an eine andere Geschichte.

5. Bitte unterbreche mich, wenn ich das schon mal erzählt habe.

6. Jedenfalls war das das Ende der Geschichte.

7. Das glauben Sie doch nicht wirklich, oder?

8. Du nimmst mich auf den Arm.

9. Das glaubst du nie.

10. Ich kam mir wie ein Trottel vor.

L. Telefonieren und simsen

L1 Hello. This is ...

Was sagt man: a oder b?

1. Sie melden sich am Telefon.
   a. Hello. Here speaks Martina.
   b. Hello. This is Martina.
2. Sie sagen, dass Sie aus Deutschland anrufen.
   a. I'm phoning from Germany.
   b. I phone from Germany.
3. Sie wollen Caroline sprechen.
   a. Can I speak Caroline, please?
   b. Can I speak to Caroline, please?
4. Sie fragen, ob Caroline am Apparat ist.
   a. Is that Caroline? b. Is there Caroline?
5. Caroline bestätigt, dass sie am Apparat ist.
   a. Yes, Caroline on the phone here. b. Speaking.
6. Sie fragen nach dem Namen eines Anrufers.
   a. Who's speaking, please? b. Who speaks, please?
7. Sie sagen jemandem, dass er sich verwählt hat.
   a. Sorry, but you're wrongly connected.
   b. I'm afraid that you've got the wrong number.
8. Sie sagen, dass Sie jemanden verbinden.
   a. I connect you. / I put you through.
   b. I'll connect you. / I'll put you through.
9. Sie sagen, dass die Leitung besetzt ist.
   a. Sorry, but it's occupied.
   b. Sorry, it's engaged.
10. Sie sagen, dass Ihr Akku fast leer ist.
    a. My battery's low.
    b. My accu is almost empty.

1	2	3	4	5	6	7	8	9	10
b									

L2 On the phone.

Ergänzen Sie.

can you tell me • I'm sorry, but
she'll be back • speak to • ~~This is~~

◆ Hello.

● Hello. (1.) *This is* Jürgen Zander.
Can I (2.) __________ Jane, please?

◆ (3.) ________________ she's not here.

● Oh. (4.) ______________ when (5.) ____________?

I'll get her • calling from Germany • is Catherine there
just hang on a moment • on the phone

◆ Hello.

● Hello. This is Annette Melzer (6.) ________________.
(7.) ________________ please?

◆ Yes, she is. (8.) _________________________.
(9.) ______________ for you.
Catherine! Annette Melzer is (10.) _______________.

I'd like to • I'm afraid • speaking • you've dialled

◆ Hello.

● Hello. This is Marianne (11.) ___________.
(12.) ______________ speak to Glenn, please.

◆ (13.) ______________ that (14.) _____________ the wrong number.

● Oh, sorry.

L3 Can you call back later?

Was passt zusammen?

1. Can you call
2. Do you want to try
3. Can I
4. Do you want
5. I'll tell her

a. again later?
b. take a message?
c. to leave a message?
d. back later?
e. you called.

1	2	3	4	5
d				

6. Can you ask her to
7. Please just tell him that
8. I'll call
9. I'll try
10. Can you give her

f. back later.
g. a message?
h. again later.
i. I called.
j. call me back?

6	7	8	9	10

L4 What's the English for 'Handy'?

Ergänzen Sie *a, e, i, o* und *u*.

1. Call me on my l_ndl_n_, will you?
2. I'm calling on my c_llph_n_.
3. Can you give me your m_b_l_ n_mb_r, just in case?

„Handy" hat zwei Entsprechungen:

4. Vorwiegend in den USA: ____________

5. Vorwiegend in GB: ___________

L5 On the phone. (2)

Ergänzen Sie das Telefongespräch mit passenden Wörtern.

◆ Weston Underwood, good morning.
(1.) H________ c________ I h________ you?
● (2.) I'd ________ to ________ to Mr Wilkins, please.
◆ (3.) Who's ________, please?
● Bertold Steinmetz from Germany.
◆ (4.) J________ a ________, please.
(5.) I'll ________ you ________.

L6 I'll just get her for you.

Korrigieren Sie.

1. ~~I just get her for you~~.
   I'll just get her for you.
2. ~~I call you back in fifteen minutes~~.
   ____.
3. ~~I find out and let you know~~.
   ____.
4. ~~I put you through~~.
   ____.
5. ~~I see what I can do for you~~.
   ____.
6. ~~I try and find out~~.
   ____.
7. ~~I ask him to call you back~~.
   ____.

8. ~~I check if anyone knows when he's back~~.

____.

9. ~~I pass your message to her as soon as she gets back~~.

____.

L7 I may not be able to take your call.

Ergänzen Sie.

a text • mailbox • message • reach • ~~take~~ • text

I may be in a meeting and may not able to
(1.) *take* your call. If you can't (2.) ______ me,
just (3.) _____ me, and I'll get back to you later.
You can also send me an email instead of
(4.) _______, or just leave a (5.) ________ on my
(6.) ________. I'll get back to you somehow!

L8 CUL8R

Was bedeuten diese SMS-Kürzel? Ergänzen Sie.

Arr 19.25.
CUL8R

1. CUL8R — *see you later*
2. FYI — for your i_ _ _ _ _ _ _ _ _ _ _
3. MSG — M _ _ _ _ _ _
4. ASAP — as _ _ _ _ as _ _ _ _ _ _ _ _
5. GR8 — _ _ _ _ _
6. SRY — _ _ _ _ _
7. THNX — _ _ _ _ _ _
8. PLS — _ _ _ _ _ _
9. ADR — _ _ _ _ _ _ _
10. ILU — I _ _ _ _ you

L9 Thank you for calling the MPC.

Entscheiden Sie.

1. You call the Mount Pleasant Centre and hear the recorded message below. The first time you don't understand it and so you want to listen to it again.
   To do this, you have to press 9.

   a. True b. False

2. You already have one of the Mount Pleasant Centre's brochures, but now you have some specific questions that you want to discuss in person.

   Which button should you press?

   a. 1 b. 2 c. 3 d. 4

Thank you for calling the Mount Pleasant Centre. In order to give you optimum service and answer your call quickly and efficiently, we ask you to choose from the following options. To make a new booking, please press 1; to change an existing booking, please press 2; to order a brochure, please press 3; for all other enquiries, please press 4. If you would like to hear the menu again, please hold. To skip this message, please press 9.

L10 Please leave a message.

Ergänzen Sie.

after the beep • ~~answering machine~~ • available
I'm sorry • leave

◆ Hello. This is Tessa and Jeremy's (1.) *answering machine*.
(2.) ________ we're not (3.) ________ to take your call.
Please (4.) ________ a message (5.) ________.

are going to be around • be passing your way
call us back on • If you remember • just wanted
we might drop in • would be convenient

● Hi, Tessa, hi Jeremy. This is Andrea Tanner. (6.) ________, we met on Ibiza last summer. I (7.) ________ to ask how you are and to see if you (8.) ________ on the weekend of the 16th to 17th of July. We'll (9.) ________ and thought that (10.) ________ if that (11.) ________. Perhaps you can (12.) ________ 0532-53189046, or I'll call again in a couple of days. Take care now.

L11 Is that Herr Stumpf's office?

Bringen Sie a.-m. in die richtige Reihenfolge, um das Gespräch zu vervollständigen.

- ◆ Hello? Is that Herr Stumpf's office?
- ● Yes, it is. How can I help you?
- ◆ (1.) *c*
- ● (2.) ...

...

Jim Tucker ◆

a. In a place called Miedenhausen.

b. You have my number?

c. ~~This is Jim Tucker speaking~~.

d. I'm afraid I can't remember. But there's a sign here to a place called Kaltenbach.

e. Yes, I'm afraid there is. My navigation system has broken down and I've lost my way.

f. That's very kind of you, thank you. This really is embarrassing.

g. Thank you. And please give him my apologies.

Karin Bayer ●

h. Oh dear. And where are you?

i. Oh hello, Mr Tucker. We're expecting you this morning. Is there a problem?

j. No problem, Mr Tucker. I'll let Herr Stumpf know.

k. Miedenhausen? Sorry, I don't know it. What was the last place you came through?

l. Yes, it's on the display here. Just give me a minute or two, then I'll get back to you.

m. Oh my goodness, Kaltenbach! Let me see. I'll have a look on Google Maps then call you back.

1	2	3	4	5	6	7	8	9	10	11	12	13
c												*g*

Check-up

Übersetzen Sie.

1. Hier spricht Senta.

   ____

2. Kann ich bitte Roger Bacon sprechen?

   ____

3. Wer spricht bitte?

   ____

4. Sie haben sich verwählt.

   ____

5. Ich verbinde Sie.

   ____

6. Frank ist leider nicht da.

   ____

7. Ich rufe aus Deutschland an.

   ____

8. Bleiben Sie mal kurz dran.

   ____

9. Können Sie ihm etwas ausrichten?

   ____

10. Mein Akku ist fast leer.

   ____

M. Termin und Uhrzeit vereinbaren

1. What time and flight number?
2. February the seventeenth.
3. Around two o'clock?
4. What time would suit you?
5. When and where should we meet?
6. I'd like to make an appointment.

Check-up

M1 What time and flight number?

Ergänzen Sie.

at 19.25 • a week later • be arriving • be there
Friday 13th • so it's Friday 20th at 19.25 • ~~what time~~

- ◆ (1.) *What time* will you (2.) ____________?
- ● (3.) ____________.
- ◆ And that's on (4.) ____________, right?
- ● No, (5.) ____________, Friday 20th.
- ◆ Ah, OK. (6.) ____________.
  And what's the flight number?
- ● BM 675.
- ◆ BM 675. OK, I'll (7.) ____________ to meet you.
- ● Thanks.

M2 February the seventeenth.

Was passt zusammen?

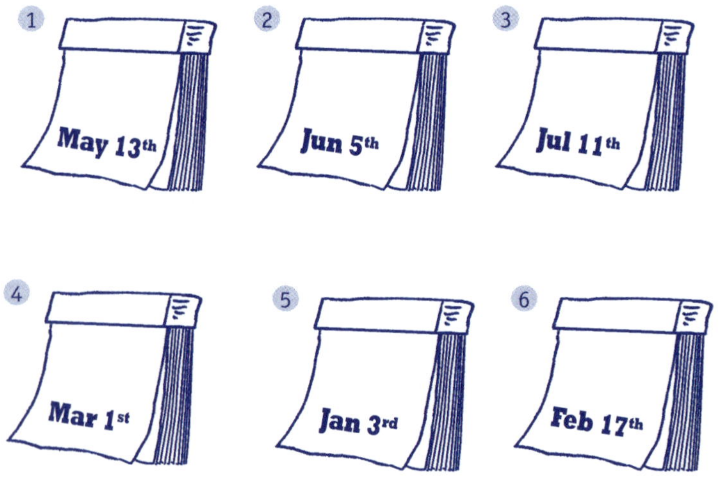

a. February the seventeenth
b. January the third
c. July the eleventh
d. June the eleventh
e. June the fifteenth
f. March the first
g. May the thirtieth
h. the fifth of June
i. the first of May
j. the seventh of February
k. the thirteenth of July
l. ~~the thirteenth of May~~

1	2	3	4	5	6
l					

M3 Around two o'clock?

Welche Lösung ist falsch?

1. When shall we meet? ... a. About two-ish?
   ~~b. Against two~~?
   c. Around two o'clock?
2. Here it's only ... a. six o'clock in the morning!
   b. six a.m!
   c. six o'clock a.m!
3. My flight leaves at ... a. one ten.
   b. ten after one o'clock.
   c. ten past one.
4. I'll see you at ... a. between eight and eight thirty.
   b. eight till eight thirty.
   c. eight to eight thirty.
5. Let's make it a bit later. So not 8 o'clock, but ... a. half eight.
   b. at half past seven.
   c. at half past eight.
6. I arrive back ... a. at Sunday 7th July.
   b. on Sunday 7th July.
   c. Sunday 7th July.
7. The project should be finished ... a. round about the end of April.
   b. towards the end of April.
   c. so about the end of April.

M4 What time would suit you?

Was passt zusammen?

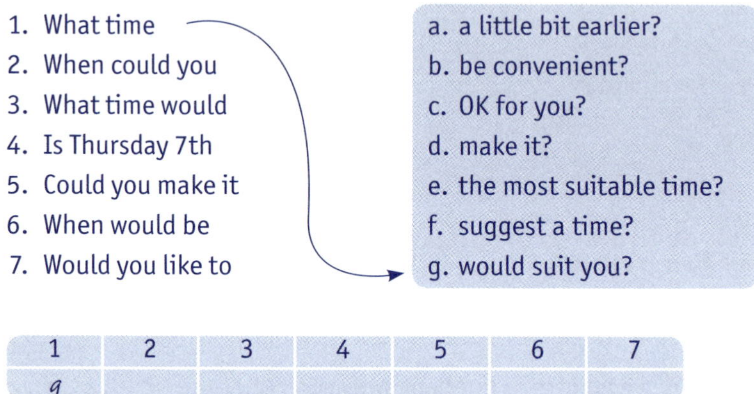

1. What time
2. When could you
3. What time would
4. Is Thursday 7th
5. Could you make it
6. When would be
7. Would you like to

a. a little bit earlier?
b. be convenient?
c. OK for you?
d. make it?
e. the most suitable time?
f. suggest a time?
g. would suit you?

1	2	3	4	5	6	7
g						

M5 When and where should we meet?

Was passt: a oder b? Oder passen a und b?

◆ When and where (a.) shall / (b.) would (1.) we meet?

● Do you know Triest (a.) at all / (b.) good (2.)?

◆ No, (a.) I'm afraid no / (b.) I'm afraid not (3.).

● Well, perhaps (a.) the easiest / (b.) the easiest thing (4.) would be if you came to my hotel.

◆ OK, and (a.) what / (b.) which (5.) time?

● (a.) Shall we say / (b.) Are we saying (6.) six fifteen?

◆ (a.) Can we do it / (b.) Can we make it (7.) a little later?

● Sure, no problem.
What time (a.) do you like / (b.) would you prefer (8.)?

◆ (a.) An half hour / (b.) Half an hour (9.) later?

1	2	3	4	5	6	7	8	9
a+b								

M6 I'd like to make an appointment.

Ergänzen Sie.

◆ I'd like to make an (1.) *appointment* for Herr Klingel to meet Mr Hargreaves at the Motor Exhibition.
I was (2.) w_________ about Tuesday afternoon.
Is that a (3.) p_________y?

● Just a moment, I'll check Mr Hargreaves' (4.) s_______e.
...
(5.) He's f___ at 4.30 for half an hour till 5 o'clock.
Would that be (6.) c________t for Herr Klingel?

◆ I'm afraid he already has a (7.) p_______s appointment then.
Does he have another (8.) s__t on Tuesday afternoon?

● No, I'm afraid he's (9.) f___y booked for the (10.) w___e of the rest of the afternoon.
What about (11.) a______r day?
He could do Wednesday in the (12.) l___ morning, or Thursday (13.) t______s the end of the afternoon.
Would (14.) e_____r of those times be (15.) s_______e?

◆ Thursday late afternoon (16.) s_____s a good (17.) o_____n.
What time?

● There's plenty of (18.) c_____e – 3.45, 4.30, 5.15.

◆ OK, let's (19.) m___ it 5.15 then.
I'll send you an email to (20.) c______m

Check-up

Übersetzen Sie.

1. Wann kommen Sie an?

2. Ich bin da, um Sie abzuholen.

3. So gegen zwei?

4. Sagen wir halb acht?

5. Möchten Sie eine Zeit vorschlagen?

6. Würde Ihnen morgens um zehn passen?

7. So gegen Ende April?

8. Wäre Donnerstag für Sie in Ordnung?

9. Können wir's ein bisschen später machen?

10. Ich schicke eine Mail, um die Zeit zu bestätigen.

N. Gast und Gastgeber sein

N1 Are you free on Saturday evening?

Ergänzen Sie.

Are you doing • ~~Are you free~~ • Do you have plans
Do you fancy • Do you want to • Would you like

1. *Are you free* on Saturday evening?
2. ________________ anything this evening?
3. ________________ for Friday evening?
4. ________________ meeting up for a drink later on?
5. A group of us are going to the pub. ________________ join us?
6. ________________ to have dinner together?

N2 I'm afraid I can't make Friday.

Ordnen Sie ein.

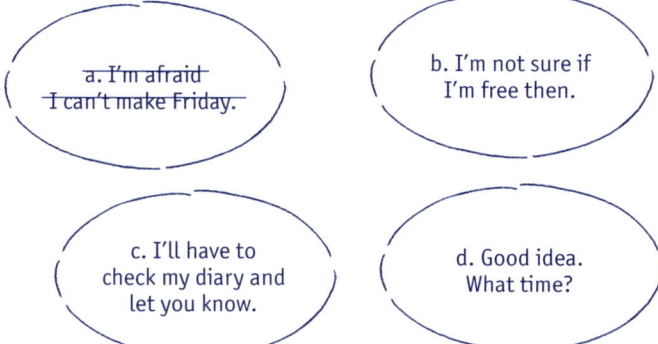

~~a. I'm afraid I can't make Friday.~~

b. I'm not sure if I'm free then.

c. I'll have to check my diary and let you know.

d. Good idea. What time?

e. Thank you for the invitation, but in fact we're away at the weekend.

f. That would be great. Thanks.

g. That's very kind of you, but unfortunately I'm busy.

h. I'd love to, but in fact I've already eaten.

1. Einladung annehmen:
2. Einladung ablehnen: a,
3. Auf Zeit spielen:

N3 That's a pity.

Ordnen Sie die Satzteile.

1. ~~Oh, / pity. / a / that's~~
   Oh, that's a pity.
2. time / another / Maybe
   ______________________.
3. mind, / another / Never / evening / perhaps
   ______________________.
4. about / instead / Thursday / How
   ______________________?
5. make / little / later / a / you / it / Could
   ______________________?

N4 We're having a barbecue party on Saturday.

Was passt zusammen?

1. We're having a barbecue
2. We're inviting a few
3. It's Janine's
4. I'm planning
5. It's very informal,
6. We'd like to invite
7. Why don't you come
8. Everybody's
9. It would be great
10. Drop in

a. friends round.
b. if you could come.
c. party on Saturday.
d. nothing special.
e. 30th birthday.
f. if you have time.
g. you and David.
h. welcome.
i. round for a drink?
j. a surprise party.

1	2	3	4	5	6	7	8	9	10
c									

N5 Dear Sarah ...

Ergänzen Sie die Sätze mit passenden Wörtern.

*(1.) **Dear** Sarah,*

Max and I are having a little dinner (2.) ________ on Saturday 17th September to (3.) ____________ our second wedding anniversary. We're (4.) ___________ some old and new friends and would be (5.) ____________ if you and Adrian could (6.) _________.

I (7.) _____ that you can make it. Please let me (8.) _____ as soon as you (9.) ____.

Love,

Jennifer

N6 Are you doing anything this evening?

Ordnen Sie die Satzteile.

◆ (1.) ~~anything / you / doing / are / this~~

Are you doing anything this evening ?

(2.) pub / ~~group~~ / for / ~~us~~ / going / are / ~~of~~ /

a / drink / to / the / ~~a~~

A group of us ____________________

● What time?

◆ (3.) work / after / straight

____

● (4.) going / where / you / are

____________________?

◆ (5.) The Crown / to / probably

____

● (6.) idea / good / you / join / I'll

__________. __________________

(7.) leaving / me / you're / know / let / when

____

N7 Lovely to see you.

Ergänzen Sie.

I'm a little late • I've brought you • ~~lovely to see you~~
some of the others haven't arrived yet
that's very kind • you really didn't need to

- ◆ Hello. (1.) *Lovely to see you*. Come in.
- ● I'm afraid (2.) ____________________
- ◆ No, no, you're not at all.
  (3.) ____________________________________
- ● (4.) ______________ a little something.
- ◆ (5.) ____________________ of you.
  But (6.) ________________________.

I hope you don't mind
the directions you gave us were perfect
would you mind
you found us all right then

- ◆ Hello, hello. (7.) __________________________?
- ● Yes, no problem.
  (8.) ____
- ◆ Good. Come along in.
  (9.) ____
  But (10.) _____________________
  taking off your shoes?
- ● Not at all. We do that at home too.

N8 ... you really didn't need to.

Welcher Satz ist falsch oder unpassend?

1. Der Gast hat sein Mitbringsel überreicht.
   Der Gastgeber reagiert.
   a. It's very kind of you, but you really didn't need to.
   b. ~~That's very nice of you, but you mustn't do that.~~
   c. Oh thank you, but you shouldn't have.
   d. You really didn't have to bring anything.

2. Der Gastgeber bietet etwas zu trinken an.
   a. Can I get you a drink?
   b. What would you like to drink?
   c. Would you like what to drink?
   d. What can I bring you to drink?

3. Der Gastgeber will den Gast mit anderen bekannt machen.
   a. Do you know anyone here?
   b. Have you met Anette?
   c. Let me introduce you to some of the others.
   d. I'll present you to some of the guests.

4. Der Gast bedankt sich am Ende des Abends.
   a. Thank you for a lovely evening.
   b. You must let me revenge myself.
   c. Next time you must come and see us.
   d. We've had a wonderful time.

5. Der Gastgeber verabschiedet den Gast.
   a. Do you really have to leave now?
   b. It's a pity you have to go.
   c. I hope you've enjoyed.
   d. It's been a pleasure to have you here.

N9 I'll have a glass of wine.

Korrigieren Sie.

1. ~~I have a glass wine, please~~.
   I'll have a glass of wine, please.
2. ~~I don't eat anything, thanks~~. I'm trying to lose a bit of weight!
   I won't eat anything, thanks.
3. ~~I try a glass of red wine, please~~.
   ______
4. ~~I don't have any more, thanks~~. I've had more than enough.
   ______
5. I just have to make a quick phone call. ~~I don't be long~~.
   ______
6. ~~I sit here if that's OK~~.
   ______
7. ~~I have one of your special cocktails, please~~.
   ______
8. ~~I don't drink any alcohol, thanks~~. I have to cut down.
   ______
9. If you ask me like that, ~~I don't say no~~!
   ______
10. ~~I don't have any potatoes, thanks~~. I'm trying to lose weight!
    ______

N10 Red or white?

Was passt zusammen?

1. A glass of wine, please. → c
2. A beer, please.
3. Tea, please.
4. Just some mineral water, please.

a. With milk and sugar?
b. Sparkling or still?
c. Red or white?
d. With alcohol or alcohol-free?

1	2	3	4
c			

N11 Starting a meal and toasting.

Welche Lösung ist falsch?

1. Für *Guten Appetit!* sagt man auf Englisch:
   a. Bon appétit! b. Good appetite!
   c. *Oft nichts.* d. Enjoy your meal!

2. Als Trinkspruch sagt man auf Englisch:
   a. Cheers! b. Your health!
   c. On our hosts! d. To Jean and Tony!

N12 Would you like to sit here?

Sortieren Sie.

a. ~~Would you like to sit here~~?
b. ~~Could I have a glass of water, please~~?
c. Would anyone like any more?
d. This is delicious.
e. More wine anyone?
f. I'm glad you like it.
g. If you don't like it, you don't have to eat it.
h. You must give me the recipe.
i. Could I have a little more, please?
j. I'd love some more, but I'm full!
k. How many coffees?
l. If anyone needs a spoon, please ask.
m. Could you pass me the salt, please?
n. No thanks. You see, I'm afraid I'm allergic to peanuts.

1. Die Gastgeberin sagt	a , ______________________
2. Der Gast sagt	b , ______________________

N13 We'll be ready to eat in five minutes.

Bringen Sie a.–i. in die richtige zeitliche Reihenfolge.

a. Can I give anyone any more before we move on to the dessert?
b. ~~Has everyone got everything? Well, bon appétit then.~~
c. I hope this dessert is OK, it's the first time I've made it!
d. Is that enough meat for you?
e. Philip. Would you like to sit here, next to Denise?
f. Please help yourself to vegetables.
g. ~~We'll be ready to eat in five minutes.~~
h. We'll take coffee on the patio.
i. Would you all like to sit down now please?

1	2	3	4	5	6	7	8	9
g					*b*			

N14 Thank you again.

Ergänzen Sie.

a fantastic dinner party • enjoyed ourselves • laughed so much
thank you again • ~~thank you for~~ • was delicious

Dear Louise,

(1.) ***Thank you for*** *a lovely evening on Saturday. We really*
(2.) ______________________.
The food (3.) ______________________,
and I haven't (4.) ______________________ *for a long time!*
It was really (5.) ______________________!
(6.) ______________________,
Denise

N15 I'm going to be in London ...

Hier sind zwei E-Mails durcheinandergeraten.
Ordnen Sie die Satzteile den zwei E-Mails zu und bringen Sie sie in die richtige Reihenfolge.

a. ~~Dear Nancy, I'm going to be in London~~
b. ~~Dear Susanne, It was lovely to~~
c. hear from you, and it's so nice
d. the week after next
e. and I wondered if we might meet up
f. that you're going to be in London soon.
g. Where are you staying?
h. for dinner one evening?
i. You're very welcome to stay here
j. The exact dates are
k. if you'd like to.
l. We have a spare room
m. Tuesday 16th to Friday 19th.
n. Let me know which evening would suit you.
o. which you are very welcome to have.
p. If you'd rather stay in town,
q. Looking forward to hearing from you and hopefully seeing you soon,
r. that's fine of course, and we'll just meet up one evening.
s. Love, Nancy
t. All good wishes, Susanne

1. E-Mail von Susanne an Nancy
a,
2. E-Mail von Nancy an Susanne
b,

N16 This is Christine.

Ergänzen Sie.

after all • and you • ~~how are things~~
I'm phoning for two reasons • it was really quite interesting
otherwise • quite a stressful day today
the first is to thank you • we were afraid that
we weren't sure • what can I do • you enjoyed it

◆ Hi, Patrick. This is Christine.
● Oh hello, Christine. (1.) *How are things?*
◆ Fine thanks, (2.) ________________?
● I've had (3.) ________________ but (4.) ________________ things are OK. (5.) ________________ for you?
◆ Well, (6.) ________________ actually. (7.) ________________ and Lila for a great evening on Friday.
● (8.) ________________?
◆ Yes, great, thanks.
● Actually, (9.) ________________ if we should have invited Montgomery (10.) ________________. He does tend to hog[1] the conversation.
◆ Yes, but (11.) ________________ listening to him.
● It was? (12.) ________________ he might have spoiled the evening for everybody.
◆ No, no. Not at all. Anyway, the second thing is ...

N17 I have lost my ...

Übersetzen Sie und vervollständigen Sie damit den Dialog.

◆ Hi Tina, this is Katie.

● Oh hi.

◆ (1.) *Ich hoffe, ich rufe nicht zu früh an.*

____

● No, it's OK. We're up, only just up, but we're up.

◆ (2.) *Ich rufe an, weil ich mein Handy verloren habe.*

____

(3.) *Vielleicht habe ich es gestern Abend bei Euch liegen lassen.*

____

Maybe it slipped out of my pocket or something.

● I haven't seen it, but we haven't finished clearing up yet.
(4.) *Wenn ich es finde, sage ich Bescheid.*

____

◆ (5.) *Ohne mein Handy bin ich verloren.*

____

● There isn't anywhere else you might have lost it?

◆ (6.) *Ich glaube nicht.*

____

● (7.) *Ach warte einen Moment.*

____

◆ (8.) *Hast du es gefunden?*

____

● Oh no, sorry. It's Kevin's. Sorry.
(9.) *Ich schaue mal und wenn ich es finde, sage ich Bescheid.*

____

◆ Thanks so much, Tina.

Check-up

Übersetzen Sie.

1. Haben Sie am Samstag etwas vor?

   ____

2. Hast du Lust, dich uns anzuschließen?

   ____

3. Das ist sehr freundlich von Ihnen, aber leider bin ich beschäftigt.

   ____

4. Am Freitag kann ich nicht.

   ____

5. Vielleicht ein anderes Mal.

   ____

6. Wie wäre es mit Mittwoch?

   ____

7. Kommen Sie doch vorbei, wenn Sie Zeit haben.

   ____

8. Ich habe Ihnen eine Kleinigkeit mitgebracht.

   ____

9. Würde es Ihnen etwas ausmachen, die Schuhe auszuziehen?

   ____

10. Ich bin satt!

    ____

O. In der Stadt und auf Reisen

1. Asking and giving directions.
2. How do we get to Covent Garden?
3. Can I try it on?
4. How many is it for?
5. Window or aisle seat?
6. At a bed-and-breakfast.

Check-up

01 Asking and giving directions.

Was passt: a oder b? Oder passen a und b?

◆ Excuse me. Can you tell me where (a.) the nearest / (b.) the next (1.) cash machine is?

● (a.) Let me see / (b.) Let's see. (2.) There's (a.) a one / (b.) one (3.) in the Guildhall Centre.

◆ And where's that, please?

● Do you see the traffic lights? Go (a.) along / (b.) down here (4.) (a.) as far as the traffic lights / (b.) until you come to the traffic lights (5.). Turn right there, and the entrance to the Guildhall Centre is (a.) on / (b.) to (6.) your left.

◆ So right (a.) at / (b.) to (7.) the lights, and then left.

● Yes, you'll find the cash machine is somewhere (a.) at the bottom of / (b.) down at (8.) the stairs in the middle of the building. There's a sign up, so you can't (a.) fail / (b.) miss (9.) it.

◆ And how do I (a.) come / (b.) get (10.) to the Quayside from there?

● (a.) Carry straight on / (b.) Go straight further (11.) through the shopping centre and (a.) out the other side / (b.) to the other side out (12.), and you're on Cathedral Square. The Quayside is the other side of the Cathedral down the hill.

◆ How far is it (a.) to go by foot / (b.) to walk it (13.)?

● Not more (a.) as / (b.) than (14.) ten minutes.

◆ Thanks very much.

● No problem.

1	2	3	4	5	6	7	8	9	10	11	12	13	14
a													

02 How do we get to Covent Garden?

Ergänzen Sie.

along there on the left • an eastbound train • change to • if you look at the map here • it's probably best • ~~on the Underground~~ • this brown line • where my finger is

◆ How do we get to Covent Garden from here?

● By tube?

◆ Sorry?

● (1.) *On the Underground*?

◆ Yes, yes.

● OK, well (2.) ____________________, the nearest station is Edgeware Road, that's here, and Covent Garden is here.

◆ Where?

● Here, (3.) ____________.

◆ OK.

● (4.) __________________ to take a southbound Bakerloo Line train, that's (5.) ________________, see it?, to Piccadilly Circus that's one, two, three, four, five stops. Then (6.) ________________ the Piccadilly Line. Take (7.) ______________, and it's just two stops.

◆ Thanks. Can I take this map?

● Sure.

◆ And where's Edgeware Road station?

● Go out of the hotel and turn right, down to the end of the street. Turn right again there, and the station entrance is (8.) ________________.

◆ Thanks.

● You're welcome.

03 Can I try it on?

Sortieren Sie.

a. ~~Can I try it on~~?
b. Can I help you?
c. Can I pay with my Maestro card?
d. Do you have anything cheaper?
e. Do you have it in the next size up?
f. How do you want to pay for this?
g. How many items have you got?
h. How much is it?
i. I think I prefer the darker colour.
j. I think I'll leave it.
k. I'm afraid I don't have that style in the larger size.
l. I'm just looking, thanks.
m. It suits you.
n. It's a bit tight. I think I need a larger size.
o. Just sign here, please.
p. That's £78.99, please.
q. That's rather more than I wanted to spend.
r. The changing rooms are through there.
s. What size are you?

1. Die Verkäuferin sagt	____________________
2. Die Kundin sagt,	a ____________________

04 How many is it for?

Bringen Sie a.–r. in die richtige zeitliche Reihenfolge (vom Augenblick, in dem die Gäste das Restaurant betreten, bis zur Verabschiedung).

a. A gin and tonic and a prosecco, please.
b. Yes, a side salad, please.
c. And the grilled salmon for me.
d. ~~And what would you like to drink with your meal~~?
e. ~~Are you ready to order now~~?
f. Fine, thank you. But could you bring us some more bread, please?
g. ~~Good evening. How many is it for? Two?~~
h. ~~Is everything all right?~~
i. Just a bottle of mineral water, please.
j. No, thanks. Just two coffees and the bill, please.
k. ~~Sparkling or still?~~
l. Still, please.
m. ~~Thank you sir, madam. Good night~~.
n. Yes, I'll have the canneloni.
o. ~~This way, please.~~
p. ~~Would you like an aperitif?~~
q. ~~Would you like anything with that?~~
r. ~~Would you like to see the dessert menu?~~

1	2	3	4	5	6	7	8	9
g	*o*	*p*		*e*			*q*	

10	11	12	13	14	15	16	17	18
d		*k*		*h*		*r*		*m*

05 Window or aisle seat?

Wo wird jeweils gesprochen? Entscheiden Sie.

1. At the check-in desk
2. At security control
3. In the departure lounge
4. In the plane
5. At passport and immigration control

a. ~~Window or aisle seat?~~
b. Anything metal in your pocket – coins, keys, ...?
c. Did you pack the bag yourself?
d. Lift your right foot please.
e. How long are you planning to stay in the country?
f. New Airlines regret to announce a delay in the departure of flight NY 298 to Amsterdam.
g. Please adjust the backrest of your seats ready for landing.
h. The cabin crew will shortly be passing through the aircraft with a selection of gifts and duty-free goods.
i. This is the final call for all passengers booked on flight BM 547.
j. What is the purpose of your visit?

1	2	3	4	5
a,				

06 At a bed-and-breakfast.

Ergänzen Sie.

as a single • can we see the rooms • double • how much is it?
I'd do the double as single • ~~I saw your sign~~
just for one night • per person • singles • we're looking for
were you planning • with a full Scottish breakfast

◆ Hello. (1.) *I saw your sign* up by the road.
(2.) ________ bed and breakfast for tonight.

● How many people?

◆ Four.

● Is that two doubles?

◆ One (3.) ________, and do you have two (4.) ________?

● I have one, but not two.

◆ Hm. Es gibt nur ein Einzelzimmer.

● I have another double if that's a problem.
You could have that (5.) ________, if it's (6.)
________. I'm afraid it's booked for tomorrow.
Was it one night, or (7.) ________ to stay longer?

◆ Just the one night.
(8.) ________

● Sixty-eight for the double.

◆ (9.) Is that ________?

● For the room, for two people. The single is thirty-five, and
(10.) ________ for thirty-five, too.

◆ That's including breakfast?

● Yes, (11.) ________, organic[1] bacon and
sausages, and home-made bread and preserves[2].

◆ That sounds good. (12.) ________, please?

● Of course. Please come in.

[1]biologisch [2]Konfitüren

Check-up

Übersetzen Sie.

1. Wo ist der nächste Geldautomat?

___

2. Sie können es nicht verfehlen.

___

3. Wie weit ist es zu Fuß?

___

4. Wie komme ich nach Covent Garden?

___

5. Am Piccadilly Circus in die Piccadilly Line umsteigen.

___

6. Ich schaue nur. [Beim Einkaufen]

___

7. Danke, ich lasse es. [Beim Einkaufen]

___

8. Haben Sie die nächste Größe?

___

9. Kein Dessert, danke. Nur die Rechnung.

___

10. Ich hätte gern einen Gangplatz.

___

Lösungen

A. Sich begegnen und vorstellen

A1 2. d / 3. a / 4. f / 5. b / 6. e / 7. c

A2 2. Nice 3. meet / see 4. I'm
5. Pleased 6. What 7. again
8. Good 9. meet / see
10. How 11. do 12. Would

A3 2. a good trip 3. go all right
4. OK 5. with your bags
6. any help 7. you a hand
8. take one of those for you
9. to Munich 10. to be here
11. see you again
12. after all this time

A4 2. Yes, it seems ages.
3. The last time was in Vancouver.
4. That must be four years ago.
5. It could well be.
6. How are things?
7. Fine, thanks. And you?

A5 1. c, g, i (besonders AE) /
2. d, f, h, j, l / 3. k

A6 2. c / 3. c / 4. c / 5. b

A7 1. This is my husband Johannes.
2. I'm pleased / glad to meet you.
3. I've heard a lot about you.
4. Sandra often talks about you / often speaks of/about you.

A8 2. introduce you to some people
3. This is 4. an old friend of mine
5. haven't we? 6. for names
7. was familiar 8. if you remember
9. It's lovely 10. I'm sorry
11. I knew 12. I just couldn't
13. Anyway 14. Good, thanks
15. not so bad 16. Can I

A9 2. f / 3. a / 4. g / 5. d / 6. e / 7. c

A10 2. How can I help you?
3. I have an appointment
4. is expecting you
5. she's still in a meeting
6. you would mind waiting
7. as soon as she can
8. take a seat
9. could you tell me
10. Certainly

A11 2. gentlemen 3. welcome
4. pleasure / honour 5. questions 6. happy / glad / pleased
7. behalf 8. wish

A12 2. Excuse 3. surprise 4. afraid
5. misunderstanding 6. mistaken
7. apologies

Check-up
1. What was your name again?
2. Are you by any chance Barbara Giles? 3. Nice to meet you.
4. How was your flight?
5. Welcome to Germany.
6. Long time no see. 7. How are things / you / you doing?
8. Have we met before?
9. I'd like to introduce you to my colleague.
10. Please take / have a seat.

B. Sich verabschieden

B1 1. b, d, e / 3. c

B2 2. e / 3. a / 4. b / 5. f / 6. h / 7. c / 8. d

B3 2. if I feel like it
3. plenty to read and listen to
4. have a safe journey home
5. you get there
6. you've arrived safely
7. thanks again for everything
8. Have a good flight!

B4 2. Give my best wishes to Michael. 3. Give my love to Ann and the children. 4. Please give my regards to your wife. 5. It's been great to see you again. 6. It was nice to meet you. 7. It has been a pleasure meeting you.

B5 2. to seeing you again soon 3. to see you again soon 4. when you come over again 5. to get in touch next time you're over

B6 1. d, e, f, i / 2. b, c, g, h, j

B7 2. afraid / sorry 3. course 4. after 4. call / phone for / order 5. covered / done / dealt with / discussed 6. forgotten / left out 7. send 8. give 9. successful / productive / good / positive 10. goodbye 11. journey / trip / flight

Check-up

1. See you later (on).
2. Take care (of yourself).
3. Have a good flight.
4. Have a safe journey home. / Get home safely.
5. Thanks again for everything.
6. Say hello to Tom for / from me.
7. We'll stay / keep in touch.
8. I('ll) look / I am looking forward to seeing you again soon.
9. I hope to see you again soon.
10. It's time I started making my way.

C. Small Talk machen

C1 2. a / 3. b / 4. c / 5. f / 6. e

C2 2. part 3. far 4. to 5. before 6. going / heading 7. family / friends / relatives / ... 8. coast

C3 2. h / 3. c / 4. i / 5. a / 6. g 7. e / 8. j / 9. d / 10. f

C4 2. b / 3. a / 4. a / 5. b / 6. b

C5 2. a / 3. e / 4. b / 5. f / 6. g / 7. h / 8. c

C6 1. b / 2. c / 3. a

C7 1. d, f / 2. e, g, j / 3. h, i

C8 2. a / 3. f / 4. j / 5. b / 6. i / 7. c / 8. g / 9. e / 10. k / 11. h

C9 2. was 3. to 4. a 5. a 6. been to 7. well

C10 2. of 3. to 4. from 5. By 6. Near 7. About

C11 2. at (AE auch on), in 3. between, at 4. out of, for 5. for 6. with, in 7. with

C12 3, 4, 5, 8, 9, 10

C13 2. We haven't decided. We may stay at home. 3. We don't usually go away in the summer. 4. I'm planning to take two weeks in May or September. 5. I had ten days off at Easter.

C14 2. play 3. go 4. do 5. do 6. play 7. go 8. go 9. go 10. play 11. go 12. go 13. go 14. do 15. go 16. go

C15 1. c, d, f, g / 2. b, e, h

C16 2. like 3. so 4. as 5. bit 6. time 7. quite 8. rain 9. change 10. terrible 11. lucky 12. brought 13. hope 14. stays

C17 B. 5+a / C. 4+e / D. 2+d / E. 1+b

C18 1. c / 2. b

C19 2. daughter 3. married 4. son-in-law 5. baby 6. granddaughter. 7. separated 8. divorced 9. re-married 10. wife 11. broke up 12. son 13. related 14. get on 15. husband 16. ex-wife 17. step-daughter 18. mother

C20 2. on 3. visit / trip 4. getting 5. all 6. well 7. been 8. went / was 9. child 10. remember

C21 2. a / 3. e / 4. c / 5. g / 6. b / 7. d

C22 2. work for 3. do you do 4. to work for 5. Have you ever heard 6. plastics 7. a year out 8. the administrative side 9. an engineer

C23 1. h / 2. b, c, e / 3. d, f, g

C24 2. He's doing 3. getting paid 4. step on the ladder 5. And the rest of the family? 6. getting by, you know 7. back in the spring 8. I'm sorry to hear that 9. for the best 10. very hard for Ann 11. can imagine

Check-up

1. Where are you from?
2. Do you know Germany at all?
3. Is this your first visit to Germany?
4. I'm / My name is Martin by the way.
5. Oh right / OK / I see. That's interesting. 6. I'm sorry to hear that.
7. I was born in Berlin.
8. I live near Aachen.
9. What do you do (for a living)?
10. I'll give you my address.
11. What's the weather like with you?
12. It's thundery.
13. I have two grown-up sons from my first marriage.
14. This/That is my step-son.
15. I'm not interested in football / soccer (AE). 16. Do-it-yourself is not my thing. / I'm not into do-it-yourself. 17. Business or pleasure?
18. I could do with a bit of /some exercise. 19. How is/are the family? 20. The first step on the ladder.

D. Nachfragen und sich verständigen

D1 2. a+b / 3. a / 4. a+b / 5. a / 6. a / 7. a+b / 8. b / 9. a / 10. a+b

D2 2. Just a little 3. Sorry, I don't understand 4. Now I understand 5. Sorry, what was the word again 6. What's that in German 7. Is that right 8. I think I've got that now

D3 2. c / 3. e / 4. b / 5. f / 6. a

D4 2. writing 3. written 4. expression / word 5. equivalent / translation / word / expression 6. forgotten 7. give 8. different 9. saying

D5 2. d / 3. a / 4. c / 5. f / 6. b

D6 2. alpha, Mike, sierra, tango, echo, Romeo, delta, alpha, Mike
3. November, alpha, India, Romeo, oscar, bravo, India 4. foxtrot, Romeo, alpha, November, kilo, foxtrot, uniform, Romeo, tango
5. echo, delta, India, November, bravo, uniform, Romeo, golf, hotel 6. bravo, echo, India, Juliett, India, November, golf

D7 2. I / 3. Q / 4. B / 5. F / 7. R/
8. T / 9. Y / 10. I / 11. C
12. X / 13. Q

D8 1. a / 2. d / 3. b / 4. c

D9 2. clear 3. screen 4. draw / close
5. blinds 6. any 7. turn 8. up

D10 2. It's the round thing that you have on your car, there are four of them. 3. It's what you do with the key when you open the door.
4. It's what you do when you go to a new place to live. 5. It's the thing at the bank where you put in your card and get money. 6. It's what you have to do when something's broken. 7. It's what you do when it's very hot. 8. It's what you need / use when you cut something.

Check-up
1. Could you repeat that / say that again, please? 2. What does 'replacement' mean? 3. How do you pronounce this word?
4. Sorry, I don't understand.
5. Can you write it down for me?
6. I don't know the English word.
7. Can you say / express it another / a different way? 8. What's that (called) in German?
9. Could you speak more slowly, please?
10. You have been / were a great help.

E. Höfliche Ausdrucksformen

E1 2. a, b, c, d / 3. a, d / 4. a, c, d /
5. a, b, d / 6. a, b, c, d /
7. a, c, d

E2 2. c / 3. g / 4. a / 5. b / 6. i /
7. f / 8. e / 9. h

E3 2. I wonder 3. I'll try
3. Can you tell me
4. You've been a great help
5. You're welcome

E4 1. Many 2. a lot 3. a million
4. very much 5. indeed
6. Thanks a million. (Oft aber auch sarkastisch gemeint) 7. Thank you very much indeed. 8. a

E5 2. course 3. ahead 4. Could
5. might 6. Sorry 7. anyway

E6 2. I'm awfully sorry.
3. I'm so terribly sorry. 4. I don't know how it could have happened. 5. I really must apologize.
6. I don't know how I could have been so stupid.

E7 2. so 3. awfully / terribly
4. sorry 5. must 6. apologize

E8 1. mind 2. could happen / could have happened to anyone 3. Don't worry about it 4. it's not the end of the world

E9 1. It's my mistake entirely / It's entirely my mistake. 2. I have only myself to blame. 3. It's my fault.

E10 1. c / 2. a / 3. d / 4. e

E11 2. Would you mind keeping it to yourself, please? 3. Would you mind not smoking, please?
4. Would you mind repeating that, please? 5. Would you mind driving not quite so fast, please? 6. Would you mind parking a little further down, please? 7. Would you mind making copies for everyone, please?

E12 2. Would you mind if I brought a friend? 3. Would you mind if I just used the phone for a minute?
4. Would you mind if I asked Alan to do that? 5. Would you mind if we changed the agenda round a bit?

Die Verwendung eines if-Satzes Typ 2, mit Vergangenheitsform (brought, used, usw.), wirkt höflicher.

Check-up

1. Please do. / Go ahead. / Sure. / Of course. 2. Thank you very much (indeed). 3. Don't worry.
4. Never mind. / It doesn't matter.
5. I have a request.
6. Would you mind moving your car?
7. It's entirely my fault / my fault entirely. 8. I wonder if you could help me? 9. Thanks anyway.
10. I really must apologize.

F. Komplimente und Nettigkeiten

F1 2. e / 3. a / 4. f / 5. b / 6. c / 7. d

F2 2. What a 3. What a 4. What an 5. What 6. What 7. What 8. What

F3 3. c / 4. i / 6. a / 7. f / 8. b / 9. e

F4 2. comfortable 3. gorgeous 4. magnificent 5. well-behaved 6. delicious 7. lovely / quiet 8. stunning

F5 3. korrekt 4. ... such a marvellous time. 5. korrekt 6. ... such enormous 7. ... such an interesting ... Vor einem allein stehenden Adjektiv steht so, vor einem (Adjektiv +) Nomen steht such.

F6 2. made 3. made 4. do 5. made 6. make 7. did 9. made

F7 2. happy 3. terribly expensive
4. incredibly original
5. fantastically clever
6. undoubtedly 7. really exciting
8. deliciously cool

Check-up

1. You look / are looking great.
2. The colour suits you.
3. It's delicious.
4. The room has a really nice atmosphere. 5. The view is magnificent! 6. What beautiful glasses! 7. What wonderful weather!
8. You look/seem so relaxed. 9. How do you manage to keep/stay so fit? 10. It sounds really exciting.

G. Freudige und traurige Anlässe

G1 2. Happy / Merry Christmas!
3. Happy New Year! 4. Happy Easter!
5. Congratulations!

G2 2. a / 3. e / 4. d / 5. c

G3 2. Oh dear 3. How did that happen?
4. What's the matter?
5. I've got the flu 6. I won't keep you
7. Get well soon! 8. What have you done to your hand?
9. That must be very painful.

G4 2. d / 3. a / 4. c / 5. h / 6. f / 7. e / 8. i / 9. b

G5 1. a + d / 2. c + f / 3. b + g / 4. e + h

Check-up
1. Merry Christmas!
2. Happy New Year!
3. Good luck with your exam!
4. Congratulations! 5. Get well soon.
6. What's the matter?
7. My sincere condolences.
8. We wish him a speedy recovery.
9. We're thinking of you.
10. That's great news.

H. Vorschläge und Empfehlungen

H1 2. What would you like
3. We could go 4. Do you really want to 5. Why don't we phone 6. if you like 7. It would do us both good
8. Let's
9. You can 10. I don't feel like it
11. I suggest 12. if that's what you want to do

H2 2. I'm afraid I don't really like fish.
3. How about a steak then?
4. I don't really fancy steak this evening. 5. Well, you could try haggis. 6. I can really recommend it.
7. Maybe I'll just / I'll maybe just have the vegetarian quiche.
8. Would you like to see the wine list?

H3 1. b / 2. a / 3. b / 4. b / 5. b

H4 2. What do you suggest doing / that we do tomorrow? 3. The hotel suggests parking / that we park ...
4. I suggest leaving ... and walking / that we leave ... and walk
5. How did they suggest sending / that we send it?

H5 2. What about coming with us?
3. What about going to the cinema?
4. How about going away for the weekend? 5. What about taking them to the beach? 6. How about hiring a car?

H6 1. wonder(ed) 2. give 3. on / about 4. by 5. on 6. start
7. depends 8. into 9. best
10. if / that 11. recommend
12. sounds

Check-up
1. What shall we do this evening?
2. Why don't we call / phone Tina?
3. How / What about inviting Anna?
4. Let's go out. 5. What can you recommend? 6. I suggest waiting / that we wait. 7. It would do us both good to get some / a bit of exercise. 8. You can if you like, but I don't feel like it.
9. I can really recommend it.
10. It depends (on) what you're into.

I. Widersprechen und sich beschweren

I1 2. c / 3. g / 4. b / 5. a / 6. h / 7. e / 8. f

I2 1. b / 2. d

I3 2. How can I help you, Mr Thompson?
3. I'm afraid there's a slight problem.
4. I'm sorry, sir. What is it?
5. The room is freezing cold.
6. It must be something to do with the air-conditioning.
7. I'll send someone right up.

I4 2. The toilet 3. The window
4. The light / bulb 5. no water

I5 2. I haven't offended you
3. I have to 4. It's very difficult
5. I hope you will understand
6. In other circumstances

I6 c, e, g, h

I7 1. f / 2. d / 3. e / 4. b / 5. a / 6. g / 7. c

Check-up
1. I'm afraid I don't agree.
2. What do you understand / mean exactly by 'soon'? 3. What's your opinion? 4. I have a complaint to make. 5. I'm sorry to have to say this, but ... 6. If you ask me, I don't think that that would be a good idea. 7. I'm afraid that is out of the question. 8. If you don't mind my saying so, it's now too late.
9. I hope I haven't offended you.
10. In other circumstances that would not be a problem.

J. Meinungen und Gefühle

J1 1. c, d, h, i, j, k / 2. b, e, f, g

J2 2. I'm not sure 3. I have my doubts about 4. I'm rather sceptical
5. undecided 6. made up my mind
7. one way or the other 8. on the other 9. certain
10. bound to be 11. totally and utterly 12. without a shadow
13. I very much doubt (whether) ...
14. I'm totally and utterly convinced.

J3 2. d / 3. a / 4. g / 5. b / 6. e / 7. c

J4 2. whatever 3. easy 4. matter
5. same 6. mind

J5 2. alarming 3. concerned
4. relieved 5. weight ... mind
6. set ... rest 7. cause ... concern
8. lose ... sleep 9. nothing ... about
10. anxious 11. sick
12. sleepless 13. look

J6 1. d / 2. e / 3. d

J7 2. live to 3. sorry 4. regret
5. do the same again 6. bitterly

J8 1. prefer, preference 2. turns, fond
3. stand, hate, detest 4. love, adore
5. care, person 6. sweet, weakness, go

Check up

1. I completely/totally disagree. / I disagree completely/totally.
2. I don't think you can say that.
3. I must admit that I'm rather/quite sceptical (AE: skeptical).
4. I'm undecided.
5. I'm completely/totally and utterly convinced. 6. Some people couldn't care less. 7. I've been worried sick. 8. We're all in a good mood. 9. I feel on top of the world.
10. I bitterly regret it. / I regret it bitterly.

K. Geschichten und Witze erzählen

K1 2. g / 3. a / 4. f / 5. c / 6. b / 7. d

K2 2. g / 3. f / 4. c / 5. e / 6. b / 7. a

K3 2. Do you know the one about
3. I don't think so
4. Well, there's this 5. Do you get it?
6. I'm a bit slow sometimes 7. Have you got it now?
8. That's a good one!

K4 1. k / 2. o / 3. m / 4. g / 5. e / 6. b / 7. d / 8. c / 9. h / 10. i / 11. l / 12. n / 13. a / 14. f / 15. j

K5 2. e / 3. a / 4. h / 5. d / 6. b / 7. f / 8. c

K6 2. did it? 3. is it? 4. did they? 5. aren't you? 6. didn't I 7. have you?

K7 2. What?! 3. apparently
4. somewhere 5. eventually
6. Wait for it
7. was having one of his off days
8. he can have cardboard
9. himself
10. apologize for any inconvenience
11. And the guy ate it?!
12. The best bit is

K8 2. as 3. dark / moonlit / moonless / starlit 4. traffic 5. almost / nearly
6. couple 7. Anyway/Well (anyway)
8. suddenly 9. to be seen
10. imagined 11. getting 12. wait

Check-up

1. Do/Did you get it? / Have you got it?
2. I can never remember jokes. 3. Do you know the joke about the elephant?
4. That reminds me of another story.
5. Please stop / interrupt me if I've told (you) this before. 6. Anyway that was the end of the story.
7. You don't really believe that, do you? 8. You're pulling my leg.
9. You'll never believe this.
10. I felt such a fool.

L. Telefonieren und simsen

L1 2. a / 3. b / 4. a / 5. b / 6. a / 7. b / 8. b / 9. b / 10. a
(Das Wort accu gibt es im Englischen nicht.)

L2 2. speak to 3. I'm sorry, but
4. Can you tell me 5. she'll be back
6. calling from Germany
7. Is Catherine there 8. Just hang on a moment 9. I'll get her
10. on the phone 11. speaking
12. I'd like to 13. I'm afraid
14. you've dialled /got

L3 2. a / 3. b / 4. c / 5. e / 6. j / 7. i / 8. f / 9. h / 10. g

L4 1. landline 2. cellphone 3. mobile number 4. cellphone 5. mobile (phone)

L5 1. How can I help you? 2. I'd like to speak 3. Who's calling / speaking 4. Just a moment 5. I'll put you through

L6 2. I'll call you back ... 3. I'll find out ... 4. I'll put ... 5. I'll see ... 6. I'll try ... 7. I'll ask ... 8. I'll check ... when he'll be / when he's 9. I'll pass ...

L7 2. reach 3. text 4. a text 5. message 5. mailbox

L8 2. for your information 3. message 4. as soon as possible 5. great 6. sorry 7. thanks 8. please 9. address 10. I love you

L9 1. b / 2. d

L10 2. I'm sorry 3. available 4. leave 5. after the beep 6. If you remember 7. just wanted 8. are going to be around 9. be passing your way 10. we might drop in 11. would be convenient 12. call us back on

L11 2. i / 3. e / 4. h / 5. a / 6. k / 7. d / 8. m / 9. b / 10. l / 11. f / 12. j / 13. g

Check-up

1. This is Senta. 2. Can I speak to Roger Bacon, please? 3. Who's speaking, please? 4. You've got / dialled the wrong number.
5. I'll connect you / put you through.
6. I'm afraid Frank is not here.
7. I'm calling from Germany.
8. (Just) Hang on a moment.
9. Can you give / pass him a message?
10. My battery's low / almost empty.

M. Termin und Uhrzeit vereinbaren

M1 2. be arriving 3. At 19.25 4. Friday 13th 4. a week later 5. So it's Friday 20th at 19.25 6. be there

M2 2. h / 3. c / 4. f / 5. b / 6. a

M3 2. c / 3. b / 4. b / 5. b / 6. a / 7. c

M4 2. d / 3. b / 4. c / 5. a / 6. e / 7. f

M5 2. a / 3. b / 4. a+b / 5. a / 6. a / 7. b / 8. b / 9. b

M6 2. wondering 3. possibility 4. schedule 5. free 6. convenient 7. previous 8. slot 9. fully 10. whole 11. another 12. late 13. towards 14. either 15. suitable 16. sounds / seems 17. option 18. choice 19. make 20. confirm

Check-up

1. When do you arrive / will you be arriving? 2. I'll be there to meet/collect you / pick you up.
3. About two-ish? / Around / About two? 4. Shall we say half past seven?
5. Would you like to suggest a time?
6. Would ten in the morning suit you / be convenient / be suitable?
7. Towards / About / Around (about) the end of April? 8. Would Thursday be OK for you? 9. Can we make it a bit later? 10. I'll send an email to confirm the time.

N. Gast und Gastgeber sein

N1 2. Are you doing 3. Do you have plans 4. Do you fancy 5. Do you want to 6. Would you like

N2 1. d, f / 2. e, g, h / 3. b, c

N3 2. Maybe another time. 3. Never mind, another evening perhaps / perhaps another evening.
4. How about Thursday instead?
5. Could you make it a little later?

N4 2. a / 3. e / 4. j / 5. d / 6. g / 7. i / 8. h / 9. b / 10. f

N5 2. party 3. celebrate / mark 4. inviting / asking 5. delighted / pleased / glad 6. come 7. hope 8. know 9. can

N6 2. are going to the pub for a drink.
3. Straight after work. 4. Where are you going? 5. Probably to The Crown.
6. Good idea. I'll join you. 7. Let me know when you're leaving.

N7 2. I'm a little late 3. Some of the others haven't arrived yet. 4. I've brought you 5. That's very kind
6. you really didn't need to 7. you found us all right then 8. The directions you gave us were perfect.
9. I hope you don't mind
10. would you mind

N8 2. c / 3. d / 4. b / 5. c

N9 3. I'll try a glass of red wine, please.
4. I won't have any more, thanks.
5. I won't be long.
6. I'll sit here if that's OK.
7. I'll have one of your special cocktails, please. 8. I won't drink any alcohol, thanks. 9. I won't say no. 10. I won't have any potatoes, thanks.

N10 2. d / 3. a / 4. b

N11 1. b / 2. c

N12 1. a, c, e, f, g, k, l / 2. b, d, h, i, j, m, n

N13 2. i / 3. e / 4. d / 5. f / 7. a / 8. c / 9. h

N14 2. enjoyed ourselves
3. was delicious 4. laughed so much 5. a fantastic dinner party
6. Thank you again

N15 1. a, d, e, h, j, m, n, q, t / 2. b, c, f, g, i, k, l, o, p, r, s

N16 2. and you? 3. quite a stressful day today 4. otherwise 5. What can I do 6. I'm phoning for two reasons 7. The first is to thank you 8. You enjoyed it? 9. we weren't sure 10. after all 11. it was really quite interesting 12. We were afraid that

N17 1. I hope I'm not calling / phoning too early. 2. I'm calling / phoning because I've lost my mobile (phone) / cell phone. 3. Maybe / Perhaps I left it at your place last night. 4. If I find it, I'll let you know. 5. I'm lost without my mobile / cell phone. 6. I don't think so. 7. Oh, wait a moment. 8. Have you found it? 9. I'll have a look and if I find it, I'll let you know.

Check-up

1. Are you doing anything on Saturday? 2. Do you fancy joining us? 3. That's very kind of you, but I'm afraid / unfortunately I'm busy. 4. I can't make Friday. 5. Maybe / Perhaps another time. 6. How / What about Wednesday? 7. Drop in / Come round/ along/by if you have time. 8. I've brought you a little something. 9. Would you mind taking off your shoes / taking your shoes off? 10. I'm full.

O. In der Stadt und auf Reisen

O1 2. a+b / 3. b / 4. a+b / 5. a+b / 6. a+b / 7. a / 8. a / 9. b / 10. b / 11. a / 12. a / 13. b / 14. b

O2 2. if you look at the map here 3. where my finger is 4. It's probably best 5. this brown line 6. change to 7. an eastbound train 8. along there on the left

O3 1. b, f, g, k, m, o, p, r, s / 2. a, c, d, e, h, i, j, l, n, q

O4 4. a / 6. n / 7. c / 9. b / 11. i / 13. l / 15. f / 17. j

O5 1. a, c / 2. b, d / 3. f, i / 4. g, h / 5. e, j

O6 2. We're looking for 3. double 4. singles 5. as a single 6. just for one night 7. were you planning 8. How much is it? 9. per person? 10. I'd do the double as single 11. with a full Scottish breakfast 12. Can we see the rooms?

Check-up

1. Where's the nearest cash machine? 2. You can't miss it. 3. How far is it to walk / on foot? 4. How do I get to Covent Garden? 5. Change to the Piccadilly Line at Piccadilly Circus. 6. I'm just looking. 7. I'll leave it, thanks. 8. Do you have the next size up? 9. No dessert, thanks. Just the bill. 10. I'd like an aisle seat.

Grund- und Aufbauwortschatz Englisch
256 Seiten
ISBN 978-3-19-109520-8

Erweitern Sie Ihren Englisch-Wortschatz!

Mit dem *Grund- und Aufbauwortschatz Englisch* können Sie systematisch und gezielt Vokabeln lernen und Ihren Wortschatz erweitern. Anwendungsbeispiele und typische Zusammenhänge verdeutlichen den Gebrauch der Stichwörter.

- 8.000 Wörter in 18 Haupt- und über 100 Unterkapiteln
- Info-Boxen mit Hinweisen auf Besonderheiten im Sprachgebrauch, grammatische Regeln und landeskundliche Hintergrundinformationen
- Übersichtliches, zweispaltiges Layout mit farbig markiertem Alltagswortschatz
- Kennzeichnung von ca. 1.000 besonders häufig verwendeten Vokabeln
- Mit englischem und deutschem Register zum schnellen Nachschlagen

Auch für Französisch, Italienisch, Russisch und Schwedisch erhältlich.

www.hueber.de/englisch-lernen

Freude an Sprachen

Grammatik einfach praktisch
Englisch
248 Seiten
ISBN 978-3-19-009901-6

Einfach praktisch – einfach gut!

Wenn Sie Englisch lernen möchten, sind solide Grammatikkenntnisse unerlässlich – dorthin führt Sie *Grammatik einfach praktisch Englisch*. Übersichtlich, leicht verständlich formuliert und mit einer »Navigationshilfe« für den Lerner ausgestattet, ist sie von Anfang an Ihr verlässlicher Begleiter zum Nachschlagen, Lernen und Üben.

- 10 Hauptkapitel mit leichten Einführungen, verständlichen Regeln, übersichtlichen Tabellen, Satzbeispielen mit Übersetzung und praxisorientierten Übungen
- Übersichtliche Lernernavigation in der Randspalte und klare Gestaltung für eine schnelle Orientierung
- Im Anhang: Verbtabellen, Lösungen zu den Übungen sowie ein Stichwortregister und Übersicht über die Grammatikbegriffe
- Zum Selbstlernen oder als Ergänzung im Unterricht geeignet

Auch für Französisch, Italienisch und Spanisch erhältlich.

www.hueber.de/englisch-lernen

Freude an Sprachen